CLAIRE TOMALIN

The Life and Death of Mary Wollstonecraft

PENGUIN BOOKS

PENGUIN BOOKS

Published by the Penguin Group
Penguin Books Ltd, 80 Strand, London WC2R 0RL, England
Penguin Group (USA) Inc., 375 Hudson Street, New York, New York 10014, USA
Penguin Group (Canada), 90 Eglinton Avenue East, Suite 700, Toronto, Ontario, Canada M4P 2Y3
(a division of Pearson Penguin Canada Inc.)
Penguin Ireland, 25 St Stephen's Green, Dublin 2, Ireland (a division of Penguin Books Ltd)
Penguin Group (Australia), 250 Camberwell Road, Camberwell, Victoria 3124, Australia
(a division of Pearson Australia Group Pty Ltd)
Penguin Books India Pvt Ltd, 11 Community Centre, Panchsheel Park, New Delhi – 110 017, India
Penguin Group (NZ), 67 Apollo Drive, Rosedale, Auckland 0632, New Zealand
(a division of Pearson New Zealand Ltd)
Penguin Books (South Africa) (Pty) Ltd, Block D, Rosebank Office Park,
181 Jan Smuts Avenue, Parktown North, Gauteng 2193, South Africa

Penguin Books Ltd, Registered Offices: 80 Strand, London WC2R 0RL, England

www.penguin.com

First published by Weidenfeld & Nicolson 1974
Published in Pelican Books (without illustrations) 1977
Reprinted in Penguin Books 1985
Reprinted with revisions, illustrations and revised notes and bibliography 1992
Reissued in this edition 2012
001

Made and printed in England by Clays Ltd, St Ives plc

ISBN: 978-0-241-96331-9

www.greenpenguin.co.uk

'An admirable biography ... In the hands of the author we are able to know much more about Mary Wollstonecraft than any one person did in her lifetime, and indeed more than she knew about herself' – *The New York Times Book Review*

'Repeatedly one wants to shout "Brava!" ... a fine piece of work ... the reader is rewarded again and again' – Mary Ellmann in the *Washington Post*

'Mrs Tomalin is a most intelligent and sympathetic biographer, aware of her impetuous subject's many failings, yet with the perception to present her greatness fairly. She writes well and wittily, and her treatment of the infinitely complex period of Paris during the Revolution shows a remarkable lucidity and understanding' – *Daily Telegraph*

'Gripping ... Illuminates Mary's courage and pioneering political foresight' – *Sunday Times*

'Mrs Tomalin's account of Mary's life and times is a vivid evocation not only of what Mary went through but also of how women lived in the second part of the eighteenth century in England and France ... Most of all, however, she makes Mary Wollstonecraft unforgettable' – Mary Kenny in the *Evening Standard*

'You have only to read Victorian biographies to realize how good our examples are. One of the best is Claire Tomalin's *The Life and Death of Mary Wollstonecraft*' – C. P. Snow in the *Financial Times*

ng and journalism for many years. She was literary editor first of the *New Statesman* and then the *Sunday Times*, before devoting herself to writing full time. She is the author of eight highly acclaimed biographies: *The Life and Death of Mary Wollstonecraft*, which won the Whitbread First Book Award; *Shelley and His World*; *Katherine Mansfield: A Secret Life*; *The Invisible Woman: The Story of Nelly Ternan and Charles Dickens*, which won the Hawthornden Prize, the NCR Book Award and the James Tait Black Memorial Prize for Biography; *Mrs Jordan's Profession*; *Jane Austen: A Life*; *Samuel Pepys: The Unequalled Self*, which was the 2002 Whitbread Book of the Year; *Thomas Hardy: The Time-Torn Man*; and, most recently, *Charles Dickens: A Life*.

She lives in London with her husband, the novelist and playwright Michael Frayn.

For Nick

Contents

List of Illustrations

WIT in women is apt to have bad consequences; like a sword without a scabbard, it wounds the wearer and provokes assailants. I am sorry to say the generality of women who have excelled in wit have failed in chastity.

Elizabeth Montagu, 1750

The more I see of radical women, the less I desire to increase their number. I went to a Radical dinner party last week, and the bold, unfeeling faces of some of the ladies, and their reckless talk, quite shocked me.

Emily Davies, founder of Girton, writing
to Barbara Bodichon in 1867

Up to the beginning of the nineteenth century the distinguished woman had almost invariably been an aristocrat. It was the great lady who ruled and wrote letters and influenced the course of politics. From the huge middle class few women rose to eminence, nor has the drabness of their lot received the attention which had been bestowed upon the splendours of the great and the miseries of the poor. There they remain, even in the early part of the nineteenth century, a vast body, living, marrying, bearing children in dull obscurity, until at last we begin to wonder whether there was something in their condition itself – in the age at which they married, the number of children they bore, the privacy they lacked, the incomes they had not, the conventions which stifled them, and the education they never received – which so affected them that, though the middle class is the great reservoir from which we draw our distinguished men, it has thrown up singularly few women to set beside them.

Virginia Woolf, 1927

Free thought has always been the perquisite of the aristocracy. So has the intellectual development of women.

Bertrand Russell writing to
Gilbert Murray, 1943

Acknowledgements

I SHOULD like to acknowledge the assistance of the staff of the London Library; the GLC archivists; the Public Record Office, London; the Dr Williams Library; the Library of the Society of Friends in London; the Guildhall Library; University College Library, London; Stoke Newington Library; the Wellcome Medical Library; the British Museum; the Bodleian; the Archives de France; the department of archives, Ville du Havre; the Kunsthaus, Zürich; the Liverpool City Libraries and the Walker Art Gallery, Liverpool; the Mitchell Library, Sydney, Australia; and the county archivist of the East Riding of Yorkshire.

I am indebted to Lord Abinger for allowing me to examine microfilms of the manuscripts in his possession.

I should like to express my gratitude to Captain Douglas King-Harman for friendly assistance in looking through his family papers for me.

Bernard Mason kindly allowed me to quote from his late brother Eudo Mason's *The Mind of Henry Fuseli*; and the Carl Pforzheimer Library and Oxford University Press permitted quotations from *Shelley and his Circle*, edited by K. N. Cameron.

I am grateful to Thomas Pakenham for drawing my attention to a reference to Mary's relationship with the Kingsboroughs in the manuscript letters of Bishop Percy of Dromore, and to Professor Gert Schiff for assuring me that there is no drawing of Mary by Fuseli in existence.

I should like to acknowledge assistance and encouragement from Edward Thompson, Professor Eric Hobsbawm, Professor D. V. Glass and Professor Richard Cobb in directing my attention to various sources of information I should otherwise have missed.

The medical aspect of Mary's death was most kindly illuminated for me by David Morris, MD, FRCS, MRCOG.

Brian Inglis most generously lent me a family tree of the Blood family, which finally cleared up the vexed question of the identity of 'Neptune': my thanks to him.

Thanks are also due to Nicolas Barker for information about Joseph Johnson's publishing practice; to Martina Mayne and Rachael Harris for translating passages of German for me; and to Eric Korn and John Bunting, both of whom tracked down rare books for me with the greatest patience and kindness. It was also John Bunting who first drew my attention to the portrait of Mary mentioned on page 126.

My debt to my editor, the late Tony Godwin, is great indeed: he left me alone when necessary, and gave me all the advice and help possible when it was needed.

Finally, it would be inappropriate to bring out a book on Mary Wollstonecraft without a domestic acknowledgement to all those who held the baby whilst I worked, the most constant being Gail Coté, Theresa McGinlay, Josephine, Susanna, Emily and my husband. To all of them, thank you.

[1]

Childhood: Spitalfields, Essex, Yorkshire

AT the ragged eastern edge of the City of London is a district known as Spitalfields. Today it is very sparsely peopled; wave after wave of immigrants has come and gone, leaving a few sad Indian faces on the streets and a floating population of tramps who build bonfires at the deserted corners on winter Sundays. The buildings are a mixed lot also: Victorian breweries and factories tower over tiny almshouses, whole streets are near derelict and the Georgian church has an even more theatrical and misplaced air than most of its fellows. Such eighteenth-century terraces as still stand are decayed and covered in grime; they have not housed families for many years.

Spitalfields has never been a particularly happy or prosperous place. Very far back, a Priory (or Spital) is supposed to have used the land as a burial ground, but in the seventeenth century it was all open fields. Then, as London drew more and more men and women from their native villages, the rows of houses began to go up, eating away the green to the north and east. Settlers came from far afield: Ireland, the north of England, East Anglia, the continent. The road from Cambridge and the north-eastern seaports ended in Bishopsgate, the busy main street of Spitalfields; behind its shopfronts and merchants' dwellings spread the warrens, alleys and courtyards of the immigrant poor. Many found work in the silk weaving trade established there, and in the 1680s came the French protestant weavers banished by Louis XIV, bringing some extra skills to the trade.

After this more and more weavers came crowding in, more and more rows of shoddy houses went up over the green lanes and along the lines of ancient meadow boundaries. By the middle of the eighteenth century the streets were dark, dirty and crammed; when the looms were humming in the houses the noise was drearily insistent, when they fell silent it meant hunger, sometimes riots. The trade was always insecure; weavers were generally despised, recognizable by their stunted height and pale faces. Their wives and children usually worked alongside them, and a whole family might be crowded into two rooms, where they laboured and lived the best they could. Outside, the street life of the apprentice boys who slept under the looms or in the cellars was brutal too: dog fights, duck hunts towards the Bethnal Green ponds, the baiting of an ox filched from Smithfield market. Here and there a weaver kept a caged bird high up at a window to whistle for his caged family as they worked, and the Huguenots tried to brighten their lives by tending narrow strips of garden: Vine, Elder and Blossom Streets still commemorate their efforts. But for the most part it was a place of stench, din and ruthless competition.[1]

As the century went by and still more workers came to the district, a few men from amongst the anonymous mass began to make considerable profits. They did it largely by remodelling the cottage industry: the old, direct dealings between craftsmen and clients were ended, and instead piece-workers were employed by the masters who organized orders and delivered on a large scale.

One of these successful capitalists was a man called Edward Wollstonecraft. Born in 1688, he had arrived in Spitalfields, probably from Lancashire,* early in the century, and settled in Primrose Alley, a turning off Bishops-

* Wollstonecraft is a Lancashire name; amongst the wills proved in Lancashire and Cheshire in the seventeenth century there are several Wollstonecrafts (and variant spellings) in the under £40 category, none richer. A gardener, Thomas Wollstonecraft of Ardwick, who died in 1693, looks like a possible father of Edward; his death might have persuaded the orphan boy to move south. Edward's mother Martha and sister Mary died in London.

gate, 'all mean and poor people'.[2] He married a wife, Jane, five years older than himself; it may have been the traditional and sensible match between the journeyman and his master's daughter. For her it meant a steady series of pregnancies, the deaths of almost all her children and the collapse of her health. Edward brought his mother and sister to live with them, and Jane died after twenty years of marriage, worn out. He took another wife, Elizabeth, continued to work hard, amassed money and invested it cleverly; he outlived his second wife also, eight of his children and several grandchildren.[3] He served as a captain in the city militia in the middle of the century[4] and acted as an officer of his parish: that of St Botolph Without Bishopsgate. By the time he reached his sixties he felt entitled to call himself not merely a man of substance but also a gentleman, and so he was described in the deeds of the house he built in 1756.[5]

Of all his sons, the only long-lived one was the youngest, Edward John, who served out his apprenticeship to his father in the days of his prosperity and became a handkerchief weaver, probably without having to apply himself too hard. When Captain Wollstonecraft moved to his splendid new establishment on the other side of Bishopsgate, Edward John remained in a cottage in what had now become Primrose Street, where his father owned half the houses. He continued to rule his family with a firm hand, but the son was chafing to escape from this domination.

He disliked his trade and he disliked London itself. He had married, whilst still an apprentice, a pretty young Irish wife, Elizabeth Dixon, and she too was reluctant to settle in the city. A son was born, followed on 27 April 1759 by a daughter, Mary.

On the twentieth of May Mary was carried from Primrose Street along Bishopsgate to St Botolph to be christened.[6] For hereditary christening gifts, she had her paternal grandfather's willpower and ambition and her mother's Irish fluency of tongue. Otherwise there was not much for her: most of the Wollstonecrafts were short-tempered and liable to fits of depression; they were not noted for intellect or good looks, and displayed no interest in anything outside their purely personal affairs. Mary's father, having lost his mother young, had been brought up with a mixture of neglect and indulgence; he was sporadically affectionate, occasionally violent, more interested in sport than work, and not to be relied on for anything, least of all for loving attention. Her mother was indolent by nature and made a darling of her first-born, Ned, two years older than Mary; by the time the little girl had learned to walk in jealous pursuit of this loving pair, a third baby was on the way. A sense of grievance may have been her most important endowment.

Another was her sense of rootlessness. She never had a word to say about her grandfather except that he was 'a respectable manufacturer';[7] and neither he nor her father could provide the anchorage into a place or a social class that a steady, solid line of male relatives might have done. She observed early that people rose by their wits and fell for lack of them; *'l'esprit seul peut tout changer'*, as Figaro sang.[8] It was to be the creed of all her contemporaries who, like her, became revolutionaries in the Nineties.

If we are to trust Mary's own account, nobody was particularly interested in her as a child. She was not a prodigy of learning like some of the bluestockings of the age who read English at two and Greek at ten; she probably spent her time penned into the backyard in Primrose Street with her nurse, teased by her father's workmen, held back from the dangers of the main street, peeping out at the world when she could from the dark little house. When she was two her mother bore a second son, Henry Woodstock Wollstonecraft.[9] He did not live long, and the loss of the baby boy must have made Ned doubly precious to his parents. It may also have helped to persuade old Edward to buy a farm out at Epping for the young family; so many of his infant sons and grandsons had died in Primrose Street. From now on the children lived partly in the country, and Edward John divided his time between business and farming.

Mary claimed that she did not know whether she was born in London or Epping.[10] Most mothers talk to their children about these things, but evidently Mrs Wollstonecraft did not; and it may also be that Mary decided very early on to remember only the farm, where she was relatively free, and forget the noisy streets of Spitalfields and the dominating figure of a stern old man whose interests were confined to church affairs and the financial future of his family. But they were still in London a good deal; in the summer of 1764 a fourth baby was born, and christened in St Botolph again: a sister, Eliza, sometimes known as Bess.[11]

The following winter old Edward settled down to compose his long and carefully considered will.[12] First he paid the protestant businessman's conscience money: extensive bequests to the parish paupers and all the inmates of three debtors' prisons. Then he made provision for a grandiose funeral. Then he divided his estate into three parts: one third for his daughter by his first marriage (already a middle-aged woman with children nearly grown up), another third to his son Edward John, and the final third to six-year-old Ned. Ned also inherited his grandfather's portrait, a solemn reminder of the ambitions that were being laid on his shoulders. There was nothing for the little girls, not so much as a silver spoon apiece.

In February 1765, at the age of seventy-six Edward Wollstonecraft died. Mary was nearly six, Ned seven; he had a good opinion of himself already, and now he came into a fortune as big as his father's. In the years ahead there were to be many wrangles over money, but for the moment Ned was almost everyone's favourite: 'the son, who is to carry the empty family-name down to posterity' as Mary wrote scornfully later.[13] The overt preference given to Ned in terms of love and money stung her quite as sharply as any of the injustices of her life.

Now, with nothing to keep them in London, the Wollstonecrafts moved further out to another farm at Barking, beside the river, and kept only a property-owning and business link with Spitalfields. Mary's aunt and cousins, if they had ever been at all close, were lost to sight; possibly Elizabeth Wollstonecraft was eager to cut their connections with the sources of their income. The satirists of the day, with their mockery of aspiring weavers and their families, encouraged such determined and absolute rejections by those who got away. In any case, Elizabeth was not a Londoner, but came from Ballyshannon on the west coast of Ireland, a pretty little town where her family lived genteelly, doing well out of the wine trade.[14] To her it doubtless looked easy enough for a family to move up the social ladder; her brothers' sons would be able to buy commissions in the army and navy;[15] she may have encouraged her daughters to turn up their noses at trade and consider themselves a cut above their origins; certainly Mary was capable of simple snobberies all her life and professed a deep contempt for business. Perhaps her mother told her tales of the delights of life in Ireland. If her father ever recalled the pleasures of his London apprenticeship, they were not calculated to win the admiration of his small curly-haired daughter, who developed an early passion for animals and a detestation of cruelty of all kinds.

At Barking, the Wollstonecrafts' neighbours and friends were the Gascoynes, sons of a lord mayor, Sir Crisp, whose money had been made in much the same fashion as theirs, albeit in larger amounts. The Gascoynes were to become members of parliament, see their family fortune increase and channel it into the aristocracy; already they inhabited an elegant country house, Bifrons.[16] More modestly, the Wollstonecrafts planned to better themselves by farming in a gentlemanly way, and intended Ned for the law. Perhaps also they hoped one day to be able to give their daughters enough to make good marriages into the country gentry, if they were lucky, and pretty, and docile.

But Mary was none of these things. It was soon observed that whereas Bess was nice-looking and polite, her elder sister was sharp in manner and often angry in appearance: her eyes bulged, the corners of her mouth turned down. From a very early age she nourished the sense that she was unappreciated and denied affection that was her due. In her fictional account of her childhood she described playing in a garden and a wood, making up songs and conversing with angels:[17] the picture suggests loneliness and an early taste for the rather one-sided dramatic exchanges she practised all her life. Slighted on grounds of inferior age and sex by her elder brother, and never a candidate for the petting that went to each new baby in turn, she looked elsewhere. A third daughter was born at Barking, Everina – Mary wrote her name Averina, which suggests the family's pronunciation – and then a third son, James. All the children flourished now and the death of Henry could be forgotten. Ned started school, Mary made toys of dogs and flowers, and 'an old housekeeper told her stories, read to her, and at last taught her to read. Her mother talked of enquiring for a governess.'[18]

At Barking, where her parents were enjoying their first freedom to do as they pleased with their money, and emulating the high style of the Gascoynes, her mother might well have thought of a governess for her daughters. But Mr Wollstonecraft had the tastes and vices of a country squire without the acreage or capital; he loved both horse and bottle but proved impatient and incompetent as a farmer. Things went badly, the prospect of a governess receded, capital was already dwindling. Almost before Mary became aware of her position as a lady, the family began to slide back down the social scale.

Her father's remedy for failure was to move on. So when she was nine they packed, said farewell to neighbours and set off up the Great North Road in a cavalcade of horses and coaches for what must have seemed like a foreign country. They were going to a farm near Beverley in Yorkshire, where the common people spoke an almost incomprehensible tongue and the land was as flat as Holland all the way to the North Sea. In those days it was not drained, and in winter it flooded and sometimes froze for mile on mile. It was good wild country for a child who preferred animals to people and liked to be out roaming in search of angels, and for some years Mary remained a solitary and a tomboy. The birth of her youngest brother, Charles, who became her favourite, reconciled her only a little to the role of eldest daughter and occasional childminder.

As time passed she began to see the attractions of Beverley too. Mr Wollstonecraft took a house in the centre, overlooking the Wednesday Market; on one side stood the huge Gothic minster that dominates the town physically. A new organ was installed soon after the Wollstonecrafts arrived, and a festival of Handel's music held to celebrate the occasion. There was also a theatre, and a new set of Assembly Rooms for dancing had just been built by public subscription. Beverley society was lively in many ways. To the west of the town a racecourse stand was put up for the crowds who attended the famous races and horse fairs, which may have attracted Mr Wollstonecraft in the first place.[19] Other local gentlemen were as interested in poetry as in horseflesh; a literary club flourished at Driffield near by. When Mary was fourteen she wrote to a friend quoting some of the deplorable doggerel turned out by the Driffield Bards, and wishing she were old enough to be celebrated amongst the beauties of Beverley; this is her earliest surviving letter.[20]

The friend to whom she addressed herself was another fourteen-year-old, a girl called Jane Arden, born in Beverley of a similarly wandering family; Mr Arden had lived in

Germany, described himself as a 'philosopher' and gave public lectures on science and literary subjects.[21] Sensitive about the failings she was beginning to perceive in her own family, and contrasting them with the dignified, sober and well-read Ardens, Mary envied Jane her entire situation and attached herself determinedly to the family of the philosopher. The lessons he gave his daughter formed a striking contrast with Mr Wollstonecraft's professed scorn for the very idea of female learning. He was becoming notorious for his temper and extravagance in the district. Drinking was the general male habit, but he took his drink badly, and Mary's stories of sleeping on the landing and shielding her mother from his blows convey her view of him. Her willpower was strengthened in the process no doubt, but at the cost of learning to despise her father and pity her mother.

The letters to Jane hinted at dissatisfactions at home but did not dwell on them. At first they were mainly given up to chat about poetry and the theatre, references to *macaronis*, arch and spiteful remarks about the failings of other girls. Then suddenly all this was swept aside in a storm of emotion. The same tone that Mary would use in her letters when she was twenty-five, thirty, thirty-five, appeared now, when she was a schoolgirl of fourteen; the voice is already unmistakable.

There was a quarrel. Mary accused Jane of neglect and of having hurt her feelings and demanded her own letters back. She then said nothing could ever be the same again but asked Jane to call as usual so that their friends should not gossip. When Jane ignored this letter, a still more frantic one followed in which Mary confessed to jealousy of another girl; the torture was the worse because the Arden parents also favoured the rival. Perhaps they thought Mary was not a suitable friend? She explained herself further:

> If I did not love you I should not write so; – I have a heart that scorns disguise, and a countenance which will not dissemble: I have formed romantic notions of friendship. – I have

been once disappointed: – I think if I am a second time I shall only want some infidelity in a love affair, to qualify me for an old maid, as then I shall have no idea of either of them. I am a little singular in my thoughts of love and friendship; I must have the first place or none. – I own your behaviour is more according to the opinion of the world, but I would break such narrow bounds.

This seems to have produced some satisfaction, for the next letter started more warmly and admitted she might have been partly in the wrong in the first place; but

Love and Jealousy are twins ... I spent part of the night in tears; (I would not meanly make a merit of it.) I have not time to write fully on the subject, but this I am sure of, if I did not love you, I should not be angry. – I cannot bear a slight from those I love.

And to round off the emotional battering she went on:

I shall take it as a particular favour if you will call this morning, and be assured that however more deserving Miss R ... may be of your favour, she cannot love you better than your humble servant Mary Wollstonecraft. P.S. I keep your letters as a Memorial that you once loved me, but it will be of no consequence to keep mine as you have no regard for the writer.

However it was Jane who preserved the letters, not Mary.

She had set up an emotional pattern she was never to break. Long before she had read Rousseau she arrived at her own conclusions about the supreme power of feelings and the divine right of the intense to cut a swathe through everything that was insipid, inadequate, conventional or disappointing; and where most of her female contemporaries insisted on the prime importance of protecting oneself by concealing emotion, Mary rejected the idea totally. She blazoned her hopes and her disappointments. She could never wear a mask or keep a weapon in reserve.

Jane's failure to respond to her affection was not the first disappointment she had suffered, as she was at pains to point out. Perhaps she had her parents in mind. How much they were really to blame for making her unhappy is hard to say; apart from the drunken episodes they seem to have been cool rather than cruel, too preoccupied with their own interests and troubles to give Mary what she wanted of them, unable to fill the roles she wished to see them in, and unappreciative of her efforts to impress them. Some of the motive power of her personality was certainly derived from resentment of their attitude. She was not able to divert her feelings into the traditionally consoling path of prayer, and she was too vehement to sustain an ironical distancing from disappointment. Both Fanny Burney and Jane Austen (and no doubt thousands of other girls) compensated for other lacks in their lives by making sisters into their chief allies and supports. Mary could not. There may have been a little jealousy of Eliza; she had moments of tenderness towards her too, and more towards Everina, but regarded them persistently as children rather than equals, and both fostered and resented their dependence on her. She could never make friends of them; they were always her albatrosses, burdensome, irritating and inescapable.

What formal education Mary received was in a day school, in Beverley or a neighbouring village: there was a grammar school with a good library for Ned, but not for the girls. She was spared being set to master the dubious accomplishments of the boarding school miss. In fact she learned little more than reading and writing, but had enough wit to flourish under this sort of neglect; she wrote of village schools later with a glow of enthusiasm that suggests she enjoyed hers. Her religious indoctrination was mercifully deficient too, product of the sleepy Anglicanism of the times: a scolding, an hour or two indoors and some perfunctory talk of hellfire was Mrs Wollstonecraft's not very rigorous way of dealing with sin.

More tedious was the machinery of becoming a woman; the necessity for controlling the hair with pins and the body with whalebone, the mysteries and limitations, discreet laundering, pins, ribbons, cumbersome and vulnerable clothes. Twelve to fourteen was thought the correct age for putting girls on their guard against the opposite sex.[22] Then the easy shifts and petticoats of childhood were supplemented by stays reaching from breast to thigh. If Mary would have preferred her brother's breeches she certainly never said so, but equally she never mentioned so much as a ribbon, a cap or a piece of lace.

Instead, she began to ask for a room of her own, somewhere in which to be herself alone; she would not quite belong to the family even if she could not leave it, as she began to dream of doing; she would think for herself, by herself. She declared that she would never marry for money. She would find something nobler and more absorbing than the way of life her father and mother had attained. She began to notice the condition in which servants and the poor lived, the workhouse children and institutionalized widows who were to be seen in Beverley, where many charitable establishments clustered in the shade of the minster. There are scenes in both her novels that suggest she came into conflict with her parents over the treatment meted out to dependents. The story in *Mary* is dramatic:

> A little girl who attended in the nursery fell sick. Mary paid her great attention; contrary to her wish, she was sent out of the house to her mother, a poor woman, whom necessity obliged to leave her sick child while she earned her daily bread. The poor wretch, in a fit of delirium stabbed herself, and Mary saw her dead body ... and so strongly did it impress itself to her imagination, that every night of her life the bleeding corpse presented itself to her when she first began to slumber ... The impression that this accident made was indelible.[23]

'Contrary to her wish': she was to be reckoned with even if she did not prevail within the family. Of course the episode may be pure invention, but it sounds true, particularly the touch about the nightmares. The pattern was one she came to know well: poverty, motherhood and death juxtaposed, the vulnerable destroyed by those who should most have helped them.

At fifteen, Mary was already a harsh judge of her parents for their social attitudes as well as their personal inadequacies; but they did not altogether destroy her faith in the possibility of domestic happiness: the ideal stayed at the back of her mind, masked for the moment by scorn. And there is no doubt that her family felt something unusual in her. So did Jane: why else keep her letters? But Mary did not know what to do with herself, and no one knew what to do with her. She was avid for life, as her grandfather and father had been, but she did not want to be settled in any way they could imagine for her; and the role of grown-up daughter at home was clearly not going to proceed smoothly.

[2]

Two Sorts of Education

IN 1774, when Mary was fifteen, her father's financial situation forced him to move again. As she wrote to Jane later,

> the good folks of Beverley (like those of most Country towns) were ready to find out their Neighbours' faults, and to animadvert on them; – Many people did not scruple to prognosticate the ruin of the whole family, and the way he went on, justified them for so doing.[1]

Despairing of success as a farmer for the time being at any rate, Mr Wollstonecraft settled the family at Hoxton, just north of his old Primrose Street home; but it was not felt as a homecoming for Mary or her younger sisters and brothers, who did not remember any London acquaintance or family and found themselves suddenly confined to a small suburban terrace house. Ned was better off; he was articled to a lawyer and came home at weekends only, to rule the roost: 'taking particular pleasure in tormenting and humbling me' wrote Mary.[2]

Somehow she had gained the impression that she was entitled to a share in her grandfather's fortune. Her father may have led her to believe this in an endeavour to lay his hands on some of Ned's money; it would explain the later quarrel between the two men. But for the moment it simply meant that she undertook to resign what she imagined was her share of the money to her father in his need, an act of supposed martyrdom that was to rankle.

With nothing congenial in her family, she looked about for new friends. Neighbours welcomed her, in particular an elderly couple called Clare who had no children of their own; he was a retired clergyman with a taste for poetry, so delicate that he almost never left the house, and mildly proud that his physical deformity was supposed to make him resemble Pope. Mrs Clare was active and hospitable, and they were both fond of the companionship of girls. They encouraged Mary to spend her time with them and gave her books to read: probably Milton and Shakespeare, Thomson and Pope, perhaps Johnson's *Rasselas*, with its message of quiet fortitude.

As it happened, it was not only her formal education the Clares took in hand, but also her sentimental education. Another protégé of theirs, Frances Blood – Fanny – had lived in their house for some time and learnt from them some of the accomplishments proper to a young lady: sewing, drawing, a little music, poetry reading and the art of writing a pretty letter. The Clares held up Fanny as a model; but she had left them lately to return to her parents in South London. Mrs Clare offered to take Mary to visit her:

> She was conducted to the door of a small house, but furnished with peculiar neatness and propriety. The first object that caught her sight, was a young woman of slender and elegant form ... busily employed in feeding and managing some children, born of the same parents, but considerably her inferior in age. The impression Mary received from this spectacle was indelible; and, before the interview was concluded, she had taken, in her heart, the vows of eternal friendship.[3]

Thus, according to Godwin, the encounter 'bore a resemblance to the first interview of Werther and Charlotte'. Fanny was eighteen to Mary's sixteen, slim and pretty and set apart from the rest of her family by her manners and talents. Mary could see in her a mirror-image of herself: an eldest daughter, superior to her surroundings, often in charge of a brood of little ones, with an improvident and drunken father (as it turned out) and a mother charming and gentle but quite broken in spirit.

Fanny was a kindred being, but she was also superior, a creature of angelic appearance and goodness. She danced before Mary's eyes with a promise of happiness, exactly as Jane had done before. Fanny's love would make up for the injustices of life at home, and she might even teach Mary to become as perfect as she was. Mary's determination to experience the ideal friendship rushed her into immediate commitment, and at first Fanny seemed eager to fill the role Mary assigned to her: there was a long initial period of discovery and enjoyment, shared enthusiasms, plans to meet whenever they could and teasing by their families over their urgent need to spend time together. What such a friendship meant to Mary we already know; to Fanny it was something much less exclusive and demanding. The fictional account Mary wrote of their relationship telescoped several years into a much shorter time, but it made clear that fairly soon she began to think she was offering her feelings at an unresponsive shrine once again; and while on the one hand she persisted in maintaining that she had found her ideal, on the other she began to complain that her hopes had 'led her to new sorrows, and, as usual, paved the way for disappointment'.[4] Fanny was no more able than Jane to sustain a passionate sentimental relationship of the kind Mary wanted; she found her eagerness greeted with an increasingly cool response. Everina and Eliza became as dear to Fanny as their sister; and there was a further barrier.

Fanny's time with the Clares had underlined the painfulness of her position at home; with them, she had appeared as a young lady, whereas in fact the Bloods were really much poorer than the Wollstonecrafts, often in desperate straits for money. Mr Blood was incapable of finding or at any rate keeping a job; he could not even raise the money to get home to Ireland where he came from. (The idea of Ireland as a refuge from trouble that presented itself to the Wollstonecraft girls on several occasions later seems to have originated with the Blood family's enthusiastic belief that everything would be all right for them once they could get back there.) Dependence on the thoroughly undependable

Mr Blood was a nightmare situation for Fanny, and to escape from such a family she knew only one way: she had to attract a man enough to make him overlook her family's deficiencies.

At the Clares' she had met and fallen in love with a young businessman, Hugh Skeys, who had engaged himself to her on impulse; but now he was frightened of what his parents would think if he married a penniless girl with improvident parents. Fanny's anxieties about the situation left her little to give Mary in return for her devotion.

> Mary was often hurt by the involuntary indifference which these consequences produced. When her friend was all the world to her, she found she was not as necessary to her happiness; and her delicate mind could not bear to obtrude her affection, or receive love as an alms, the offspring of pity.[5]

She coped with the situation by assuming her natural dominance; if she could not be beloved, at least she would be the lover. She told herself that the very strength of her feelings gave her the edge over milder, more conventional people. And since Fanny was one of these mild, conventional people, Mary assumed the position of a chivalrous suitor: she worshipped, but presently she began to condescend too, like a Victorian bridegroom. She realized, for instance, that although she lacked accomplishments she was much cleverer than Fanny. She continued to idealize her; she said she cherished her better than anyone in the world; and she began to make plans for living with her – 'the height of my ambition'.[6] But it was clear that the dream rested on Mary's needs rather than Fanny's real qualities.

All the while the Wollstonecraft family fortunes continued to deteriorate. After two years at Hoxton Mr Wollstonecraft carried his family off once again, this time to Laugharne in Wales, where they were consigned to a farm whilst he spent most of his time in London, 'on business or pleasure' as Mary put it. The separation sharpened her feelings for Fanny – it is easier to idealize by post – and when he decided to bring them back she persuaded her father to take a house at Walworth, near the Bloods, instead of the more familiar northern suburbs. On their return Eliza and Everina were sent to a boarding school in Chelsea, perhaps in the hope of making them more marriageable than Mary. At about that time Ned married, set up house in St Katharine's Dock, began to practise law and detached himself firmly from his family's fortunes. Mary was now eighteen. Her plan to set up similarly with Fanny was not very likely of realization but was at least a distraction from envy of Ned and the prospect of her father's repeated cycle of failures. Once Mary threatened to leave home and was dissuaded by Mrs Wollstonecraft's tears, but then she announced decidedly that she was going to work as a companion to a Mrs Dawson, a widowed lady chiefly resident in Bath and Windsor. She had found the job for herself, probably by consulting the Clares, and she was not going to give up the prospect.

It was an adventure, a way of earning and saving some money for her future with Fanny, and an escape from the oppression of semi-idleness at home; but it was also a brave move for a girl not absolutely obliged to leave home and earn her living. Fanny Burney called the work of a companion 'toad-eating' and painted a horrifying picture of the degradation involved in selling oneself to the bidding of a bad-tempered and ill-mannered rich woman.[7] It meant the loss of freedom and dignity – a paid companion had to swallow her pride before she took up her post; she had to be entertaining on demand and efface herself when not wanted; she was likely to receive insults from servants and be the butt of gentlemanly witticisms, if indeed she ever came across any gentlemen. But Mary was evidently quite prepared; Mrs Dawson had the reputation of a formidable employer, and she regarded this as a challenge to her own temper.

And she made a success of it. When she wrote to Jane, with whom she still corresponded intermittently, she mentioned her earlier sufferings at home but sounded cheerful enough about her current life. She described some of the things that amused her: a coach journey with talkative companions, sea bathing at Southampton, the crowds at Bath, and her own sense of superiority over Mrs Dawson's nieces, who thought of nothing but fashion, a preoccupation Mary despised with the confidence of the deliberately dowdy intellectual woman. She was too discreet to comment in writing on her employer, but aimed her satirical touches where she felt free to do so; for instance, at the old maids of Windsor keeping a sharp eye on the Prince of Wales's taste in girls:

> ... all the damsels set their caps at him, and you would smile to hear how the poor girls he condescends to take notice of are pulled to pieces: – the withered old maids sagaciously hint their fears, and kindly remark that they always thought them forward things: you would suppose a smile or a look of his had something fatal in it, and that maid could not look at him, and remain pure.[8]

To Jane, Mary also wrote lyrically about her feelings for Fanny and plans for the future with her. 'The roses will bloom when there's peace in the breast, and the prospect of living with my Fanny gladdens my heart: – You know not how I love her': perhaps Jane was meant to feel a little jealous. But Fanny herself was pining. Hugh Skeys was now away in Lisbon, increasingly negligent, and her health was beginning to deteriorate. Mary blamed and despised Skeys but profited by his neglect of Fanny to busy herself with her alternative ideas; sometimes these were transformed into accompanying her to Lisbon, but more often she seems to have expected to have her to herself:

> I have now given up every expectation and dependance that would interfere with my determination of spending my time

with her. – I know my resolution may appear a little extraordinary, but in forming it I follow the dictates of reason as well as the bent of my inclination; for tho' I am willing to do what good I can in my generation, yet on many accounts I am averse to any matrimonial tie.[9]

Not all these accounts were to do with Fanny. Mary brooded over what it meant to be the wife as well as the daughter of men such as her father and Mr Blood, and she also seems to have doubted her own ability to attract a husband. There was a good deal of talk in her letters about wrinkles and prematurely aged appearance, as though she had decided to make a virtue out of her ugliness as well as her plain clothes, proudly disclaiming any wish for what she feared she would not be offered.

There were also mysterious references to something that had happened to shock her: 'painful circumstances, which I wish to bury in oblivion'.[10] An anecdote taken from her autobiographical novel, *Maria*, may possibly offer a clue to this remark: a young girl asks a middle-aged lawyer, 'a man of the world, with rosy face and simpering features', to assist her in a charitable exercise, and finds herself being kissed and fondled in return for his help, without understanding what he is about. If something of the sort had happened to Mary it doubtless took on a disproportionate importance in her imagination for a while, and confirmed her suspicion that men were more likely to be predators than supports.

She may have been impressed too, as so many women were, by the elopement of Lady Eleanor Butler with Sarah Ponsonby, in 1779; their behaviour caused a furore of admiration. The strong-minded Lady Eleanor saved her friend from the unwelcome attentions of a male guardian, and the escaping pair set up a temple of friendship for themselves in a Welsh valley, Llangollen Vale; here they received selected visitors in an exquisitely arranged house and garden, and became the envy of many women with no taste for the ordinary arrangements of society. Nobody thought of characterizing their friendship as perverse, in writing at any rate, until the twentieth century. Women of the world knew perfectly well what lesbianism was, but regarded it as a dirty little vice of servant girls, boarding schools and actresses, and did not think of applying it to cultivated women of decent unbringing.* Mothers were warned against allowing their daughters to form such relationships, but they did not associate them with the emotional bonds of friendship; they came into the category of gross behaviour.

So Mary was perfectly easy about her feeling for Fanny, which 'resembled a passion' as she said, and was almost (but not quite) that of an intending husband. She wanted to dominate and monopolize her, and she had begun to feel patronizing towards her. But she also wanted to serve, and not to use her; and at this stage of her life this may well have seemed the crucial difference between men's and women's love.

In spite of these emotions and professions, a certain secret disloyalty to Fanny did take place. It is rather a relief to discover it. In Bath a good-looking young Cambridge don called Joshua Waterhouse found Mary, although a mere lady's companion, piquant enough to embark on a flirtation with her. He was a farmer's son who had attended the university and latched on to a rich young baronet with whom he travelled about to smart resorts. Waterhouse turned out to be vain, cantankerous and snobbish, but initially, at any rate, he and Mary appear to have enjoyed one another's conversation. Her admiration tickled his

* Mrs Piozzi, for instance, spoke freely enough in her diary about the lesbianism of actresses, and the medical manuals written for women, e.g. *The Lady's Dispensatory*, warned mothers against allowing their daughters to be corrupted, with the implication that such corruption was most likely to come from the lower classes.

vanity, and she allowed herself to build some hopes on his interest in her. They embarked on a correspondence.

Her love letters to him were found at the time of his death, many years after hers.* They were destroyed. She never mentioned the affair to Godwin; Waterhouse's character may have been reason enough for wishing to forget that she had dreamed of him as a possible husband, but a more cogent one perhaps was that she preferred to remember herself as entirely devoted to Fanny during these years. In any case, he clearly disappointed her and the correspondence lapsed after a time, though it left her bitter and regretful. In certain moods she expressed to Jane a ferocious rejection of traditional femininity: 'It is a happy thing to be a mere blank, and to be able to pursue one's own whims, where they lead, without having a husband and half a hundred children at hand to teaze and controul a poor woman who wishes to be free.'[11] This is the bitter root of feminism, a determination to reject the other sex, an insistence that one sort of life must be denied if the other were to develop: a woman could not be a free agent and enjoy family life. Later Mary abandoned this position, and specifically rejected it in the *Vindication*, but for the moment she was driven to assert it.

* Waterhouse led an eccentric life: he tried to rig his own election as master of his college, but was driven out and became a miser. He was murdered by a thief in 1827 and a sackful of love letters from various women was found by his nephew, who destroyed them as of no interest. A contemporary report mentions that some were 'ardent' and some 'prudent', and goes on:

'Amongst the many fair ones to whom the singular rector of Stukeley paid his addresses was the once-famous Mary Wollstonecraft, distinguished during the period of the French Revolution for her democratical writing, and afterwards united to Mr Godwin, author of *St Leon*, &c. How far the reverend gentleman sped in his wooing with this intellectual amazon we have not been able to ascertain; but, like all his other attachments, his passion for the author of the *Rights of Women* was destined to evince the truth of the poet's observation, the course of true love never did run smooth.'

Since leaving her own family they had in fact shown little interest in her; and she was hurt by this indifference, as a letter to Eliza from Windsor expressed clearly enough.

You don't do me justice in supposing I seldom think of you – the happiness of my family is nearer my heart than you imagine – perhaps, too near for my own health or peace – For my anxiety preys on me, and is of no use to you. You don't say a word of my mother. I take it for granted that she is well – tho' of late she has not even desired to be remembered to me. Some time or the other, in this world or a better, she may be convinced of my regard – and then may think I deserve not to be thought so harshly of.[12]

The 'better world' was often evoked in Mary's letters when she was depressed, and this one seemed to offer no cheerful prospects to those she loved or indeed to herself. She did not intend to stay with Mrs Dawson for ever, and the problem of what to do next must have obsessed her. It was all very well to speak of pursuing one's own whims: a whim did not provide a living. Jane was now a governess and planning to run a school with her sisters; but Mary had not half their qualifications. The questions that mocked every unprovided and intelligent spinster were before her: what can I do with my life? How can I earn my living in a tolerable way? How can I be independent and respectable? To these questions neither Fanny nor Waterhouse could offer answers.

[3]

Eliza

In the autumn of 1781 the traditional, unpaid labour of a daughter presented itself to Mary again when she was summoned to nurse her ailing mother. The family had moved once more, to Enfield, a Middlesex village some way out of London, and here Mary came to watch over Mrs Wollstonecraft's slow and painful wasting. She died in the spring of 1782 and was buried on the nineteenth of April in the pretty churchyard of St Andrew's.[1] Before her death she had at least the satisfaction of seeing a granddaughter and namesake born to Ned's wife at St Katharine's Dock.[2] And she could feel some pride in her children: Ned, the darling of her heart, established in his profession and marriage; Mary independent but finally dutiful and affectionate; Eliza pretty, Everina and the boys sturdy. She was young to die, only just into her fifties, but had nothing to live for apart from her children: she had been able neither to manage nor combat her husband; she had no profound religious belief to support her, no intellectual capacity or training to occupy her as she aged. Her whole existence had been bound up in her femininity. Mary retained enough tenderness for her mother to dwell on her last words, 'A little patience, and all will be over', and enough residual resentment to write out, five years later, a fictional death-bed scene in which the dying mother is made to apologize for her unfair treatment of her daughter.[3]

Mrs Wollstonecraft's death produced an access of grief and remorse in her husband, but in the nature of things this could not last long. For the moment Eliza and Everina went to Ned and his wife; at twenty-one and eighteen they were expected to help in the house and to find husbands.

James decided to go to sea. Mr Wollstonecraft left Enfield, taking Charles, and went back to Laugharne, where he had kept a farm. Here he spent the rest of his life, and here he probably married his second wife, Lydia.[4] She had no children, and we know little about her but that Mary held her in contempt, using the phrase 'an artful kind of upper servant' about her,[5] and suggesting in a letter to Eliza that it might 'blister the tongue' to name her Mrs Wollstonecraft.[6] But Mary's contempt came easily, and Eliza had a kinder word for Lydia; evidently she did her best to be a good wife.

Mary did not choose to return to Mrs Dawson; instead she went to live with the Bloods at Walham Green, near Fulham, where she spent the next eighteen months. It proved a dreary time. She was living with Fanny at last, but it was no Llangollen Vale dream of friendship and cultural activity. A cramped suburban cottage with too many people crowded into it and not enough money was more like a degraded version of life with the Wollstonecrafts. Mr Blood had to be managed. Mrs Blood was pleasant enough but ignorant, and she and Fanny and Mary would work through the night sometimes at a sewing job to earn a little, till they felt sick and half-blind from stitching. The younger children were not properly educated, Fanny looked ill, and in spite of Mary's remarks to Jane Arden about expecting to go abroad with her, Hugh Skeys seemed ever reluctant to come to the point with Fanny herself, let alone invite her bossy and disapproving friend to join them in Lisbon. Mary had managed to find and read some medical books; she understood enough to realize that Fanny was consumptive and what the outcome of the illness would almost certainly be, but she allowed herself, as most people are apt to do under such circumstances, to know and yet not fully to face the knowledge of the future.

And Fanny was not at all the companion she had hoped for; their minds were not congenial, 'nor did she contribute to her comfort in the degree she expected'.[7] This too was tormenting. Nevertheless, in their poverty and wretchedness, Mary came to identify herself very closely with the whole Blood family, as is clear from her later letters to Fanny's younger brother George, in which she speaks of Mrs Blood as 'our mother'.[8] This identification and fierce championing had its emotional attraction for her, partly no doubt because both Ned and the Skeys family disapproved of the Bloods so much and regarded them as spongers and generally inadequate; and also because she was to them 'the princess'[9] (George's term, which pleased Mary), bringing them help from a superior position and defending them against the accusations of the world. They were her special, pet underdogs, who depended on her.

Six months after Mrs Wollstonecraft's death another family event took place, apparently a more cheerful one: this was Eliza's wedding, in October 1782. Mary was pleased with the marriage in spite of some bitter remarks about the institution in general, and told Jane Arden that Eliza had found 'a worthy man' with a 'truly eligible situation', adding a faintly rueful joke about her younger sister now taking precedence over her as a matron. She did not name the bridegroom or reveal his occupation, possibly for snobbish reasons; none of the sisters ever mentioned it. He was in fact a young boat-builder from Bermondsey across the river from Ned, and his name was Meredith Bishop.[10] Ned evidently approved of the match because he was a witness to the wedding at St Katharine by the Tower on 20 October, when the bridegroom nervously (or perhaps tipsily) signed his name 'Merideth': an arresting slip which the other witness, who was the parish clerk, left alone.[11]

Within a month pretty, ladylike Eliza with her beautiful brown eyes and Chelsea boarding school manners was pregnant. A month later, at Christmas, Mary called on her to borrow £20 from the obliging Meredith to tide the Bloods over the festive season. Perhaps she did not much like what she saw of her brother-in-law on this occasion and prepared to pity Eliza; after a few weeks of marriage, she wrote to Jane Arden, 'the raptures have subsided, and the dear hurry of visiting and figuring away as bride, and all the rest of the delights of matrimony are past and gone and have left no traces behind them, except disgust'.[12]

Meredith however not only lent Mary the money but decided she was a reliable and obliging woman, a decision that probably wrecked his chances of happiness in life for good.

Ten months after the wedding, on 10 August 1783, Eliza gave birth to a daughter who was christened at the age of one week in Bermondsey parish church.[13] There was no question of Eliza herself being allowed up for the ceremony so soon after her delivery, but Mary and Fanny probably came over from Fulham to be godmothers and saw the tiny baby given the names Elizabeth Mary Frances. According to Mary at any rate the child was known as Mary.

During the months after the birth Eliza suffered some sort of breakdown; no one in Bermondsey seemed able to do much to help. The baby was looked after by a nurse, but Meredith had no women in his family to call on to supervise the house, the care of the child or the management of Eliza. By November he was in despair and sent for his sister-in-law.

The winter of 1783 was very cold; there were nine weeks of frost in southern England. Life with the Bloods must have become especially grim and monotonous. Mary answered Meredith's summons immediately and left them, never to return. Instead she involved herself in a painful and complicated drama whose outcome was disastrous in one way or another for everyone concerned in it, except perhaps herself. As far as she was aware at the time, her motives were of the highest, but she may possibly have grown uneasy about what happened later, since she never mentioned the affair to Godwin and we know about it only from letters preserved by Everina.[14]

When Mary arrived at the Bishops' she found Eliza in a severely disturbed state, talking disconnectedly but saying enough to suggest to her sister that she had been very ill-used by her husband. Whether this was a delusion of her breakdown or based on some real grievance is hard to say; Meredith would not have sent for Mary if he had felt too guilty, and most married couples can find some grievances, especially during the first year. Eliza and Meredith were more than likely casualties of their upbringings, she innocent and squeamish, he boorish and crude in his wooing. Mary's remark that 'he can't look beyond the present gratification' suggests a simple explanation for their trouble; if Eliza's sexual experience was confined to inept husbandly assaults, uncomfortable pregnancy and excruciating childbirth, she may have taken refuge from the situation in her breakdown (which never, as far as we know, recurred). It would also help to explain Meredith's alternations of anger and conciliatory gestures.

Mary decided her sister was well enough to be taken out for a coach ride, and then sat down to write to Everina:

> I cannot yet give any certain account of Bess [i.e. Eliza] or form a rational conjecture with respect to the termination of her disorder. She has not had a violent fit of phrenzy since I saw you – but her mind is in a most unsettled state and attending to the constant fluctuations of it is far more harassing than the watching of those raving fits that had not the least tincture of reason.

Her next letter asked anxiously whether Everina also had something preying on her mind, and exhorted her to patience and resignation, as though she too might suddenly go mad. Then Mary inquired whether Ned would consider taking in Eliza; Mary herself was in such a state that she talked of her own brain turning. Should she not ask Ned herself, she wondered, and would Everina please not let him discuss the business with Meredith, 'for it would only put him on his guard, and we should have a storm to encounter that I tremble to think of'. Already it sounded as though she was plotting to counter a male conspiracy with a female one.

Eliza herself now uttered the fatal words 'she had rather be a teacher than stay here'; Mary added, rather surprisingly under the circumstances, that she expected her sister soon to be deprived of her reason. 'B [Bishop] cannot behave properly – and those who attempt to reason with him must be mad or have very little observation. Those who would save Bess must act and not talk.' The baby, cared for and fed by a nurse, seemed an insignificant person at this juncture.

Presently the wretched Bishop fell ill too, after trying to reason with Mary, who had by now, at whatever cost, assumed her usual dominant position over the whole household. She wrote to Everina:

> My spirits are harried with listening to pros and cons, and my head is so confused that I sometimes say no when I ought to say yes. My heart is almost broken with listening to B. while he *reasons* the case. I cannot insult him with advice which he would never have wanted if he was capable of attending to it.

Meanwhile Eliza was in fact recovering, though still very depressed; but she was well enough to receive a visit from Fanny, who was at once drawn into Mary's plan to rescue her sister from her husband.

And so, in a state bordering on hysterical high spirits, Mary crept out of the Bermondsey house, with Eliza but without the baby, during Meredith's absence one day in January. They took a coach into central London and then another to the village of Hackney, far north of the river, where they installed themselves in lodgings under false names – Mary called herself Miss Johnson – and awaited developments.

She had taken on her family before in acts of defiance,

when she left home to work for Mrs Dawson and again to live with the Bloods; but this was her first open and general challenge to the conventions of society. It probably felt like a blow against all tyrannous husbands, against her father and her unloving and bullying brother, against Hugh Skeys who threatened to take Fanny from her but was too craven even to do so, against Mr Blood who gave his wife too many children and failed to support them, against all the men who claimed God-given superiority and enjoyed inheritances, education, professional careers and the right to choose or reject women. There was no thought of asking for help or shelter from Laugharne or, at this stage, from Ned; everything was to be done in defiance of their natural protectors.

All the way across London Eliza in her distress had been biting her wedding ring. Mary's first letter from the Hackney lodgings sounded both terrified and exultant: she asked Everina to apply for Ned's advice on Eliza's legal position. Could she be forced to return? She herself now feared Meredith more than Eliza did, she added.

Left to herself, there seems little doubt that Eliza would have returned to her repentant husband and innocent baby; she was soon sighing for the little creature. 'The poor brat! it had got a hold of my affections; some time or other I hope we shall get it,' said Mary; but she knew the baby was Meredith's trump and prepared to fight him, even though she herself was now ill with swelled legs and a stomach disorder. She and Eliza were both also suffering from an inconvenient shortage of chemises, handkerchiefs and aprons, but all this had to be borne. Ned was to be told that Eliza was 'fixed in her resolution of never returning'.

Having got so far in the drama, Mary's next step was to establish herself, her sister and friend as an independent female community; Fanny could be detached from her family and sell her sketches for a living, and Ned might after all be persuaded to provide furniture if he did not take refuge in his customary 'prudence'. But Ned was obviously furious about Mary's intervention in the Bishops' marriage; and he had further distractions. His wife had just given birth to a son, yet another Edward, in September, so he was perhaps even less inclined than usual to give away his inherited household goods.

Fanny knew perfectly well that Ned disapproved of her and her family, and she wrote an anxious letter pointing out the practical difficulties of Mary's plan and stressing her own reluctance to be a nuisance to anyone. Her suggestion was that Ned might set up his sisters in a small shop. Mr Blood now also intervened with an invitation to Mary, Eliza and the baby to share his humble home. But it was impossible to imagine them all crammed in with the Bloods, and his moods were not always so expansive and generous as his offer suggested. Mrs Clare, offering her advice, backed Fanny's plan for a shop, called on Mary in Hackney and expressed cautious approval of her action in regard to Eliza so far, but she wound up by saying a reconciliation with Meredith and return home must be the eventual solution. Mary's tone to Everina began to grow significantly fiercer when friends criticized:

> I knew I should be the Mrs Brown The *shameful incendiary* in this shocking affair of a woman leaving her bed-fellow ... In short 'tis contrary to all the rules of conduct that are published for the benefit of new married Ladies by whose advice Mrs Brook was actuated when she with grief of heart gave up my friendship.

Whatever the cost in disapproval, she was determined to remain in control of the situation and impose her will on everyone else. When Meredith showed signs of turning nasty she grew more cheerful, because it spared her feeling sympathetic towards him. She wrote to Everina carefully explaining that she felt 'some pain in acting with firmness, for I hold the marriage vow sacred'. It was a surprising statement at this stage, and probably intended for Ned's eyes, but his furious disapproval did not waver.

Fanny sent for news of the baby but was given none; no doubt by now Meredith had hired a whole troop of nurses. Mary wondered whether to go to Ireland to run either a shop or a school. The nights were freezing and by day it rained steadily.

This state of affairs – cold weather, uncomfortable lodgings, increasing disapproval and uncertainty over the future – continued into February. Eliza never went home to Bermondsey and almost certainly never saw her little daughter again. No one has ever thought to ask what happened to Elizabeth Mary Frances Bishop, but we need only turn to the pages of the parish register for St Mary Magdalene, Bermondsey, to find out. On 4 August 1784, just before her first birthday, she was buried in a vault in the churchyard. Her funeral was an exceptionally fine one, her father paying ten shillings and tenpence for the coffin, shroud and dues, whereas the normal rate for a Bermondsey baby was only three and tenpence.[15]

Whatever feelings of guilt and unhappiness Mary and Eliza suffered at that moment are not recorded. Thereafter Mary alternated between maternal and protective feelings for her sister and exasperation at her infuriating characteristics: she accused her of snobbery, and of a tendency to 'turn up her nose and ridicule'. When Eliza complained, Mary reminded her that her lot could have been worse. Later, when Mary was thinking of sending her sisters to America, she so far forgot Eliza's married though separated state as to discuss the probability of her finding a husband in the United States. But Eliza did not forget, and her later bitterness and sarcasm about Mary must be attributable to her having helped to destroy her marriage before it had a chance to establish itself, and in so doing deprive her of the child she bore and the possibility of ever bearing any more. It is even likely that Mary's own daughter Fanny Imlay suffered the last effects of the incident, when her aunts refused to have her to live with them in Ireland many years later. Why should Mary's brat be succoured when Eliza's had been left to die?

[4]

Newington Green and the Dissenters

For Eliza and her small family, the events of the winter were a disaster; for Mary there was a compensation. They enabled her to escape from the dead end she had worked into with the Bloods. The last two years had seen her trapped by her affection for Fanny and the entire family's dependence on her; all she had gained from the experience in return was an insight into the way in which poor women, clinging to respectability by taking in work at home, were paid at starvation rates and crushed in health and spirit. It was enough to ensure that she would neither return to the Bloods nor let Fanny remain at home longer than could be helped. But money was running out, she and Eliza could not stay idle in lodgings much longer, and the male members of the various families were ready to pounce and force a simple, humiliating conclusion if she showed signs of distress or wavering. That was out of the question. In February she announced decisively that she and Eliza and Fanny were going to keep a school together.

The decision was to involve her in two more years of unhappiness and exhaustion, punctuated by further tragedies, but she began to plan with her usual energy and, under the circumstances, a remarkably cool head. Her companions were not in a state to be of much help, and from the start she was the only real driving force in the household of women. She had to borrow money to begin with, as well as to find rent and furnish a house with the basic necessities for a school. Since neither Ned nor Mr Wollstonecraft, who did not offer to intervene in his daughters' troubles, were likely candidates for a loan, she must have persuaded someone else to put up the money: possibly the Clares, who were concerned for their girls, and conveniently near at hand at Hoxton.

They may have helped in the house hunting too; the first place Mary decided on was at Islington, and for a few bad weeks pupils were awaited there in vain. There were too many would-be teachers about; because teaching required no qualifications and even less capital than shopkeeping – the very thing that made it attractive to Mary – it had become the traditional last resort of the penniless.* And like most others who put up optimistic boards announcing 'An Academy' or 'Young Ladies Educated', Mary had no vocation, no theories of child care, no special liking for children even: they were luxuries she could not yet afford. Still her mind was made up. Threatened failure, mounting debts, and the nervousness of Fanny and Eliza only emphasized her sense of responsibility as head of the enterprise; she was now as intent as a queen bee, determined at all costs to establish her group of frail dependants somewhere and renew their strength, if possible, from her own.

As soon as she realized that the prospects at Islington were hopeless, she prepared to move again. She heard of a better possibility, not far away, at Newington Green; a large house was standing empty and a few pupils actually guaranteed. Everything was bundled up once more, and Everina, who could not get on with Ned and his wife, came to join the venture too. They plunged at once into a routine of daily lessons with the girls available, grateful for all comers. Most were day pupils; nothing sophisticated could be offered in the way of instruction, but Fanny could teach drawing and sewing, and Eliza and Everina hopefully pass on whatever expertise their Chelsea boarding school had given them. They could all cope with reading, writing and

* Wendeborn, a German observer of English life in the 1780s noted how many schools were set up by failed tradesmen, or 'a woman, who never had a proper education herself, or whose moral character cannot very well bear a strict enquiry'.

nature study. Mary had to organize as well as teach; maids and cook had to be given orders, timetables arranged, bills paid and sent out. She managed after a fashion, and she looked around the district and even began to make friends.

Newington Green was a village south of Hackney and east of Islington, a leafy suburb far enough from the City to offer the pleasures of country life without being comatose. The Green itself was bordered by trees, and the trees sheltered solid, handsome houses, one of which was Mary's school. It had the air of a propitious place. Ever since Defoe had lived at Newington a hundred years earlier it had attracted dissident intellectuals, pedagogues with reforming ideas and Dissenters. From her windows Mary could see both the Dissenting chapel and the home of its minister, Dr Richard Price, a man famous far beyond the confines of his own village.

She was soon introduced to him. He was the first radical intellectual she had encountered in her life: a small, bewigged man in black whose prim and dusty air concealed an intense idealism outrageous to his political opponents. In his presence, the words Whig, democrat and reformer began to take on flesh for her. As a political theorist he had favoured the American rebels and had been courted by the Whig politicians of England; he claimed that his primary concern was always with theology and ministering to his congregation, but he had devoted himself to agitating for parliamentary reform during the Seventies, and indeed written enough on the subject to fire the enthusiasm of many younger reformers: 'levelling republican principles' were what Tory churchmen suspected him of.[1]

Price was in correspondence with the most eminent scientists and philosophers of his day, in England, France and America – men such as Franklin, Jefferson, Condorcet and Joseph Priestley, a fellow-Dissenter – and was looked to with respect by all who were not too blinkered by religious or political prejudice. But he remained an unpretentious man, and when Mary met him he was in fact in a subdued and quiescent state. He was in his sixties; the recent death of his closest friend and neighbour at Newington, James Burgh, a writer and schoolmaster who had worked with him for reform, had upset him badly, and the failing health of his wife was imposing limitations on his activities. Lately he had turned down both an invitation from the newly established American government to settle in the United States and another from Lord Shelburne, on becoming head of the English government in 1782, to become his private secretary.[2]

As a neighbour, he was kind and particularly responsive to the young, the vulnerable and those in difficulties. He always had time for children and there were many stories current concerning his humanity to animals that must have appealed to Mary: he was said to free netted birds when he found them on his long country walks, and set upturned beetles carefully back on their legs. This was exactly the sort of quixotic goodness she liked, and though as an Anglican she was not officially one of his flock, it made no difference to his interest in her or her response to him. The opportunity to hear him preach was not to be missed, and she began to attend his chapel as often as her own church on Sundays.

A network of men and women with ideas and ambitions a little outside the common run clustered about Price; Mary found herself made welcome on the Green by many Dissenting households. They included the large family of the banker Thomas Rogers, whose son Samuel was a poet – 'the Poet' Mary called him – and much under Price's influence politically.* Then there was the widow of James Burgh, an

* Sam Rogers was twenty at this time; his fame as a poet later led him to be offered the laureateship by Queen Victoria, in 1850, when he was eighty-seven. According to tradition in Newington, he sat in the pew adjoining Mary's when she attended the chapel, but in his respectable old age he was not inclined to include this amongst his pleasant memories.

energetic and cultivated woman who took it upon herself to be particularly helpful to Mary; she was seconded by another schoolmaster's widow, a Mrs Cockburn. Yet another family on the Green offered Fanny's younger brother George a job, at the request of the Clares, and George became something of a pet for Mary, uneducated and unsteady as he was. He worshipped her, and she found it easy to lavish uncritical affection on him in return.

There was none of the usual village domination of squire or parson at Newington, but a more equal sort of society in which Mary, her sisters and Fanny could take their place with some dignity. Still, in any village day-to-day life is largely a matter of petty interests, quiet friendships, small irritations; if it is to be enjoyable there must be the temperament and the leisure to relish small change and a jog-trot pace. But Mary's temperament was geared to drama, violent emotion and struggle: when she was angry with Mrs Cockburn it was (temporarily) a boiling hatred; when she defended George from attack it was without reservation. She had no capacity for nuance or irony; and then she was always busy, too busy to pause and smile. The foreground of her attention was filled with cares that demanded constant exertion: the running of the school, the ever-pressing problem of money. The Blood family as a whole remained a drain on her from the other side of London; she had responded indignantly to Ned's warnings about their spongeing, but there was no doubt that the parents clung to her and had lost any inclination to help themselves. Throughout her time at Newington she had the steady burden of providing them with money, and she was never able to afford it.

A few more pupils arrived. Seeing how things were, Mrs Burgh pointed out that the house was far too big for its inmates, and suggested that the gaps might as well be filled with lodgers, who would at least contribute to the rent and the servants' wages. Mary had not imagined herself as a lodging-house keeper, but she was in no position to be anything but grateful for the proposal, and Mrs Burgh triumphantly produced a friend who needed rooms, and installed her with her three children. This was a Mrs Disney, almost certainly connected with more Dissenting females: John Disney was a Cambridge clergyman who left the established church in 1782 to join his brother-in-law Theophilus Lindsey, founder of the Unitarian chapel at Essex Street, close to Newington.

Mary did her best as a landlady; as a schoolmistress she was a failure. Her letters, which discuss neighbours, callers, servants and lodgers freely enough, do not mention so much as the name of a pupil, although the ideas she had begun to acquire about education, filtered down from Rousseau and Thomas Day,* required close and constant supervision of each child. It was an approach that must have had its difficulties in a newly and uncertainly established school, and was perhaps more likely to lead to exasperation and frustration than any short-term success.

When Everina and Eliza ran a school together in Dublin much later, Eliza was regarded with great affection by her small pupils, who remembered her gentleness and sugarplums for years, but Everina had the reputation of a tartar: judging from Mary's own account of an ideal teacher in her *Original Stories,* she came closer to Everina. She might have dispensed justice, one feels, but never sugar-plums, unless they were intended to demonstrate the ill effects of gluttony.

Even where pupils were not in question, the atmosphere of the house was uncertain. Eliza pined for her baby through the spring and summer, and mourned her after her death. Fanny's illness made her listless by day, and in the evenings put her into a state of febrile gaiety that seemed inappropriate to Mary. Everina was beginning to establish her lifelong

* Thomas Day was an old resident of the Green; his *Sandford and Merton* began to appear in the Eighties, and his educational ideas, with their emphasis on character training, impressed Mary very much.

reputation for shortness of temper. Privacy was lacking, as always in villages and institutional houses; everyone knows who calls on whom, who has quarrelled, who is in love, who is slighted. The kindest neighbours are not above treating one another as peepshows. When Mary received calls, as she began to, from local schoolmasters and clergymen who were disposed to admire her intelligence and battling spirit, it was observed. When she wished to talk on what she called rational subjects, she found the track of the conversation lost in the chatter of the other women of her household, drawn like steel filings to the room where the magnetic male presence was lodged. There were times when Fanny, her sisters and her lodgers all appeared quite simply as a crew of infuriating distractions and liabilities.

Very occasionally she got away. A young schoolmaster called John Hewlett, who kept his establishment at Shacklewell near by and had ambitions to become a writer, found her interesting enough to carry her off early in her first summer at Newington to visit the great Dr Johnson, who was staying at Islington in the hope that the clean air of the suburbs might mend his health. Johnson was impressed by her conversation too, so much so that he invited her to visit him again. During this last year of his life, when he was seventy-four, he enjoyed the company of argumentative young women and liked to tease them, as old men often do. Boswell does not mention Hewlett or Mary, but records several other spirited conversations with women: 'Women have a perpetual envy of our vices; they are less vicious than we are, not from choice, but because we restrict them' the doctor informed the daughter of an Oxford friend shortly after his stay in Islington; he may have tried the idea out on Mary. But as it turned out she was more interested in Dr Price on natural virtue than Dr Johnson on natural vice. The two men had deeply opposed views on most subjects, and it was Price who won and kept her allegiance. She never saw Johnson again; by the time he returned to London he was too ill for callers, and he died in December 1784. She cherished the memory of meeting him, but turned decidedly against his view of life.

Mary wanted to believe that individual willpower and energy could better the state of the world, and that human nature was improving, as Price and his friends thought. It seemed to her far preferable to hope that men might grow less vicious as the circumstances of their lives grew gentler, rather than accept that women were given an appearance of virtue only by the crack of the whip; and both the example and the stated beliefs of the Dissenters who surrounded her on the Green encouraged her in this optimistic view. Rational Dissenters, or Unitarians, worshipped reason and Locke; they represented the critical and sceptical tradition of protestantism without its black insistence on guilt.* They had thrown out the doctrine of the Trinity, the idea of original sin and the concept of eternal punishment, explaining them all as purely poetic myths. James Burgh's book *The Dignity of Human Nature* breathed the spirit of prudent optimism in which they were inclined to view this world and the next.[3]

There was a blend of enthusiasm and gravity about the Rational Dissenters that was congenial to Mary; they were domestic, sober in the strict sense, hard-working, humane, respectful to their womenfolk. Whatever cynicism she had picked up earlier about the relations of the sexes was softened a little at Newington, where she began to hear the names of Dissenting women writers who were not afraid to tackle a variety of subjects: Ann Jebb, the wife of Price's friend and fellow reformer John Jebb, who wrote political articles for the press,[4] and Anna Barbauld, daughter of the

* This particular brand of nonconformity was something quite distinct from Methodism, of which Price thoroughly disapproved, describing it as a faith that ascribed 'particular feelings, without reason, to supernatural suggestion'.

Dissenting Doctor Aikin, was a successful poet and educational writer. Mrs Burgh too, though her husband had preached the essential inferiority of women and the necessity of obedience to husbands, was a living example of a strong-minded and independent widow who could cope with life and deal with men on equal terms where practical matters were concerned.

This provided an undercurrent of inspiration and hope for Mary even if it did not have very much effect on the continuous anxieties and problems of her day-to-day life. She knew that her own energy and willpower were the only things that kept the household going, and that the prospect of the school paying its way remained distant, but she could at least dream of becoming an intellectual woman.

Fanny's health was growing steadily worse; the winter of 1784 threatened to bring as much distress as its predecessor. Then, providentially, Hugh Skeys made up his mind to summon her to Lisbon for the wedding. What prodded him to action after so many years is mysterious; it may have been Mary's persuasion.

Fanny set off in January. In her sickness she had become increasingly difficult, and it was a relief to see her going to a better climate, but Mary missed her and feared for her once she was gone. This was indeed the end of the dream she had lived with for seven years; at least half the point of setting up the school had been that she and Fanny should live together. 'I could as soon fly as open my heart to Eliza or Everina' she wrote; and 'without someone to love this world is a desert'.[5]

The question of whom she might reasonably love was a difficult one. Soon after Fanny's departure, George also set off hastily for Ireland. He had abandoned his job without giving proper notice because he was accused, not for the first time, of fathering a child: Newington Green begins to look less and less like a Jane Austen village and more and more like a corner of Hogarth's world as one reads on in Mary's letters. The pregnant servant girl who accused George was more probably the victim of her employer, said Mary; but the Clares fussed lest their good name should become involved in this deplorable business, gossip proliferated, and Mary was obliged to 'assume the Princess', she wrote to George, when faced with rudeness from local busybodies. At least her sisters and the Poet shared her faith in George's innocence of paternity.

Deprived of Fanny, and determined in her defence of George, she wrote him a series of tender letters, using him as her confidant. Her mind was harassed, she said, her heart broken, and she often wanted to die. In her illness, she had herself bled and blistered, neither process likely to raise depressed spirits.* Another blow fell when Mason, a favourite maid, had to leave. The Green had become a Deserted Village, she lamented, and her description of her state of mind did at times sound like that of someone about to break down altogether: 'my heart sometimes overflows with tenderness – and at other times seems quite exhausted and incapable of being warmly interested about anyone.'[6]

Not all her grief was for Fanny, or her remorse for Eliza. There was trouble over several men too. What she thought of as tendrils of affection could evidently look like tentacles to those at the receiving end. She had grown fond of the clever and attractive John Hewlett, who was only three years her junior; there were many mentions of his kindness in her letters, and alongside one the wistful remarks that she knew herself to be 'too apt to be attached with a degree of warmth that is not consistent with a probationary state, as I have learned on earth and have been *sorely hurt*'. Several times she compared Hewlett with Rousseau, whom

* They were the two standard all-purpose medical procedures at the time nevertheless: one involved drawing blood from a vein in the arm, and usually produced fainting; the other meant the application of scalding cups to the skin.

she had begun to read and worship. When Hewlett married, she burst into a series of acid remarks about his wife – 'how he is yoked!' and so on; but he himself seems to have been perfectly satisfied with his choice, and only poor Mary suffered on his behalf.

Another man mentioned in her letters to George was Neptune Blood, a cousin of her Bloods;[7] of him she says, 'perhaps I was as much to blame for expecting too much as he in doing too little – I looked for what was not to be found'. Then a Mr Church, a frequent caller during her first year on the Green, disappointed her too; he hardly came any more, offered Mary his opinion that she would never thrive in this world, and earned from her the description 'prudent Church' (although he lent her money). 'Prudent' was always one of her favourite terms of disparagement, often applied to her brother Ned, but there is no doubt that her own over-enthusiastic behaviour was sometimes responsible for an access of prudence in others. She remained baffled and hurt by her inability to find the ardently responsive friends or lovers she dreamed of.

Fanny's letters from Lisbon were less than ecstatic about married life. Advanced tuberculosis did not prevent her from becoming pregnant immediately, and it was not comfortable to be dying and breeding at the same time under the sun of Portugal. The expected confinement was referred to only as 'a certain occasion' but loomed dreadfully in her and Mary's minds. Mary decided to go out to Lisbon. Skeys, whom she again castigated as ungenerous and conceited, was not consulted and she had to find the money for her passage. Mrs Burgh, learning of the problem, produced the fare for her and urged her to go; Mary suspected the money came from Dr Price, and prepared to set off with such encouragement. Mrs Cockburn, on the other hand, advised her not to go and even warned some prospective lodgers to keep clear; and from a practical point of view she may have been right, because Mary's presence was essential to keep things running even tolerably well in her household. As soon as she had gone Eliza and Everina quarrelled and were quite unable to manage either the school or the lodgers.

The voyage to Lisbon in late November would have been wholly unpleasant to anyone without Mary's passion for travel, but she had her father's love of moving on, and treated the condition on board as a challenge:

> We were only thirteen days at sea. The wind was so high and the sea so boisterous the water came in at the cabin windows, and the ship rolled about in such a manner it was dangerous to stir.[8]

Mary stirred constantly. Her fellow travellers were a sea-sick woman and a consumptive man,

> so opprest by his complaints that I never expected he would live to see Lisbon – I have supported him hours together gasping for breath, and at night if I had been inclined to sleep his dreadful cough would have kept me awake.[9]

It was a cruel enough reminder of what she was travelling towards, but she rose to the occasion and spent thirteen days and sleepless nights nursing. Evidently there was a rewarding side to this devotion, since she used her experience of tending a feverish man as the basis for a mildly erotic episode in her first novel.

Once the ship docked at Lisbon she forgot everything but Fanny, and when she arrived at her bedside she found her already in labour. It was obvious that she was past any help. Dismissed from the room where the double process of birth and death was struggling to complete itself, Mary tried to assume a religious resignation that did not come easily to her. She sat down to write to Eliza about Fanny, carefully avoiding any words that might seem 'like signing her death warrant'.[10]

A moment of hope came when the baby was born, frail but miraculously alive, and had to be found a wet-nurse. But within days first Fanny and then the child too were indeed dead; its life was of so little moment that Mary did not say whether it had been a boy or a girl.

Mary's passionate love for Fanny, which had long since settled into a lesser, protective emotion, now flared up again; she could be restored to her position as ideal romantic friend and mourned with bitter sincerity. Mary and Skeys were drawn together for the first time in their common grief, and revised their views of one another after so many years of hostility: perhaps they both now realized they had more in common in their relationships with Fanny than they could acknowledge.

Mary stayed on in Lisbon for several weeks, looking about with an intolerant eye at the Portuguese and English society, nuns and colonial-style ladies, neither to her taste. She and Skeys became lasting friends; but she had to return to her school, and she set off again in the New Year of 1786.

This time her passage was longer, stormier and still more dramatic. At one point she took it on herself to force the reluctant captain to take aboard some French sailors whose own ship was in trouble. She was rightly proud of her strength of character on this occasion: sea-captains are not notorious for listening to a woman's bidding. They did not reach London again until February, and her first sight of her home town was as grim as anything she had seen in Portugal or at sea: the dockland prostitutes falling upon the sailors like so many birds of prey, a scene of 'complicated misery' that a young woman of her background should have affected not to notice at all. It impressed itself upon her and was not forgotten.

She had been rushed through too many emotions and exhausting experiences in too short a time; but there was to be no relaxation at Newington. The school had dwindled in her absence almost to nothing, while her sisters quarrelled both with one another and with the lodgers. Mrs Disney left, disputing her bill and leaving it unpaid. Mary wrote to George that she was in extreme distress for money, and could therefore no longer help the Blood parents. She added that her eyesight was impaired – she took to wearing glasses – and her memory gone, and, once again, she hoped to die.

At this moment Ned disclaimed responsibility for any of his sisters: they had chosen to defy him, and they must bear the consequences. George wrote suggesting that Mary should flee her creditors and join him in Ireland, and she did wonder again whether to try to set up a school in Dublin. But she rejected the idea in favour of a better one of her own: she would send the Blood parents across, so that George could take over responsibility for them.

And in spite of her own desperate and deteriorating situation, she came up with one of her bursts of energy and inventiveness, and produced within weeks the £10 necessary for shipping Mr and Mrs Blood across the Bristol channel. The sum was an advance on a book, and it came from a friend of John Hewlett's, a publisher called Joseph Johnson, of St Paul's Churchyard. Johnson was another Dissenter with radical leanings who had published some of James Burgh's works, and who had a special interest in educational books. He was to become the most important man in her life, but for the moment Mary viewed him rather condescendingly, as a tradesman and a useful person to know. His money however solved one of her problems, and his acceptance of her manuscript encouraged her in the hope she might one day make a career as a writer.

Like almost all her subsequent books, *Thoughts on the Education of Daughters* was written at high speed. It may well have been inspired in part by James Burgh's copious educational writings, which took small account of girls but did at least acknowledge the importance of encouraging them in rationality.[11] It is easy enough to imagine Mrs

Burgh urging Mary to fill in a few gaps left by her late husband. Mary's tone in her book fluctuated in a way that suggests there may have been some conflict in her own mind as to whether she represented the Dissenting tradition or the school of Rousseau and Day. On the one hand she adopted a deliberately severe pose over such matters as cosmetics, hair powder, card-playing and the theatre, and added that it was better for girls not to marry young (announcing for good measure that it was 'sufficient for women to receive caresses, not to bestow them'). On the other, she held forth against the bad effects of teaching by rote, and premature Bible reading: better to read animal stories, she said, recommending one called *The Perambulations of a Mouse*.

A striking omission from her book, as from her letters, was any mention of her own pupils. There were plenty of personal references, but they were almost all to herself. She never could write without inserting more or less veiled remarks about her own emotional state, and though they read a little curiously in the middle of an educational manual, they make it abundantly clear that she was far more interested in the state of her own life and the prospects that lay ahead of young women than in their years at school.

Burgh had not thought it necessary to mention the subject of female employment at all, but it is the one point in Mary's book in which her arguments take fire. In the case of men, Mary said, 'if they have a tolerable understanding, it has a chance to be cultivated', but not so with women; and then, 'few are the modes of earning a subsistence, and those very humiliating'. They were listed: companion, schoolteacher, governess, and a few trades which were 'gradually falling into the hands of men, and are certainly not very respectable'. Probably she meant occupations such as hairdressing, millinery, mantua-making, midwifery and dentistry; all were undertaken by women, especially if they were the widows of men who had practised them, but none would have been considered suitable for someone of Mary's background. Governesses, she pointed out, had nothing to live on when they grew old unless 'perhaps on some extraordinary occasion, some small allowance may be made for them, which is thought a great charity'. Schoolteachers might scrape together some money by taking on too many pupils if they had the chance but, as she knew full well, they would be lucky if they did.

She had established the facts, which were indeed to be taken up and insisted on by many more writers after her;[12] she was the first to state what came to seem obvious – then she collapsed. She had not yet learnt the courage of her anger; she fell into religious platitudes and spoke of the good that arose necessarily from the trials of life; the main business of existence after all was to learn virtue, not to have an interesting or well-paid job. She even called one chapter 'The Benefits which arise from Disappoinments' (*sic*). And it was also during this period that she wrote a letter in which she volunteered that she was trying 'to do my duty in that station in which Providence has placed me',[13] the most conventional and cowed remark she ever made. Had such Christian resignation prevailed with her there would have been no *Vindication*, but luckily she continued to find difficulty in accepting what Providence had to offer.

For the moment there was nothing very pleasant in store, apart from her book's acceptance. In May the Blood parents left, and soon Mr Blood wrote pressing Mary to join his household once again. Her answering letter went to George, declining the offer; although she loved Mrs Blood, she 'could not live with your father and condescend to practise those arts which are necessary to keep him in temper'.[14]

Everina and Eliza were trying to find jobs as teachers or companions; Mary, her 'debts haunting her like furies', was preparing to sell the furniture and take a small, cheap lodging with no servant at all, and try to keep on a handful of pupils. Presently – miserable defeat – Everina went back to Ned, who relented just enough to allow that. Mrs Cockburn took in Mary and Eliza, and Mrs Burgh found Eliza a teaching post in Leicestershire. Now that the worst had happened and the physical presence of her sisters was removed, Mary's spirits rose slightly again; anticipation had been more horrible than the event. And a job was being found for her by her friends – only she needed French for it, and started wrestling anxiously with the language which she did not know at all.

She was going to Ireland after all, neither to the Bloods nor to run a school in Dublin, but to be governess to the daughters of Robert, Viscount Kingsborough, heir to an earldom and master of many thousands of Irish acres and peasants.

It was a world of which she had no experience, and she considered it with a mixture of exhilaration and nervousness. She wrote to George that she was short of clothes and asked him to send her some material; her old maid Mason came to help her make a greatcoat, and Mrs Cockburn gave her a blue hat. Weeks passed in a frenzy of dressmaking and French verbs; and she was still teaching eleven pupils in August. In September she had her last recorded contact with her elder brother: 'Edward behaved very rude to me and has not assisted me in the smallest degree' she told Eliza in a letter.[15] At the same time she mentioned the particular friendliness of Dr Price; his wife was dying, but he still had time to think of Mary's welfare. The contrast between the kindness shown by most of her Dissenting friends and the indifference or hostility of her own family was not lost on her during those last weeks at Newington.

She was never tempted to abandon her comfortable and easy-going Anglicanism for Dr Price's faith, nor was he interested in making converts: his own wife had remained an Anglican throughout thirty years of devoted marriage. But Mary learnt a great deal from Dr Price all the same; he had set her on certain paths and prepared her to think critically about society. The actual position of the Dissenters, excluded as a class from education and civil rights by a lazy-minded majority, was something for an embryonic feminist to brood on. Later, she was to draw a direct comparison between the disabilities of women and those of Dissenters, and attribute the character defects of both groups to the oppression they had to endure.[16] There can be no doubt that she identified with them, and that their views on human rights and equality of opportunity encouraged her to think of her own sex and its problems in the same light. Although she did not become a Dissenter, she learnt from them some of the ways of dissent.

The Dissenters in fact had turned their disabilities to good purpose; debarred from the universities, for instance, they had set up their own academies which proved markedly superior to anything Oxford or Cambridge had to offer: in particular, and alone, they taught history, science and economics, suggested a critical approach to the text of the Bible and encouraged speculative thought and debate on points of religion. A true intelligentsia was developed through the academies at Warrington, Daventry, Northampton, Hoxton and later Hackney; a great many of Mary's later friends and acquaintances were to come from them. They were indeed nurseries for revolutionaries, turning out students trained to approach all subjects with a critical rather than a reverent eye, and consider institutions on their merits rather than the authority they derived from tradition. The Dissenting parliamentary reformers derived their democratic ideas from the concept of God-given rights, the principle of the greatest happiness of the greatest number (Priestley's before it was Bentham's) and the more basic proposition that all taxpayers should have a say in their own government. James Burgh had laid particular stress on this point, and his last work, *Political Disquisitions*, had led Wilkes to introduce the idea of universal male suffrage in his reform project in 1776; in the same year Price's *Observations on Civil Liberty* had proposed the abolition of the House of Lords as well.

Mary would return to London to take up all these ideas and more, but for the moment she had to leave Dr Price's circle for outer darkness. It had been arranged that she should join the brothers of her future charges at Eton, where the boys were at school, and travel to Ireland with them. Although she had old friends from her Windsor days to stay with – their name was Prior and he was a master at Eton – she looked around sourly at the company of 'witlings' she found there, and dismissed the conversation of the masters and their wives as shallow and frivolous after what she had been lately used to. 'Puns fly about like crackers' she noted disapprovingly; if this was the atmosphere in which the sons of the rich, future members for parliament and lords were brought up, so much the worse for the country. Her experience of high-minded and plain-living Dissenting life had equipped her with the Dissenting brand of snobbery too, which looked down on the manners of social superiors. 'There is not only most virtue, and most happiness, but even true politeness, in the middle classes of life,'[17] was a dictum Mary was prepared to subscribe to even before she arrived at Lord Kingsborough's; an understandable and almost certainly justified attitude, but not the easiest state of mind in which to approach her new job.

She remained at Eton, disapproving, for longer than had been expected, because of delays and muddles over the arrangements for her journey, and in the end she made the crossing to Ireland alone. On the boat she had a small adventure that cheered her up; she met a young clergyman who, like her, was going over to be a tutor in an aristocratic family. His name was Henry Gabell, and he was a future headmaster of Winchester and teacher of Thomas Arnold;[18] for the moment, however, he was nothing more than a good-looking young man who fell into enthusiastic religious chat with Mary. He did not feel obliged to mention – why should he? – that he was already engaged to be married; and Mary, who knew only too well how ready she was to form sudden and imprudent attachments which ended in disappointment, was charmed by him. They agreed to correspond and hoped to meet again in Dublin should his employers visit town at the same time as the Kingsboroughs. And with this prospect at least to look forward to, Mary arrived in Ireland.

[5]

Ireland

In Dublin Mary parted from Henry Gabell, with a promise to exchange letters, and was greeted by the Kingsborough's butler, whom they had sent, with great civility, to escort her on the last part of her journey. Mitchelstown Castle was 120 miles to the south, and the coach journey was something of an ordeal, given the state of Irish roads and inns and the November weather. Wrapped in her home-made greatcoat and with her blue hat on her head, she braced herself for her reception at what she called the 'Bastille': it was in fact a newly built Palladian house.

Mary's self-pity, always liable to swell to huge proportions, was never so indulged as during her stay with the Kingsboroughs; but, upheld by a consciousness of moral superiority, she was rarely in danger of succumbing to despair. There are even moments when some sympathy for her employers is added to the pity we feel for her. It was a complicated ordeal for all concerned, the first battle on record in which a governess emerged with at least equal honours from the field and revenged herself in print, instead of being simply crushed and swept aside.

A governess's position was undoubtedly awkward and lonely, the treatment handed out to her reflecting the ambiguity of her employers' expectations. She was neither servant nor one of the family. Ideally, she would be a well-bred girl whose father had suffered financial disaster, putting her thereby at the disposition of those upper-class households where a little assistance might be needed in bringing up younger and more fortunate daughters; but since it was not always easy to find a ready supply of suddenly impoverished young ladies, many governesses were less perfect than they ought to have been. Lord Palmerston, for instance, considered it entirely appropriate to obtain a position as governess for his cast-off mistress, and she found that her charges' father felt free to make automatic advances to her.[1] In fiction, the governess was always as yet a subsidiary character, often morally equivocal in her role. Occasionally, in life, she edged forward: Lord Halifax, posted to Dublin as Lord-Lieutenant, decided to take his daughter's governess with him as his proclaimed mistress, breaking off the prospect of an advantageous second marriage to do so, though not of course going so far as to marry the governess.

Mary, with her unsullied reputation and respectable references, scarcely expected trouble (or success) of that kind. Her misgivings related to the loss of freedom and friends, the sense of going into exile and isolation with almost nothing by way of compensation. At one time, it is true, she had longed to visit Ireland, and professed to know and admire the Irish character; while she was living with the Bloods in 1782 she had written to Jane:

> ... of all places in the world, I long to visit Ireland and in particular the dear County of Clare – The women are all handsome, and the men agreeable; – I honor their hospitality and doat on their freedom and ease, in short they are the people after my own heart – I like their warmth of Temper, and if I was my own mistress I would spend my life with them: – However, as a friend, I would give you a caution, the men are dreadful flirts, so take care of your heart, and don't leave it in one of the Bogs. – Preserve your cheerful temper, and laugh and dance when a fiddle comes in your way, but beware of the sly collectors.[2]

Her account of the pleasures and dangers of Irish life is knowing enough to suggest she had already made a visit, but if so she never spoke of it apart from this one inconclusive reference.

Mrs Prior's gossip had warned Mary of Lord Kingsborough's notorious extravagance, disposing Mary to a sisterly sympathy for his Lady. But her reputation for finicky perfectionism where her daughters' education was concerned made Mary nervous about her own inadequate French and lack of skill with the embroidery needle. She winced at the thought of disappointing; however she was never criticized on these scores.

The trouble that arose had deeper roots. Caroline Kingsborough and Mary, though their positions were officially unequal, had something in common: they both needed to establish ascendancy over their companions in order to be happy. They very soon became violently jealous of one another, and not only as concerned the children, orthodox battle ground between mother and governess. Things might have been easier had the Kingsboroughs simply oppressed and neglected Mary; had they been only frivolous, thoughtless and occasionally brutal, she could have kept within a defensive shell of formality. Instead, they tempted her out with shows of friendship; they seemed spontaneous and sympathetic, they made jokes, extended invitations to the drawing-room and introductions to their friends, a whole sequence of well-intentioned gestures she could not resist. It was because she found them attractive at times that things became intolerable for her.

She might have been better armed against them had she known something of their history.[3]

Robert, Viscount Kingsborough and heir to an earldom, and Caroline, his wife and cousin, were only a little older than Mary; they were just into their thirties. Their large brood of children was headed by a son of fifteen at Eton and a daughter of fourteen, Margaret. Robert and Caroline had been married themselves at sixteen and fifteen; in fact he had been taken out of Eton for the ceremony, and a tutor from the school, Mr Tickell, appointed to live with the young couple for several years after the marriage.

In their portraits they look very much what they were: spoilt, beautiful, fine-boned children dressed up in wigs and pearls and party clothes to enact the roles laid upon them by family ambition. Their marriage had made them jointly the biggest landowners and possibly the richest family in Ireland, though the income from Irish estates was always larger in theory than in practice. There was some though not much true Irish blood in their veins. The King family had arrived in Ireland during the reign of Elizabeth I in the person of Sir John King, a Yorkshire squire eager, like most of his fellow English, to drive out the barbarous natives and grab their land for himself and his heirs. He fathered a long line of soldiers and administrators of the Protestant ascendancy. Various branches of cousins flourished during the seventeenth and eighteenth centuries, sending their sons to Eton and Oxford and then on the Grand Tour when it became fashionable, marrying their daughters into other Protestant landowning families, picking up quite impartially a knighthood from Cromwell and a peerage from Charles II.

Caroline's great-grandfather, the third Baron Kingston, had married a pretty and persistent Irish scullery maid; their one son, James, in turn produced a single daughter who married a Richard Fitzgerald and died when her only child Caroline was nine. Thus Caroline Fitzgerald found herself heiress to huge rent rolls and vast estates, including the ruined castle of Mitchelstown. Her grandfather, seeking some way of securing the future – that of the estates rather than the little girl perhaps – decided that the best course would be to marry her to her third cousin Robert King before some other dynasty snapped her up.

Robert was too young at this stage to record his own opinion, but his father was charmed with the arrangement. 'I have procured for Him one of ye Prettiest Heiresses in ye British Dominions' he wrote. A man of dogged tenacity of purpose where family aggrandizement was in prospect, he had married money himself and pestered the authorities for titles shamelessly and without ceasing. His hard work was rewarded: in 1764 he was created Baron, in 1766 he rose to Viscount and finally, with a last mighty effort, he achieved an earldom in 1768. When Robert and Caroline were married in December 1769 the King family had arrived at the peak of its success: Robert King had become Viscount Kingsborough and would in due course be upgraded to Earl of Kingston.

The young couple went to live amongst their various in-laws: Mitchelstown had to wait till they came of age. They were given £6,000 a year to play with and had nothing to do but get a family. George was born in 1771, and Margaret followed in the summer of 1772. Then there were problems; Caroline could not endure her mother-in-law's interference with the babies, and found the company of her own father, Colonel Fitzgerald, who had acquired a second wife and family, equally trying. Robert's father, the Earl, managed to absent himself as much as possible from the household of squabbling women, and Robert's earliest letters as a married man are boyish apologies to his father about Caroline's rude and improper behaviour. Since things showed no signs of improvement, he decided to take his family to England. In December 1772, still accompanied by his tutor Mr Tickell, they departed, determined not to return until they were of age. They took a house in Hill Street in the West End, at £360 a year.

The Earl continued to bombard his 'dear Robin' with exhortations not to quarrel with his wife, not to drink too much porter and not to forget his prayers, either at morning or evening. Robert sent back ever patient and respectful replies. In the summer of 1773 a third baby, politicly named Robert Edward for his grandfather, appeared; and in October Robert, Caroline, Mr Tickell and little George set off for the continent with a train of nurses, footmen and maids, leaving the two small babies in the care of four more maids at a house outside town, near the Kensington gravel pits.

In Paris, Robert and Caroline attended dinners, balls and masquerades and visited the court of Louis XVI and Marie

Antoinette at Versailles. Then they travelled on through France, Italy and Germany. At this time the Earl wrote a curious letter to Robert asking for the sum of £12,000 as a payment for having arranged his marriage for him; Robert agreed, docile as ever, only stipulating that he could not pay until he and Caroline had reached their majority. (It was after all largely her money he was handing over.) The Earl meanwhile had been giving her father large sums of money to compensate him for the financial loss he had suffered in letting his rich daughter marry so early. All the Kings understood perfectly that marriage was fundamentally a business matter of money and land. They were also lavish spenders who found it hard to grasp the idea that the cash might ever run low; in Robert's case it seems to have been part of his 'finish of a perfect gentleman', as Arthur Young put it, to spend without thought or calculation.

Caroline stayed in Geneva while Robert continued his tour through France. She was pregnant again as she approached the age of twenty-one. In five and a half years of marriage she had produced four babies. Her father-in-law was not entirely satisfied with this record; his Countess was still bearing children herself, and he wrote to Robert:

> It gives me great pleasure to hear that Caroline is again breeding, I should be glad, if it was God's will, that you should have a numerous family, but besides I was apprehensive that her bad state of health might be the cause of not having children as fast at first as we had reason to expect.

Caroline however continued to do her duty, and bore the Earl twelve grandchildren during his lifetime. She did not lose her looks; even Mary commented on her 'perpetual prettiness' when she was in her thirties. She was not very tender to her children, but this is not so surprising in a girl married off at fifteen, eager to enjoy the pleasures her money and rank and good looks could provide, and constantly hampered by pregnancies. The accepted system of wet-nurses and nursery maids naturally estranged her further from the small creatures she bore whether she wanted them or not. Caroline was ambitious for her children as her family had been for her, but she seems to have had little patience or love for them and Mary observed at once that they in turn feared rather than loved her.

Her eldest daughter Margaret has left a description of her childhood, written from the perspective of her own middle age:

> My father Robert King Earl of Kingston, was married very young to his relation Caroline Fitzgerald ... I was the second of their twelve children and being born in that rank of life in which people are too much occupied by frivolous amusements to pay much attention to their offspring I was placed under the care of hirelings from the first moment of my birth – before three years old I was subjected to the discipline of governesses and teachers whose injudicious treatment was very disadvantageous to my temper. As I advanced in years I had various masters (for no expense was spared to make me what is called accomplished) and at a very early age I was enabled to exhibit before my mother's visitors, whose silly praises would probably have injured me if I had not suffered so much in acquiring the means of obtaining them that they afforded me no pleasure. With this sort of education it is not extraordinary that I should have learnt a little of many things and nothing well.[4]

Her parents came of age when Margaret was three. Now they could spend their money and do exactly as they pleased. They returned to Ireland, eager to turn Mitchelstown into a fashionable earthly paradise. The house was to be entirely rebuilt as a Palladian mansion, the gardens also designed on classical lines. So the medieval ruins gave way to a large square house with wings at each side, its ceilings adorned with frescoes executed by an Italian artist. However, a touch of the past was retained at the young Viscount's insistence: the thirteenth-century White Knight's tower was incorporated into the structure of the building, and a second tower which had formed part of the outworks of the castle was converted into a library.*

Twelve hundred acres of land were enclosed by a thick wall six and a half miles long (it is still standing today), and gardens were laid out, acres of vineries and conservatories established, thousands of oak, ash and beech trees planted. Robert also had mulberry trees put in so that a silk industry could be started; he was eager to do something to improve conditions amongst the wretchedly poor peasantry in their mud huts, now sited outside the walls of his estate, but still a burden to his conscience. Whatever his defects, he was not going to be the light-hearted absentee landlord of Irish tradition, spending rents in London whilst his tenants starved and his agent grew fat. In fact, eager to command the best of everything, he invited the celebrated agricultural expert Arthur Young to come and be his agent and reform the management of his estates altogether. Although Young had formed a very unfavourable impression of the Irish gentry when he toured the country the year before, he was tempted by the large sums of money offered him and accepted the position.† His account of his time at Mitchels-

* Unfortunately the house Mary knew was pulled down by the third Earl in 1820 and replaced by an enormous mock-medieval structure. This was burnt during the Troubles in 1922 and the stones carted off to build a fake Gothic church. A cooperative dairy stands on the site today. The square of small, terraced town houses built by the Kingsboroughs for 'decayed Protestant gentlefolk' early in the nineteenth century, known as College Square, is their most handsome legacy to Mitchelstown.

† Young's stories of Irish life perfectly illustrate the atmosphere in which Mary found herself. One concerns Sir James Caldwell, who decided to entertain Lord Shelburne by enacting the meeting of Captain Cook and the New Zealand savages on his own ornamental lake with two hundred of his men suitably dressed to represent the opposing groups. Lady Caldwell pointed out that the harvest was in full swing, and that they could ill spare the men, but he brushed her objections aside and called for the men, tailors to dress them and boat furbishers to disguise his boats in the appropriate styles. As it

town is funny in its own right; it also throws some light on Mary's later experience.[5]

When he arrived everything seemed pleasant enough. There was a temporary house for him on the estate but he had been promised a new one to be built to his own specification. As a rule he dined at the castle and generally played chess with Caroline after dinner for an hour or two. 'I learned by report that her Ladyship was highly pleased with me, saying that I was one of the most lively, agreeable fellows.' Young found Lord Kingsborough 'of a character not so easily ascertained' and feared that he was too easily influenced by 'persons of inferior abilities'. Soon it became clear that the situation was far more complicated than anything Young could have expected. The castle hummed with conspiracies.

Young's first aim was to persuade Lord Kingsborough to let his lands directly to the cottagers, without using any middlemen at all, and this had indeed been Robert's plan in the first place. But now it appeared that a Major Thornhill, one of Caroline's relations, was casting covetous eyes on the position of agent; and worse, his wife, 'an artful designing woman', had embarked on a plot to secure the job for her husband.

Mrs Thornhill's plot was in the style of Feydeau: it hinged on the current governess, a Catholic girl called Miss Crosby, whom she persuaded Caroline into believing to be the object of Robert's attentions. Caroline decided to sack her and asked Young to draw up some sort of agreement whereby she should be paid an annuity of £50 a year; it was an exceedingly handsome sum for a discharged governess who cannot have been with the family for long and must have been still young, and makes one wonder just what she had done or suffered to be rewarded so handsomely. But

---

turned out Lord Shelburne was obliged to cancel the visit and the hay harvest was lost too.

that was no concern of Young's; the actual drafting of the agreement however obliged him to be at the castle more often than usual. This gave Mrs Thornhill a pretext for persuading Robert that Young was in love with the Viscountess. At the same time she worked on Caroline until *she* believed that Young was plotting to further the supposed affair between Miss Crosby and Robert.

The outcome of this preposterous intrigue was the dismissal of the innocent Young, who departed thankfully in October 1778. In one respect he did very well out of the episode: when he asked to be paid, Robert found himself short of ready cash, so Young proposed that he should have (like Miss Crosby) an annuity of £72 a year in lieu of payment. As far as we know he continued to draw it until his death. If Miss Crosby did likewise she was a uniquely lucky member of her calling. When Mary came to her more arduous task with the children ten years later she was offered only £40 a year.

When she arrived finally at Mitchelstown castle, Mary was told that Lady Kingsborough was confined to her room with a sore throat, but a score of surrogates appeared to greet her: Caroline's widowed stepmother, Mrs Fitzgerald, her three big daughters ('just going to market' as their brother put it) and the King girls, Margaret, Caroline, Mary, little Jane and Louisa. The three eldest were to be Mary's especial charges. There were 'Mrs and Misses without number' she wrote to her sister later, a little dazed by the size and clamour of the household.

Lord Kingsborough turned up also to take a look at another of Miss Crosby's successors. Mary dismissed him mentally for the moment: 'his countenance does not promise much more than good humour, and a little fun not refined'.[6] Soon she was summoned for an interview with his Lady in her room. The bed was a turmoil of satins and pet dogs; Mary perceived that the human occupant was a beauty and she established herself, through the yapping, as a woman to be reckoned with. She was clever – better read than her governess in fact; Mary was more intimidated by her than she had expected to be. To keep her courage up, she decided at once to disapprove of the dogs, who were obviously receiving affection that should have gone to the children.

Leaving Lady Kingsborough to her dogs, Mary found she had been given a comfortable room with a view over the mountains. There was even a fire burning; she could spend her first evening alone. She sat writing to her sisters, and heard a new sound stealing up the stairs towards her closed door: the fiddler was playing below. To her it was not a cheering noise. It served to emphasize the peculiarity of this great house, the contrast between its Italianate splendours and the miles of desolate Irish bog around, the fact that the servants with their different gradations were all, from fiddler to governess, there to serve one end alone: the pleasure of My Lord and My Lady.

But when daylight came again there was little time to brood. The children left her alone for scarcely a moment. They told her very frankly that they had been determined to plague and annoy her, but finding her to their liking they changed their minds and merely hung about her with affectionate demands. And she herself, rather to her surprise, began to feel a maternal emotion.

> The children cluster about me. One catches a kiss, another lisps my long name – while a sweet little boy, who is conscious that he is a favourite, calls himself my son. At the sight of their mother they tremble and run to me for protection. This renders them dear to me – and I discover the kind of happiness I was formed to enjoy.

For the moment the power of children to 'plague and teaze' was forgotten; and indeed it is considerably reduced where there is a household of servants to share the burden. Almost at once she made a favourite amongst the big girls; Margaret, the eldest, responded with the enthusiasm of adolescence. This is more of Margaret's own account:

> ... the society of my father's house was not calculated to improve my good qualities or correct my faults; and almost the only person of superior merit with whom I had been intimate in my early days was an enthusiastic female who was my governess from fourteen to fifteen years old, for whom I felt an unbounded admiration because her mind appeared more noble and her understanding more cultivated than any others I had known – from the time she left me my chief objects were to correct these faults she had pointed out and to cultivate my understanding as much as possible.[7]

However deficient the society at Mitchelstown appeared to Margaret and her governess, the situation seemed happy enough all through November, and Mary wrote to George Blood that 'the whole family make a point of paying me the greatest attention – and some part of it treat me with a degree of tenderness which I have seldom met with from strangers.'

She confided some of her family troubles to the Kingsboroughs and felt that her confidences were respected and encouraged. In December she wrote to Eliza about plans to bring both her sisters over to Ireland; Lady K said she would help to find them places in reputable schools, and Mary had the impression they might even be invited to stay at Mitchelstown. Wollstonecrafts and Kingsboroughs were to be equally delighted with one another in Mary's new dream, and she grew almost exultant at this point in her delight at being such a great favourite with her employers.

She tried in turn to be useful to them, writing to Joseph Johnson to ask if he could suggest a respectable clergyman's family who might take on the education of Mrs Fitzgerald's wild young son ('his temper is violent and his mind not cultivated'). Johnson does not seem to have been able to oblige; but his exchange of letters with Mary, whose book was now printing, grew increasingly friendly.

One of the reasons for the immediate favour she found with her employers was a dramatic illness that afflicted Margaret: 'my poor little favourite has had a very violent fever – and can scarcely bear to have me for a moment out of her sight – her life was dispaired of – and this illness has produced an intimacy in the family which a course of years might not have brought about.' Warm-hearted and dictatorial, Mary made a good nurse. Margaret recovered quickly enough and intensified her devotion to a governess who gave her the tenderness and attention her mother could not spare. And at Mitchelstown in midwinter the new governess was of course a distraction, a new source of amusement for all the ladies, who were certainly bored, cooped up in their country paradise with nothing to do but read, chatter, play chess and spend five hours a day dressing, applying rouge and washing in asses' milk. The men were as likely as not to disappear, fishing or hunting or visiting the tenants; there was not much to keep them interested at home. Mary, shocked by the rouge and the asses' milk, described them carefully all the same for Eliza's benefit, adding an admonishment not to become too curious about the habits of titled people. She herself, she announced, intended to go out visiting the poor in their cabins.

Her letters to Everina were more caustic on the subject of the conversation and manners of the ladies of the family; all matrimony, dress and dogs, but without any feeling, she said, adding that her own temper was considered 'angelick'. 'If my vanity could be flattered by the respect of people, whose judgment I do not care for – why in this place it has sufficient food.'

Her moods and her estimate of her surroundings rose and fell from day to day: called on to perform an exceptional task, such as nursing Margaret, she felt a sense of purpose and satisfaction with herself and looked more kindly on those about her: when things settled down again, she had more time to brood and think of herself as a 'poor Melancholy wretch'. She often felt unwell with what she herself called a nervous complaint. To Johnson she even wrote that 'it is with pleasure that I observe my declining health, and cherish the hope that I am hastening to the land where all these cares will be forgotten'.

Before dismissing remarks of this kind as pure self-dramatization intended to evoke sympathy, it is worth remembering that she had lately seen her mother and Fanny die, neither of them old women; she had the news of the death of Mrs Price; Eliza and Fanny's babies were both dead, Margaret's life had been in danger. To George Blood she wrote: 'life is but a frightful dream', and in a mood like that it might well seem worth exchanging one frightful dream for another sort of sleep.

Fortunately a new distraction appeared on the scene. There were visitors to Mitchelstown; Robert invited a fellow MP and privy councillor, George Ogle, with his wife and sister. Ogle was a man in his forties, good-mannered and intelligent; and he was a poet. His arcadian lyrics had won the praise of Burns:

Shepherds, I have lost my love, –
  Have you seen my Anna?
Pride of every shady grove
  On the banks of Banna.

I for her my home forsook,
  Near yon misty mountain,
Left my flocks, my pipe, my crook,
  Greenwood shade and fountain.

Never shall I see them more
  Until her returning;
All the joys of life are o'er –
  From gladness changed to mourning.

Whither is my charmer flown?
Shepherds, tell me whither?
Ah! woe for me, perhaps she's gone
For ever and for ever?

Heavenly, said Burns, and the verses are certainly accomplished; this Anna bathed in asses' milk without a doubt and did not herd sheep from a mud hut outside the walls. But if Ogle worked within the limitations of his class, he still made a great impression on Mary; he was 'a *Genius*, and *unhappy*: such a man, you may suppose, would catch your sister's eye'. Unfortunately he had already caught Lady Kingsborough's eye. Mary was delighted by his attentions; he found her worth talking to, and she probably told him about her forthcoming book; he made her feel that she was at least as interesting as her employer. Caroline was not so pleased.

For the moment she gave the governess a few days' holiday. Mary paid a brief visit to Tipperary, where she stayed with an uncle and aunt of Fanny's; she was not impressed by them, finding them chilly and correct. She returned to Mitchelstown to travel with the children to Dublin, ahead of their parents. The Kingsboroughs had a new house in Merrion Square, where the governess was installed in a suite of rooms that included a drawing room furnished with a harpsichord, which she could not play (but no matter), and a parlour in which to receive male visitors. The idea sent her into one of her maidenly flurries of underlining and exclamation marks, and she could not resist adding that the last governess had been treated quite differently, like a servant. However, there was now no longer any talk of bringing her sisters over to join her.

The letters from Dublin continued to alternate between skittishness and deep, despondent self-pity and hypochondria. Fanny Burney said that to find the true meaning of a woman's letter you must always look to the post script; Mary's ran to rows of dashes and references to being in love, but she offered no names and probably she was ready to consider herself in love with any one of at least three candidates: Henry Gabell, who turned up in Dublin for a while and who exchanged letters with her; Neptune, who also appeared in Dublin in May; and George Ogle. He took the trouble to call on her before the adult Kingsboroughs arrived in town, and presented her with a poem of his own composition. There was nothing sentimental about it, but it was still something for Mary to receive such an attention, and she copied out the lines carefully for her sister:

> Genius – 'tis th'ethereal Beam –
> 'Tis sweet Willy Shakespeare's dream –
> 'Tis the muse upon the wing
> 'Tis wild Fancy's magic ring –
> 'Tis the Phrenzy of the mind –
> 'Tis the eye that ne'er is blind –
> 'Tis the Prophet's holy fire,
> 'Tis the music of the lyre
> 'Tis th'enthusiast's frantic bliss
> 'Tis anything – alas – but this.

A real rivalry with Caroline began; Mary noted that her employer 'wishes to be taken particular notice of by a man of *acknowledged* cleverness' and later she said that Ogle was in fact Lady K's 'flirt'. She cannot have been delighted when her flirt took to calling on her children's governess, encouraging her moodiness, which he professed to find interesting, and offering her poems.

Still Caroline made efforts to get on with Mary; she took her to the Dublin Handel festival, and persuaded her into attending a masquerade. Mary wore a black mask and indulged herself in satirical talk as interpreter for another woman dressed, probably not too accurately, as a female from the newly discovered islands in the South Seas. But these distractions did not help matters much. In March Mary was ill and Caroline called her own doctor; he confirmed

Mary's diagnosis of a nervous complaint and charged her an aristocratic fee, which outraged her. Margaret also fell ill again. This time Mary was critical of her mother's treatment, fearing it would bring on a consumption, something she always feared after Fanny. Probably she did not express herself with much tact to Lady Kingsborough.

From Caroline's point of view Mary's fault as a governess was not just that she won the affections of the children too obviously or even attracted the attention of her own admirer. It was that she allowed herself to behave with all the capriciousness and displays of sensibility that were meant to be the prerogative of the leisured classes. If she thought Caroline had been rude she would sulk in her room. In March a deputation of Mrs Ogle, her sister and Caroline herself had to persuade Mary to come downstairs in order to meet the old Earl, and they had considerable difficulty with their mission. Caroline was just not prepared to keep up this sort of special treatment. Why should she have to worry constantly about the governess's nerves or wounded pride?

Soon she was busy planning a ball to be given at Mitchelstown; her dress had to be prepared with artificial flowers, and the whole household 'from kitchen maid to Governess' was required to make wreaths of roses for it. Mary's short-lived enthusiasm for Ireland was now well and truly over; she disliked the place with all her heart and longed to be back in England. The King family was 'proud and mean', and Mrs Fitzgerald had failed to find jobs for Everina and Eliza as she had promised.

When Mrs Fitzgerald left the house for a while, matters grew still worse: 'You know, I never liked Lady K., but I find her still more haughty and disagreeable now she is not under Mrs Fitzgerald's eye. Indeed, she behaved so improperly to me once or twice, in the Drawing Room, I determined never to go into it again.' Snubs or scoldings Mary would not take. She also worried about her clothes and the expense of hairdressing and hats, but when Caroline offered her a poplin dress Mary refused it and there was an explosion of anger from her employer. Mrs Fitzgerald arrived back to soothe everyone's feelings, and induced Caroline to apologize to her prima donna of a governess. Mary stayed in her room as much as she could, working on a novel.

In the middle of March she wrote to Everina about her 'spasms and disordered nerves' and incurably broken heart. There was talk of a 'constant nervous fever', violent pains in the side, difficulty in breathing, fits of trembling, a rising in the throat and faintness. Caroline was accused of tormenting the children and Mary, in an access of priggishness, exclaimed, 'Thank heaven I am not a Lady of Quality.'

But she could not maintain her aloofness. Persuaded once more into the drawing room, she found herself facing George Ogle again:

> As he had not seen me lately he came and seated himself by me – indeed his sensibility has ever lead him to pay attentions to a poor forlorn stranger – he paid me some *fanciful* compliments – and lent me some very pretty stanzas – melancholy ones, you may suppose, as he thought they would accord with my feelings. Lord K. came up – and was surprised at seeing me *there* – he bowed respectfully – a constellation of thoughts made me out-blush her Ladyship's rouge. Did I ever tell you she is very pretty – and always pretty. Such is the style I live in ...

What made Mary blush? Lord Kingsborough's gallant bow on discovering her engaged in intimate conversation with his wife's flirt? Mary's knowledge, surely acquired by now, that Lord K had in the past been accused at any rate of a love affair with a governess? Her sensation of mixed triumph and confusion at finding herself in the drawing room attended by Caroline's husband and admirer all at once? Or her wish that she could indeed steal men's hearts and attentions from pretty Caroline, and not just in the drawing room?

The fact is, Mary was later accused of having wanted 'to Discharge the Marriage Duties' with Caroline's husband.[8] And perhaps Robert's ideas of 'a little fun, not refined' included routine attempts on the virtue of all the governesses his wife produced, though it is scarcely conceivable that Mary encouraged him: she had everything to lose by doing so. And yet she seems to have felt guilty about something, even if it was no more than envy or a half-formed inclination to join in a way of life she censured. A letter to Everina confessed:

> You know not, my dear Girl, of what materials this strange inconsistent heart of mine is formed, and how alive it is to tenderness and misery. Since I have been here I have turned over several pages in the vast volume of human nature, and what is the amount? Vanity and vexation of spirit – and yet I am *tied* to my fellow-creatures by partaking of their weaknesses. I rail at a fault – sicken at the sight – and find it stirring within me. New sympathies and feelings *start* up. I know not myself.

None of this can have meant much to Everina, but she was accustomed to Mary's cryptic style where certain subjects were concerned; for Mary, it was a way of unburdening herself for her own relief, and it certainly suggests that she had become vulnerable to someone or something in the Kingsborough circle. In May she was talking about Ogle's *great* faults, balanced by his genius and sensibility; and pointing out the dreadful life of Society couples, 'seldom alone together but in bed – the husband perhaps drunk, and the wife's head full of pretty compliments that some creature that nature designed for a man paid her at the card table.' It was not the sort of observation expected of governesses.

In June the whole family crossed over to England to take the medicinal waters at Bristol Hot Wells. They stayed for several weeks. And here, in August, the inevitable rupture came, and Mary was dismissed.

In her account of the affair to Godwin she attributed the dismissal entirely to her too obvious success in winning the children's affections from their mother. She also recalled Ogle as 'the most perfect gentleman she had ever known',[9] a remark Godwin printed with the additional comment that Ogle's later opposition to Catholic emancipation had disappointed Mary. But if we turn back to the letters we see Ogle had disappointed her on an earlier occasion. Something in his behaviour upset her enough to produce some odd and incoherent scrawled remarks to Eliza in a letter from the Hot Wells dated June 1787:

> Lords are not the sort of beings who afford one amusement – nor in the nature of Things do they – poor half-mad Mr Ogle was the only Rt. Honourable I was ever pleased with – and I pity him – I am sorry to hear a man of sensibility and cleverness talking of sentiment sinking into sensuality ... such will ever I fear be the case with the inconsistent human heart when there are no principles to direct and sustain it.

She went on to quote Paley severely, complain of the bad weather and the way she was treated by the 'little souls' about her, and mention a sum of money which 'A *friend* whose name I am not *permitted* to mention has lent me.'

Evidently the friend was not Ogle, whom she now disapproved of; nor was it Mrs Fitzgerald, whose loans to her were freely mentioned, or Church (of Newington) who had also advanced her money. It is usually assumed that it was sent to her by Joseph Johnson, and this is a probable enough explanation, although there was no particular reason for discretion about the payment of advance royalties from a publisher. One further possibility remains: Lord Kingsborough himself may have felt the governess had been ill-treated by his wife, and decided to assist her. He had after all given an annuity to a former governess; and the King men liked to regard themselves as patrons of needy literary women; his uncle Robert had been much involved with Laetitia Pilkington.*

* Laetitia Pilkington, usually described as an 'adventuress' (so she still stands in the DNB), was in fact a talented *divorcée* of a genera-

If he did in fact assist Mary, it would help to explain Caroline's later accusations against her; in that household there were always plenty of tale-bearers about, and if any of the servants learned that money had passed hands between his Lordship and Miss Wollstonecraft they would be very likely to jump to conclusions and pass their information on where it would do most damage. Caroline's jealousy was certainly aroused by some means, and although she could scarcely adopt a self-righteous pose over Ogle's small attentions to Mary, she felt herself fully entitled to be angry over any of her husband's.

So Mary departed in disgrace. Only Margaret remained in a state of violent, rebellious loyalty to her governess. But she took her revenge with her: the manuscript of her completed novel, *Mary*.

Mary is primarily an attempt at self-analysis, a portrait of a heroine equipped with intelligence and the social virtues in spite of an inadequate upbringing. She cannot

---

tion earlier than Mary who tried to earn her living by her pen. She suffered much persecution; gentlemen who took an interest in her assumed she was eager for their advances and simultaneously abused and tried to take advantage of her. She had a witty pen but took to drink and died at the same age as Mary, thirty-eight. One of her last patrons was Robert Kingsborough, our Robert's uncle, to whom she addressed this somewhat ambivalent complimentary poem in 1748:

> The Peers of Ireland long have been a jest,
> Their own, and every other climate's pest:
> But King shall grace the coronet he wears,
> And make it vie with Britain's noblest stars;
> And when, in time, to grace his nuptial bed
> Some chaste, illustrious charmer he shall wed:
> May love, and joy, and truth the pomp attend,
> And deathless honour to his race descend.

But Laetitia's verses were not prophetic: the subject of her poem died unmarried.

help being a little conceited and feeling that life owes her something more than the trials she has to endure. She finds herself at odds with her parents, with her status as a married woman and even to a degree with Ann, the friend (based on Fanny) to whom she devotes herself until her death from consumption in Lisbon. So far it is straightforward enough. The curious feature of the book is the way in which Wollstonecraft and Kingsborough characters are combined. The heroine's mother is called Elizabeth (and father Edward); but she is clearly a hostile sketch of Caroline, preferring dogs to children, jealous of her growing daughter and of her husband's affections (he spends a good deal of time visiting those of the tenants on his estate who have pretty daughters). Elizabeth's ancestors inhabited a romantic ruined castle, she was married under family orders without affection, and her own daughter 'Mary' is married off whilst still a child in order to join two estates. Thus in the novel the real Caroline, transformed into Mary's mother, is annihilated; whilst Mary herself is raised to the freedom and power of her social position and able to rectify in her own person the weaknesses and follies of her 'mother'.

The fictional Mary is attractive to men and enters into flirtatious relationships with several; her husband, dispatched abroad immediately after the marriage ceremony, plays no part in her story except as a barrier to other possibilities. She likes the awkward manners of literary men, men 'past the meridian of life, and of a philosophic turn'; she is moved by an ugly, sensitive invalid, Henry, who plays simple Scottish ballads on his violin; and she enjoys some passionate embraces with him. 'Have I desires implanted in me only to make me miserable?' she asks, and 'can I listen to the cold dictates of prudence, and bid my tumultuous passions cease to vex me?'[10] One of her sneers at the character of 'Elizabeth' is that she is too prudent and cold to betray her unloved husband except in imagination. Nowhere in *Mary* is adultery openly defended, but the contrast between Elizabeth and Mary implies that feeling rather than prescription is the right guide to behaviour. Sensibility, 'the most exquisite feeling of which the human soul is capable',[11] is not to be confused with gross sensuality, but the distinction becomes rather a fine one, maintained in the book largely by the device of making Henry a dying man.

'I have drawn from Nature,' Mary told Henry Gabell in a letter,[12] but she was probably not directing his attention to her views on the matrimonial bond, since he had lately told her he was about to be married himself. The novel ended in fact with the death of the fictional Henry, and with Mary, heartbroken, retiring to her country estates determined to run them on model lines: she 'established manufactories' and 'threw the estate into small farms', a course of action not entirely unlike that of Robert Kingsborough in his younger and more idealistic days. Several other touches relate to the Kingsboroughs, and it must certainly have caused considerable displeasure to Caroline if it ever fell into her hands. No doubt the idea gave Mary some legitimate satisfaction.

Mary's departure from the Kingsborough household did not bring it much relief from family disputes. Within two years, in 1789, Caroline insisted on a formal separation, accusing Robert of persistent ill-treatment, its nature unspecified though it is easy enough to guess at. They lived their lives apart thereafter; she became known as 'the good countess' around Mitchelstown and he busied himself with the militia as Ireland grew increasingly restless and violent; he is credited with the particular brutality of inventing 'pitch-capping', a form of torture in which short-haired (and therefore politically suspect) peasants had burning tar and gunpowder applied to their heads.

The many Kingsborough sons took up conventional careers in the army and the church. Two of their daughters however retained a streak of wildness, for which some people held their governess responsible. Margaret kept up a short-lived clandestine correspondence with her.[13] When she was nineteen she married her neighbour, the young Earl of Mountcashel, not because she loved or admired him but to get away from home, and confident that she could manage him.[14] She bore him rows of children, in whom, like her mother, she seems to have taken little enough interest. Instead she became absorbed in Irish republican politics, to the considerable annoyance of her husband. By her late twenties she was

> a democrat and republican in all their sternness, yet with no ordinary portion either of understanding or good nature . . . uncommonly tall and brawny, with bad teeth, white eyes, and a handsome countenance . . . with gigantic arms, which she commonly folds, naked and exposed almost to the shoulders.

(This description comes from Godwin, who became her firm friend, although he did not meet her until after the death of his wife.)

Margaret Mountcashel spoke up loyally in defence of Mary when popular opinion credited her with having corrupted her charges,[15] but she never attempted to make contact with her again and did not even name her in the autobiographical note she left. Perhaps while Mary still lived the younger woman was embarrassed by the memory of an intense relationship, which would have been impossible to revive; and later she may have had doubts about Mary's wisdom. 'Misfortune must ever be the lot of those who transgress the laws of social life,' she wrote for the benefit of her own youngest daughters. She was referring to her own personal transgressions: in 1803 she decided to leave her husband and settle in Italy with a lover, George Tighe. There she lived out her life, calling herself 'Mrs Mason', apparently contented with her calm exile in the sun and her respectable Irish companion, who busied himself growing potatoes in pots on the window-ledges of their *palazzo*. In time she befriended Shelley and the ladies who buzzed about him, preferring Claire Clairmont to the daughter of her old governess. She was a tender mother to her own extra-matrimonial daughters and even wrote a book on child care, *Advice to Young Mothers by a Grandmother.* Sadly, her Mountcashel children remembered her always as a harsh and unloving parent.

Another scandal, far worse than Margaret's discreet elopement, involved the third King daughter, Mary, and Robert Kingsborough himself, and was followed eagerly by the whole newspaper-reading public of England and Ireland. The story belongs later in this narrative, but the fact that Mary's name was brought up when it happened, that she was accused of having corrupted her charges, and that Caroline herself joined in the attacks on her, indicates something of her success in ruffling the feelings of the good countess.

Mary parted from the Kingsboroughs in haste, muddle, defiance and unhappiness. She had offended a peeress and become convinced that the ladies of the aristocracy were irredeemably frivolous and arrogant. No doubt other governesses had come to the same conclusion in silence. But her case was a little different. She was not an isolated figure, and she was moving back into a world of allies: the Dissenters, the London intelligentsia. Soon she would have Henry Fuseli's account of how he had boxed the ears of Lord Waldegrave's son and thrown up his tutorship; she might hear Joseph Priestley's strictures on Lord Shelburne, whom he had served as librarian for seven years but parted with coldly enough in the end. She would meet Thomas Holcroft, the playwright and translator, who had just brought the names of Beaumarchais' Figaro and Susanna to London. Their message spoke directly to Mary's experience: My Lord, the man of empty honour and sexual obsession, and My Lady, the spoilt slave of his despotic whim, could not continue to hold the centre of the stage much longer.

[6]

Joseph Johnson and St Paul's Churchyard

All the same, Mary was homeless again, without a job or a reference; she had nothing to live on, and she was in debt to several people. She had no marriage prospects. She was twenty-eight, with a face that looked as though it had settled permanently into lines of severity and depression around the fierce eyes. In her heart she knew herself for an enthusiast, but so far life had handed her more opportunities for contempt than enthusiasm, and her most remarkable trait was still that she had refused to learn the techniques whereby women in her situation usually attempted to make life tolerable for themselves: flattery, docility, resignation to the will of man, or God, or their social superiors, or all three.

To turn to her family was out of the question. Her father was in Wales with his Lydia, and in any case down to his last penny; James was at sea, Charles indentured to Ned at St Katharine's Dock, Ned himself implacably hostile. She had to find somewhere to live and some means of earning money. The ladies of Newington Green would certainly have been willing to find her a post in a girls' school like her sisters, both now teaching again, but Mary was not prepared to be grateful to any more women, even well-intentioned ones, for the time being.

She had one other resource: her publisher, Joseph Johnson. When she stepped out of the Bristol coach she made straight for his shop in St Paul's Churchyard. It was by far the best thing she ever did. Johnson was probably the only person she knew who was in a position to offer her an alternative to the treadmill turned by governesses, companions and schoolteachers, but better still he was ready to believe in the unusual and behave unconventionally.

For us, Johnson is not an easy man to approach. We know that he was a successful businessman and a Dissenter with no love for the establishment; he was also wary, self-effacing and remarkably efficient at obscuring his own tracks. Put in the witness box during the treason trials of 1794, he contrived to appear almost wholly ignorant of the workings of his own business, which was all the more a feat as he ran it virtually single-handed.[1] His cautiousness induced him more than once to abandon printing books already set up in type: the first part of Tom Paine's *Rights of Man*, Blake's *French Revolution*, Beckford's *Travels*. In each case his first instinct as a publisher was sound, but blocked by anxieties about political or other repercussions; he never betrayed a friend, but he had no desire to be a martyr either.

His uncommunicativeness persisted even after his death: he contrived to leave scarcely a scrap of his own writing to the world, and his correspondence, which must have been one of the most extensive and interesting of his day, disappeared too; probably he destroyed it himself. Even the compliments he received run to the impersonal. The nineteenth century hailed him as 'the father of the book trade', which shows in what respect he was held but scarcely throws a flood of light on his character. His most famous author, William Cowper, ventured the private opinion that, 'though a bookseller, he has in him the soul of a gentleman'.[2] Booksellers, like governesses, were scarcely expected to cultivate their souls, and in any case the tribute was paid sight unseen, on the basis of letters and contracts. (The poet did invite Johnson and Fuseli to visit him at Olney in February 1789, but there is no record of the visit taking place.)[3] Cowper's friend Newton, who did meet Johnson, allowed that 'though not a professor' he was not absolutely ignorant either.

His obituarist, the journalist Nichols, drew a little closer to the man, giving him the character of a good and generous friend: 'the kindness of his heart was ... conspicuous in all the relations of his life' and the calls of 'friendship, kindred and misfortune' always found him ready to answer. But on the other hand he possessed 'a temper the reverse of sanguine ... a manner somewhat cold and indifferent' and was 'not remarkable for the encouragement he held out to his authors'.[4] The picture is one of caution and benevolence in roughly equal parts.

Johnson was a bachelor. He suffered from chronic asthma. He had begun his professional career as a specialist in medical books, branched out into general literature and become concerned to produce cheap, plain editions of whatever he published in order to reach as large a public as possible; clearly he took the Enlightenment view of publishing as an efficient means of raising the general intellectual and moral tone of society. He became official distributor of the literature of the Unitarians[5] and this kept him in constant touch with the Dissenting Academies and various provincial centres, with the result that his shop became a focus for the intellectual activities arising in them. It meant that he was in the thick of reforming and radical ideas from early days.

By the time Mary appeared on his doorstep he was already a figure of influence, a better patron than any lord. Mary's very evident need of practical assistance touched his humanity; her emotional and dramatic personality must have appealed to him too: he sought and enjoyed the company of talkers and enthusiasts. She had the recommendation of her friendship with Dr Price and her recent bitter experience at the hands of the aristocracy, for whom Johnson had no more love than she did. It seems unlikely that he judged her a genius on the basis of *Thoughts on the Education of Daughters* or even her new manuscript, *Mary*. All the same, when she arrived in his shop he at once invited her to stay with him. And almost in the next breath he proposed to set her up in a house of her own, and keep her for an indefinite period. Her payment was to be the work she undertook for him.

It was an extraordinary proposal for a middle-aged businessman (he was forty-nine) to make to a youngish woman; perhaps he was in a manic moment such as come to certain asthmatics. Mary, whose emotions most certainly ran in cycles, accepted without inquiring into his motives, and a state of joint euphoria descended on them both. Johnson became at once her best friend, sole support, banisher of gloom and obliterator of the stinging humiliations inflicted by the Kingsboroughs. With his encouragement she could take a completely fresh view of her future: free of money troubles and with an assured supply of useful and interesting work, she was to become a new kind of professional woman – 'the first of a new genus'.[6] Only a few months before she had been writing, with careless condescension, of 'little Johnson' in her letters; now her need and his generosity dissolved the phrase and the feeling away entirely.

Purely as a physical description the 'little' was apt. Johnson was short and slight, and his asthma had not been helped by breathing the smoke of the City for the past thirty-six years. But in spite of poor health and deficient stature, he was an attractive man: a neat, curled wig presided over large, dark eyes; the jaw was strong, clean-shaven but shadowed with black beard, a narrow top lip above a full and smiling lower one. His clothes were dark too, and severely cut, though not without traces of conscious elegance. And indeed he was neither ostentatious nor mean in any aspect of his life.

Like other ambitious publishers, he knew the value of keeping a welcoming dinner table, and his three o'clock gatherings were eagerly attended: 'a sort of Menagerie of Live Authors' they were called.[7] The domestic arrangements at St Paul's Churchyard were in the care of a housekeeper; a few years before a Miss Johnson, no doubt his sister, had been with him, but she had now departed.[8] A young man named Rowland Hunter, nephew by adoption only, was also part of the household and gave a hand with the business. Johnson's interest in women as anything other than friends was either extremely discreet or, more probably, non-existent. Still he was obviously inspired by the idea of what he could do for Mary; her presence charmed him; together they set up for a while that society for mutual admiration which is a good part of love. They played at fathers and daughters.

She was not his only new friend. He had just been persuaded into another departure from caution by a dazzlingly clever young Scotsman of twenty-five, Thomas Christie; Mary's arrival coincided with Johnson's decision to partner Christie in setting up a new monthly magazine. It was to be called the *Analytical Review*, and was to play an important part in Mary's life.

Mary told Everina that she found her patron's manner rather stiff at times. She also felt obliged to keep discreetly quiet the fact that she was lodging under his roof; probably she was awkward about how their association might be interpreted, and he may have wanted to reassure her that his intentions were businesslike. Still, nothing was too much trouble for him. He offered to send for one of his own cousins from the north to come and live with her and act as her maid, and was even prepared to interest himself in the fates of her younger brothers and sisters. Kindly and delicately, while the summer weather lasted, he sent her off to visit first Everina in Henley and then Eliza at Market Harborough; and while she was away he prepared the small house he found for her at 45 George Street, just south of Blackfriars Bridge, within easy walking distance of St Pauls.*

Her letters flew back from this trip out of town, chatty and even exuberant; by the time she returned to London in September she was ready to confide her most intimate

* Now called Dolben Street, it has been almost entirely demolished to make way for a railway.

emotions to him, and took to addressing him directly as 'a father and a brother'. George Street was to be her home for the next four years, but 72 St Paul's Churchyard was the centre of her existence, the place where she was in touch with work and friends, where she dined almost daily and met more and more people with backgrounds and ideas resembling her own; the place where she could always turn even when depression and self-hatred plagued her again, as they inevitably did from time to time.

For his part, Johnson shrugged off any misinterpretations there may have been about his setting up a young woman in a rent-free house. If reasons were required, there were sound business ones: the market for books aimed at women and children was expanding rapidly and the loyalty of a promising new female writer was worth gaining early in her career. He persuaded the elderly Mrs Trimmer and Mrs Barbauld, both of unimpeachable respectability, to call on Mary and encourage her; Anna Barbauld was already a model contributor to his educational list as well as a poet. He knew he would need editorial staff and reviewers for the *Analytical*; this was the sort of work Mary could usefully undertake.*

* The *Analytical Review* was the first British literary and scientific monthly aimed at the general public and made up almost entirely of book reviews. The leading reviews took the form of long and serious essays, but there were also shorter notices; medical books, poetry, art, history, fiction and a good deal of what would be called sociology today were covered. Reviews were anonymous or signed with initials only, usually not the initials of the writer but some arbitrarily chosen ones such as 'Y.Y.'; it makes attribution difficult. The *Analytical* never sold well, though it had a better reception in Scotland than England, probably thanks to Christie's connections; Mrs Piozzi commented on its 'Scotch' affiliations and speculated that most of the reviewers were of that nation (in her diary in 1790). But Fuseli, Cowper and Dyer were all contributors and most of Johnson's authors seem to have been pressed to work for it; its bias was of course towards radicalism. The first number appeared in May 1788 and it died in June 1799, six months after Johnson had been forced

And finally, it seems clear enough that he had a real interest in the advancement of women. Injustice and oppression of all kinds were repugnant to him; here was an opportunity of demonstrating his belief in their capacities in a practical way.

His own life provided a good enough example of how to break out of a constricting framework and make a career on a new pattern. He was the second son of a farmer at Everton, near Liverpool; born a Baptist, he had suffered under the usual educational disabilities of Dissenters, and lacked the physical strength for farming even if he had enjoyed the prospect of inheriting his father's land. So, at the age of fourteen, he had come to London as an apprentice to the bookseller George Keith, stuck out his seven years and in 1760 set up his first shop, selling medical books in Fish Street, close to Guy's and St Thomas's hospitals. His interests widened rapidly; he was one of the cooperative group who commissioned Samuel Johnson's *Lives of the Poets*. In the Sixties he formed a close and crucially important friendship with a young Swiss writer who had just arrived in London, and whom he invited to come and live with him: this was Johann Heinrich Fuessli, better known as Henry Fuseli (his own adaptation of the name to suit his adopted country). Fuseli's scholarship and multitudinous enthusiasms – for ancient and modern poetry, for painting and sculpture, for art history and entomology, for Rousseau, for the English theatre – impressed Johnson and must have spurred him on to a much greater adventurousness in what he published, notably in the direction of producing translations of modern works. One of the first was Fuseli's own translation of Winckelmann's *Reflections on the Paintings and Sculpture of the Greeks* (in 1765); and in 1767 he also published, anonymously, Fuseli's *Remarks on Rousseau*, a witty, splen-

to withdraw his support. In format it was a small, thick magazine, with close-set, tiny print; the size was roughly that of the *Reader's Digest* today.

etic apologia written in the aftermath of the quarrel between Rousseau ('the purest moralist, the most penetrating politician – and a good man') and Hume (a 'c – – –' according to Fuseli).[9]

Another aspect of the early friendship between Johnson and Fuseli could throw some light on the relationship of both men with Mary later. Fuseli was without doubt bisexual in his youth; he has left letters and poems in German that make this clear.[10] Johnson, having left no personal records, has made it impossible to be precise about his private emotions, but it seems at least likely that he shared some of Fuseli's inclinations. The problems and fears of male homosexuals in England in the eighteenth century were very great; in 1780 two men convicted and sentenced to the pillory for sodomy were pelted to death by the crowd. When Burke, to his eternal credit, tried to intervene to mitigate such sentences he was accused of a personal interest and felt obliged to bring a libel action to clear his name.[11] Beckford, whom Johnson and Fuseli both had dealings with, ran into enough trouble to force him to become a recluse; the rich and the aristocracy were not altogether immune from public disapproval, and found it wiser on the whole to go abroad at least as far as Rome to indulge such tastes. In France even the *philosophes* took the view that sodomy was unnatural and reprehensible, although they did not approve breaking on the wheel by way of punishment.[12] Such a climate of opinion meant that men with any tendency towards homesexuality were forced at the very least into outward conformity, and often into concealing even from themselves what they felt.

There is no direct evidence that Johnson was a homosexual by inclination; failure to marry, close friendship with Fuseli and the adoption of a young protégé (Rowland Hunter ultimately inherited a substantial sum of money and a share in the business)[13] are all perfectly explicable in other ways, and I do not want to labour the point beyond suggesting that, if Johnson was lacking in sexual feelings for women, it may have helped him to respect and love those women who aspired to something more than a purely sexual role in life (much as Edward Carpenter, for instance, did later).

In fact his relationship with Mary might not have remained as smooth as it did if he had allowed her to eye him as a possible husband; the subject of marriage was an awkward one between them. Mary cracked jokes about 'the world' having married her to Johnson; and when he tried to marry her off to a young man she reacted with hysterical anger:

> I will not be insulted by a superficial puppy – His intimacy with Miss – – – gave him a privilege, which he should not have assumed with me – a proposal might be made to his cousin, a milliner's girl, which should not have been mentioned to me. Pray tell him that I am offended – and do not wish to see him again! – When I meet him at your house, I shall leave the room, since I cannot pull him by the nose. I can force my spirit to leave my body – but it shall never bend to support that body – God of heaven, save thy child from this living death! – I scarcely know what I write. My hand trembles – I am very sick – sick at heart.[14]

The mistake was not repeated, though Johnson was clearly pleased when Mary did acquire a husband and children of her own initiative.

Early in their relationship he realized he must exercise a controlling discipline over her if she was not to overpower him; she was the sort of person, he remarked, whose mood preceded her into the room whenever she arrived, an extra presence that could not be ignored. The observation is affectionate, but he sometimes told her off for over-indulging herself emotionally; she in turn was quick to feel his disapproval, and struggled to apologize. One of her sorrowing and penitent letters ends disarmingly, 'Allow me to love you, my dear sir, and call friend a being I respect.'[15]

For the New Year holiday of 1788 he offered to have her two sisters to stay with him. She decided however to find a spare bed for them to share in her George Street house; she wanted to be good to them, but perhaps preferred that they should not trespass too much on her territory. Eliza departed reluctantly again in late January for Market Harborough, but Everina remained in London until February, when Mary dispatched her to Paris to learn the language with a family of well-to-do shopkeepers. At this point Mary made one of her many resolves never to have her sisters living with her again; she found them harder to bear than Johnson found her, or them. To Everina indeed he sent a merry postscript in a letter of Mary's, written as they walked to deliver it at the mail coach soon after she had gone to Paris: 'You see what room she has left me, not to make love surely! only to express my good wishes for your happiness J.J.'[16] The prim joke could be risked safely to Everina at a distance; but there was to be no lovemaking at close quarters.

The first phase of Johnson's friendship with Fuseli had ended abruptly when fire ravaged the house they were sharing in Paternoster Row in 1770, destroying everything they owned. Fuseli used this as a spur to leave for Rome to study painting, and Johnson was fortunate enough to have other friends who were ready to assist him in acquiring new premises in St Paul's Churchyard. Here, without any partners, and supervising every aspect of the business himself, he began to build up his large list. By the mid-Seventies he was already publishing political pamphlets; the effect of one on a Bristol election was sharply noted by the Dean of Gloucester. He had also embarked on his educational list, and was publishing everything written by Joseph Priestley, through whom he would make his contacts with other members of the Lunar Society later: R. L. Edgeworth and Erasmus Darwin, and then through them the next generation, Maria

Edgeworth and Thomas Beddoes, the fiercely radical feminist doctor who became Maria's brother-in-law.[17] He was also publishing in partnership with the Warrington Academy press. But Johnson's biggest single commercial triumph was with William Cowper, whom he took on when he was wholly unknown and helped to make into the most widely distributed poet of his time by a policy of progressively cheaper reprints.[18]

This sort of success made it easier for him to expand further in the direction of publishing humanitarian and radical writings: a perfect example of a publisher using his flair as a businessman to promote the causes he had at heart. There were not many oppressed groups among his contemporaries who did not find a champion under his imprint: slaves, Jews, Dissenters, women, victims of the game laws and press gangs, little chimney sweeps, college fellows barred from matrimony, animals ill-used, the disenfranchised and the simply poor and hungry. Names associated with reform projects and sympathies studied his list: not only Priestley, Beddoes and Thomas Christie, but also John Horne Tooke and John Cartwright the parliamentary reformers, William Roscoe of Liverpool, Thomas Cooper of Manchester, George Dyer of Cambridge, Tom Paine, William Godwin, William Blake, Mary Hays, Anna Barbauld, William Wordsworth, Samuel Coleridge, the American Joel Barlow. Some were also published by other firms, but all appeared under Johnson's imprint at one time or another. And there is little doubt that he was active in seeking political works. In 1794, for instance, he wrote to Anna Steward, who was not one of his authors but was a leading poet of the day, asking her for a poem deploring the political condition of the country. She refused: the interesting thing is that he took the trouble to ask her.[19]

So Johnson's shop was a place for the radical and unconventional to gather, both Londoners and provincials passing through. The upstairs rooms became something like a club, where they were sure of a welcome and could talk in comfort late into the evening. For Mary there could have been nothing more congenial. She told George Blood: 'You would love Mr Johnson if you knew how *very* friendly he has been to the princess ... Whenever I am tired of solitude I go to Mr Johnson's, and there I meet the kind of company I find most pleasure in.'[20] The Green had given her a foretaste of such people and talk, but here there were fewer elderly widows and clergymen to set the tone, and the younger generation was a good deal more inclined to kick its heels intellectually and push away all the old props. Price and Priestley had read the French *philosophes*, and corresponded with some of them too, without losing their religious faith; but their disciples, more intoxicated than they allowed themselves to be by a diet of Helvétius, Holbach, Voltaire, Turgot, d'Alembert and Rousseau, showed a distinct tendency to throw out religion. Price and Priestley preached the perfectibility of the human race as a philosophical adjunct to political reform; for others, the creed of perfectibility came to replace all other creeds, and the good of posterity became at least as important as the fate of the individual soul. Advances in education and a reshaping of the formal structure of society were expected to level everything up and bring about a golden age in the future. In America such a golden age was thought to be beginning already, and those who found English church and government too despotic began to emigrate across the Atlantic; during the next decade many Dissenters from all over England and Scotland were to go, still more to dream of going. There were even already a few canny American businessmen who realized there were profits to be made out of such dreams, by selling land in the wilderness to European idealists.

Dr Price, who did so much to popularize this dream of America, had himself moved house following the death of his wife, but only as far as Hackney – about a mile from

Newington Green – where a large congregation was devoted to him. Privately, as he grew older, even he began to query the immortality of the soul.[21] Priestley was not afflicted with doubts on that score, but expected the Day of Judgement to arrive shortly, and retained an endearingly secular vision of eternal bliss: the company of wife and children, plenty of books and the conversation of friends. Both these good men were kind to Mary and there is a description in William Beloe's memoirs that mentions Mary, Price, Priestley, Mrs Barbauld and several others at a gathering that took place at the house of 'an austere and rigid Dissenter of the old school'. According to Beloe he was

> the devoted friend of Priestley and Price and of consequence took a most active and zealous part in what he was pleased to call the cause of political religious liberty, and what was a very customary and favourite phrase among them, the general melioration of the state of man.[22]

Like many Dissenting women, Anna Barbauld was a fierce champion of democracy as well as the rights of her co-religionists; Johnson published her political pamphlets, and she attended political dinners. She wore a perpetual and rather alarming grin on her face, according to Mrs Chapone, but it may have indicated social diffidence as much as optimism on the subject of human perfectibility. Priestley loved her dearly – he had known her from her childhood – and paid her the compliment of criticizing what she wrote seriously (he once scolded her for likening the love of God to the love between man and woman; she took the reprimand meekly).[23] But although she was fierce about the rights of man, she was not prepared to champion her own sex; in fact she had turned down a proposal to run a college for young women on the grounds that such an institution was unnecessary. At this stage Mary had as yet said and done nothing to alarm her Dissenting friends, and they were very cordial towards the unpretentious, enthusiastic and hardworking young woman in her decent black dress. She in turn continued to find their mixture of optimism and social concern attractive and impressive.

She had not lost her own eye for the London scene, and the wretchedness she saw as she walked about the streets filled her with horror. In her *Original Stories*, a children's book that came out in 1788, the poor emerged as the most salient feature of every landscape. Callous landlords, rotten housing, inadequate diet, lack of medical care, the fate of unmothered children and the sufferings of unnecessarily bereaved parents roused her to indignation she did not hesitate to express to her young readers. And when a second edition was called for, Johnson invited an unknown artist, William Blake, to illustrate it, and she found that he entered fully into her rage at the sight of oppression and despair. She had a new ally: Blake was no perfectibilist, but his politics and Mary's sprang from a common feeling.

Blake had even less behind him in the way of family fortune than Mary. He was one of several friends she made at this time who had risen dramatically out of poverty and ignorance by their talents alone. Another was George Anderson, a civil servant of her own age: the son of Buckinghamshire farm labourers, he had been discovered amusing himself with geometrical problems scratched on the walls of a threshing barn, and sent to Oxford by a local vicar to receive a delayed education. Refusing to go into the church, as had been planned for him, he was found a post in the Board of Control and quickly rose to the top.[24] Then there was the painter John Opie, who came from a family of Cornish carpenters and was born in a two-room cottage; now a court painter, he remained simple in his tastes and manners, and he and Mary took to one another at once.

Presently she was to meet Thomas Holcroft,* the trans-

* Holcroft, son of a London cobbler, spent his childhood roaming and sometimes begging with his impoverished parents, taught himself to read, became a Newmarket stable boy and then decided to try

lator of *Figaro*, and then his friend, William Godwin, philosopher and lapsed Dissenter. Their enthusiasm for perfectibility was such that they envisaged the end of all superstition, crime, war, illness and even (in their wilder moments) sleep and death itself. Unkind friends suggested that Holcroft's faith in perfectibility stemmed from too complacent a view of his own progress through life, and there is an element of truth in the notion that the English perfectibilists were the meritocrats of their day: but kindly, not ruthless meritocrats.

Few who gathered at St Paul's Churchyard, Dissenters or others, were enthusiastic in their religious observance. Johnson himself seems to have lacked any fervour (although the *Analytical* always stuck to a loosely Christian line). Fuseli, a lapsed Protestant priest, professed a brand of Christianity so primitive as to require no observance. Blake's angelic visions were unconnected with any formal brand of faith. Paine, born a Quaker, returned from America half-way to atheism. Holcroft's aggressive atheism was notorious, and Godwin's years of study at Hoxton Dissenting Academy had prepared him efficiently to become an unbeliever. In such an atmosphere Mary too gave up church attendance, though she retained a tenuous but stubborn belief in God.

Of all the new friends she was to make during the next few years, the one who represented most perfectly the intellectual atmosphere in which she now lived and worked was Johnson's partner in the *Analytical*, the young Scot Thomas Christie. His father was a banker and provost of

---

his luck as an actor. He had some success writing plays, learned French and German and lived as a hack translator, turning out novels as well. His most dramatic achievement was the memorizing (with one friend to help) of *Le Mariage de Figaro* in Paris, in order to bring it to London, where he played the part of Figaro himself on the first night in 1786. Alas, his version is not very good and cuts out altogether the intrigue involving Marceline and the comments on women's rights.

Montrose, and he and his sister Jane had been nurtured in the first Unitarian Church to be set up in Scotland.[25]* Young Christie was too turbulent in spirit to remain in his father's business; he gave it up for medicine, studying in Edinburgh and London and planning to specialize in obstetrics, where he rightly perceived the need for much improvement; but he grew bored with that too and turned to journalism instead. In 1787 he made a tour of England, calling on all the provincial intellectuals he considered worthy of his attention, and expressing *en passant* a wish for an improvement in ballooning that would enable him to breakfast in the north and dine in the south. He won general approval for his 'sprightly wit, scientific acquirements, ingenuous manners and literary ardour'.[26]

Then he brought his sister Jane, who shared his restlessness, to live with him in England; he took up the study of foreign languages, entered into correspondence with a number of French and German writers and persuaded Johnson into the *Analytical* venture with the idea of bringing continental ideas into better circulation in England. By now his faith in God was on the wane, though he remained discreet in expressing himself on the religious issue. His politics were of course radical, but he was also intent on making money, and he was one of a small band of business adventurers who were excited by the possibility of making fortunes for themselves by encouraging and working for the revolutionary movement.

With Johnson, Christie and Fuseli all keen to bring foreign ideas and literature to the notice of the British pub-

* The link between Dissent and radicalism appears here, for the Montrose Unitarian Church was founded under the guidance of Priestley and its first minister was a young Eton and Cambridge divine, Thomas Fysshe Palmer, who remained in Scotland to work with the radical movement there and was later tried and sentenced for sedition; Dundas, the Secretary of State, called him 'the most determined rebel in Scotland' and had him shipped to Australia for seven years.

lic, Mary was set to translating from the French – Necker's *De l'importance des opinions religieuses* – and later from the German, a book of edifying stories for children to which she added her own touches (the author, Christian Salzmann, was pleased enough to return the compliment and translate the *Vindication* into German later). Johnson also asked her to tackle Italian, but she found it too much of a strain and gave it up. Translating was a highly competitive affair; several of the works she started on were not published in the end because of rival translations appearing first (her Lavater, for instance: Holcroft beat her to it, Fuseli was rude about his translation in the *Analytical*, and there was a small literary row).

She worked hard; in spite of outings with Anna Barbauld and dinners at St Paul's Churchyard, the life of the hack reviewer and translator was essentially a lonely grind. And she imposed a stringent economy on herself. All her life she travelled light, and even in George Street, where she settled for a relatively long time, she did not accumulate much – a few sticks of furniture, a few clothes. The only worldly goods she ever fretted about were her books. Johnson saw that her household repairs were carried out and bills paid; domestic chores were in the hands of her maid, a necessary fixture who remained in the shadows and was never named in any letters, although Mary believed in democratic household arrangements and probably took her meals with her when she was at home: 'I do not know a more agreeable sight than to see servants part of a family ... We must love our servants, or we shall never be sufficiently attentive to their happiness' she wrote later.[27] In 1788 she may not have achieved quite this degree of love, but she was dependent on her maid for the basic organization of her life, the sweeping, washing and fire-lighting; probably she fetched what food was needed too. Mary could not afford to entertain and was largely indifferent to what she ate, preferring vegetables to meat although meat was the staple food of her class. London women who had no cook had most of their meals brought in from bakehouses, and no woman thought of cooking as a creative activity. Sewing on the other hand was supposed to be an ennobling as well as a necessary activity for women, but Mary detested and avoided it. She was still dedicated to looking as plain as possible, all the more defiantly perhaps after her experience with Caroline Kingsborough's rouge, poplin and asses' milk.

One of her main personal preoccupations was with settling her debts and her family's affairs. Her father's money had dwindled almost to nothing, Ned was not interested, and she tried to take on some of the financial burdens involved in assisting her younger siblings. Her brother James, whose current chances of promotion on merit alone in the Navy looked very slim, came to live with her at George Street while she arranged for him to go to Woolwich Academy to study mathematics under George Bonnycastle, a friend of Johnson's who had kept a school at Hackney before being appointed to his professorship. It was hoped that his coaching would improve James's prospects. Eliza was brought closer (but not too close) and installed in a Putney school run by a Frenchwoman, Madame Bregantz, and when Everina returned from Paris she joined Eliza there. Presently Johnson acquired a country house to the west of London at Purser's Green in Fulham; Mary could visit both establishments by taking a boat up the river to Putney Bridge, where the meadows came down to the water's edge. It was a pleasant trip and became a familiar one.

She kept up other old links and obligations, writing to George Blood in Ireland, and for some months using him to deliver clandestine letters to Margaret King. This did not persist for long, but George continued to be useful, carrying out small commissions for both Mary and Johnson. The chief topic of her letters to George soon became the fate of his sister Caroline, whom Mary discovered in a wretched state in a workhouse in December 1787: she offered to pay the parish authorities half a crown a week for Caroline's keep, and saw that she was found work as a servant and decently lodged. But she did not attempt to take Caroline in herself; perhaps by now she was beginning to concede that the Bloods were a hopeless cause, for they failed to send Caroline money and made no effort at all to rescue her. Her prospects in a London workhouse cannot have been bright, and she was still there when last heard of in January 1792. Mary was prepared to be dutiful to Fanny's sister, but no more; her tone to George grew more patronizing as the months went by, and the correspondence petered out.

But George never forgot Mary; in 1791 he proposed to Everina, the 'princess' being beyond his reach, but Everina turned him down. She pleaded sisterly feelings and also probably considered the Wollstonecrafts a cut above the Bloods. Many years later George, a middle-aged man with a large family, called on Mary's daughter Fanny in London and spoke to her reverentially of her mother. Fanny expressed surprise to her sister at his lack of education. For a while Mary had raised the Bloods in her imagination above their capacities, but not even her daughter could see them as she had done.[28]

Although she would not take on Caroline, Mary did want to have someone in her charge whose character she could mould; and presently a small orphan girl, Ann, a cousin of Hugh Skeys, was brought to her. But this fostering experiment proved a failure: Ann was not as tractable as Mary hoped, and reports in her letters refer mostly to her unsatisfactory behaviour. She does not seem to have made much of a dent in her foster-mother's time or consciousness, and when Mary had had enough of her she was passed on to Everina, then to another friend, and then who knows where. It was a common enough way of handling children, but still a sad one, and it is hard not to feel that Ann, like Eliza, was a victim of Mary's egocentric imagination. Those who came into her power and could not play the roles she had planned for them were not let off lightly.

This thread in Mary's character, a very faintly sinister one, is hinted at in parts of her *Original Stories*, where the virtuous governess, Mrs Mason, deprived by death of her husband and child, is endowed with absolute confidence in her power to direct the children in her care along the paths of virtue. She is entrusted with two orphan girls of twelve and fourteen (Mary and Caroline – again) and leads them through various lessons in sincerity, control of the appetites, punctuality, contempt for personal beauty and fashionable appearance (they learn of a young woman whose character has been much improved by a disfiguring attack of small-pox), kindness to servants and so on. She also takes them unhesitatingly into scenes of frightful misery in order that they shall appreciate the necessity of charity. On the whole they are chilly lessons. Mrs Mason does not scold when she is displeased, but the girls come to fear the expression in her eyes; one has the alarming feeling that the revolutionary eye of vigilance is already at work.

There are battling impulses at work in *Original Stories*: some talk of conscience and prayer, balanced by a definition of goodness that would satisfy a nonbeliever: '"Do you know the meaning of the word Goodness?" asked Mrs Mason. "I see you are unwilling to answer. I will tell you. It is, first, to avoid hurting any thing; and then, to contrive to give as much pleasure as you can."'

Another problem faced her in the stories: she wanted to show women in a variety of roles, single, married and widowed, living equally useful and dignified lives and able to maintain themselves. But to do this she had to falsify reality: one woman, for instance, is presented as earning her living by selling the pincushions she makes. It is hard to believe that the girls who read *Original Stories* and absorbed its solemn warnings against marrying out of ambition or for fear of the prospect of spinsterhood could really have believed they might earn a satisfactory living by pincushions alone.

She prepared a characteristically tart introduction to the stories, suggesting that parents who had done their duty by their children would not stand in any need of her book as an adjunct to their education. Johnson asked her to tone it down, but Mary refused, and Johnson gave way on this occasion.

They had come to a pretty good general understanding of one another. Taking Mary on had been a rash act; coping with her as well as he did showed Johnson's real strength. He knew when to give way and when to defend himself against her personality, and he was able to give her the opportunities she needed. He seems never to have regretted his first impulse towards her, and long after they were both dead, Rowland Hunter would sometimes recall to the aged Everina the happy times and deep affection he and Johnson and Mary had shared together.[29]

[7]

Fuseli

1788, 89 and 90 were years of hard work and relative obscurity for Mary: her life was manageable at a practical level, thanks to Johnson, and her ideas were developing, but she was not making any great mark in the world. When bouts of depression overcame her she accounted for them by saying she was still mourning the loss of Fanny.[1] Probably this was no more than a way of focusing the grief she felt for herself, the passing of her youth, the lack of major achievement, the sexual failure.

Johnson remained her emotional mainstay, but he was not able to answer all her needs. She knew her capacity for sustaining a grand passion, and was prepared to seek one out. Eventually she alighted on a man who did seem to promise everything she was hoping for: he was Johnson's most intimate and respected friend, Henry Fuseli, artist, scholar and self-proclaimed genius.[2]

Fuseli had the bravura of a great man. Whenever he appeared in St Paul's Churchyard he dominated the company; he expected to be admired and deferred to, and he was confident of his genius and the respect to which it entitled him. He had the healthy vanity of the artist who values his own achievement because he knows what it costs him, what struggles, what discipline; and he studied and worked unremittingly. But he despised mere technique in art just as he despised the merely decorous life. Like Mary, he was a born romantic. Byronic heroes yet undreamed of were to be built on his model: vain, sardonic, lecherous, treacherous, bisexual, given to much declamation on the subject of his own desires and feelings, bored by other people's. He liked to play the moralist, and preened himself when it was suggested he received diabolical inspiration.

He produced for his own pleasure, and probably for private clients too, a steady stream of pornographic drawings, detailed but chilly in their eroticism. His most famous public picture, *The Nightmare*, showed a sleeping woman, head and shoulders dropped back over the end of her couch in an attitude of abandon that is in fact quite hard to imitate, visited by demons – in one version the ghostly head of a horse, in another a grinning goblin crouched on her chest. The story was that he had eaten raw pork in order to stimulate his imagination before taking up his brushes; he appreciated the notion. *The Nightmare* made Fuseli's reputation in England when he showed it in 1782.

From then on the applause of the world justified his opinion of himself, and in 1788 he was elected associate member of the Royal Academy. He was temperamental and touchy, and could be naive in his conceit, as when he boasted of being invited to all the best houses in London. Still he was at St Paul's Churchyard as often as anywhere else, and a special place was kept for him there. For decades he had been so much the most welcome and regular guest that his absence sometimes cast a gloom on the other diners. On introducing new friends to Fuseli, Johnson would advise them, 'If you wish to enjoy his conversation, you will not attempt to stop the torrent of his words by contradicting him': on the torrent came crushing sarcasms, obscene jokes, erudite references and, on occasion, direct rudeness. His voice was loud, he had a heavy German accent; someone described his wit as 'a formidable force of gunnery'.

Fuseli knew eight languages and derived much of his inspiration as an artist from classical mythology and from literature; he painted numbers of scenes from Shakespeare and Milton, and many of his drawings sought to catch histrionic moments of despair, horror or sublime emotion, expressed in faces with staring eyes, in slumped bodies, the flared nostrils of a woman or the tensed thigh muscles of a man. Some of the portrait heads of women are simple and beautiful, but his female figures are more often grotesque. He never drew Mary.[3] Like Blake, he imagined human figures floating and moving in the air as fish move in water; the two men admired one another's work and respected one another's character, though they had not much in common beyond their fantasies of human flight. Blake's tribute to Fuseli is probably the best-known thing about him:

> The only man that e'er I knew
> Who did not make me almost spew
> Was Fuseli: he was both Turk and Jew –
> And so, dear Christian friends, how do you do?

If he had the crafty, miserly and savage streak Blake attributed to him, it did not stand in the way of their friendship or prevent Fuseli from persuading Johnson to commission Blake as an illustrator.

Fuseli's concern for Blake in his poverty must have been one of the things that impressed Mary; but his whole personality and reputation were made to appeal to her: the legends of his fiery temperament, the learning which would have been pedantic had it not been leavened with jokes, the long years of struggle before success. The vehemence of his manner did not frighten her so much as excite her, and she felt herself quite capable of holding her own; even when she was low-spirited she was not timid.

They must have met not long after she had settled in George Street; both were constant callers at Johnson's and early contributors to the *Analytical*. What she saw was a small-boned and graceful middle-aged dandy, a few inches above five feet tall, wearing his own straight, unpowdered hair; the same illness that had whitened it had afflicted his hands with a perpetual trembling. His eyes were set far apart; at times his face took on the look of a cat, and his movements were catlike and quick, his glance bright and piercing.

Like Mary, he needed glasses; like her, he was too vain to be seen wearing them.

What Fuseli observed was 'a philosophical sloven, with lank hair, black stockings and a beaver hat', but piquant enough to capture his attention.

According to the account given by the Scots writer Allan Cunningham, who wrote about Fuseli in his *Lives of the Painters* at a date when there were still living witnesses of his behaviour, Mary fell in love with him the first time she ever set eyes on him,

> and he, instead of repelling, as they deserved, those ridiculous advances, forthwith, it seems, imagined himself possest with the pure spirit of Platonic love – assumed artificial raptures and revived in imagination the fading fires of his youth.

Fuseli was forty-seven, an age when fires are not always entirely extinct, and Mary twenty-nine; Cunningham however could not resist adding his opinion that 'the coquetting of a married man of fifty with a tender female philosopher of thirty-one can never be an agreeable subject of contemplation'. And unfortunately for Mary, Fuseli was indeed married; or rather, he was in the process of getting married at the very time they met. His bride was an uneducated woman from Somerset called Sophia Rawlins, who had been earning her living as an artists' model, and was very likely endowed with the mixture of prettiness, shrewdness and determined respectability that often goes with successful modelling. (After Fuseli's death she piously gathered up all the pornographic drawings that were still in the house and burned them.) Perhaps he married her for domestic comfort and to put his life on a regular footing: *se ranger,* the French term for this sort of marriage, expresses it perfectly. He maintained a clear demarcation between home and his social round, from which Sophia was as often as not excluded; evidently she was not chosen for her qualities as an intellectual companion.

A man who marries for the first time at forty-seven may experience a panic resentment at the moment of committing himself, and if he meets just then a woman in almost every respect the opposite of the one he has just tied himself to, she may take on twice the appeal she would otherwise have had. Something of this sort seems to have occurred with Fuseli; by flirting with Mary he simultaneously reassured himself and teased Sophia. It was by no means the first time in his life he had set out to shock his friends and indulge a perverse streak in his own nature.

He was born neither Turk nor Jew but a respectable Swiss protestant from Zürich. His father was a painter who had determined that the elder of his two boys should become a minister of the church; Fuseli said he was flogged into learning and had to draw in secret to satisfy his longing for art. At the age of eleven, inspired with a passion for English poetry by a teacher, he attempted to translate *Macbeth* into German. The protestant sect to which the family belonged was that of Zwingli, a little less rigorous than Calvinism; Fuseli was ordained when he was twenty and spent a year preaching in Zürich. His best friend was Johann Lavater, ordained at the same time and also destined to become famous for inventing a pseudo-science that became the craze all over Europe: the earliest form of phrenology, which he called physiognomical studies. The young Fuseli's feelings for Lavater were intense: even allowing for the vocabulary of German romanticism, there appear to have been unequivocal declarations of erotic passion and reproaches addressed to Lavater's timidity.

In 1763 the two young men, joined by a third friend, Hess, launched a political attack on a corrupt city judge, and as a result were asked to leave Zürich. They went north to Germany, and for six months lived a life of idyllic happiness in a cottage in Prussia, writing poetry. Then Lavater and Hess decided to return to Zürich, trusting rightly that things would have blown over. But Fuseli was now set on a different course and did not want to go tamely home; instead he went on to Berlin, where under the guidance and patronage of the English ambassador he translated Lady Mary Wortley Montagu's letters into German. While he was busy with this first attempt to come to terms with an English bluestocking, he addressed a series of letters to Lavater, in which he described himself as 'a soul in love, but not ignobly in love':

> You ask for my 'Complaints' [his collection of poems] – I may not send them, for they are only for the Lavater with whom I slept, and I fear they might fall into the hands of him who wrote the two letters I am now answering. What does your sedateness want with words that burn? ... But my brain catches fire, I grow too excited, I must stop here – O you who sleep alone now – dream of me – that my soul might meet with yours, as through the lattice the hand of the Shulamite met with her dew-drenched beloved.[4]

When Lavater announced his marriage a few years later, Fuseli could not resist sending messages to his bride urging her to bring Lavater back from the land of disembodied spirits, and suggesting that his own spirit would hang about their lips when they kissed. Later he sent the bridegroom himself a poem expressing his own readiness to give up all the pleasure provided by women for 'your embrace'. Fuseli's attitude to women remained ambivalent.

Once the Wortley Montagu letters were published he set off for London, in March 1764. He managed the feat of translating Winckelmann into English during his first year of residence; he met Johnson and they took to one another at once: 'My first and best friend' Fuseli called him. He had still not touched a paintbrush and regarded himself as a writer, and soon he found the traditional employment of the penniless man of letters, as tutor to a young aristocrat. In December 1765 he set off with Lord Chewton, son of the Earl of Waldegrave, for the Grand Tour. Fuseli put his opportunities to good use and managed to meet Rousseau in Paris, but Lord Chewton's education demanded that they travel to Lyons. Here the tutor became so enraged with his charge that he brought his engagement to an abrupt end by boxing his ears.

A brief stay in France followed, then London and journalism. He managed to review his own book on Rousseau; he lived with Johnson. Still later came the decision to become a painter, and the departure for Rome; he spent seven years in Italy. Typically, he boasted that the many weeks lying flat on his back on trestles under the roof of the Sistine chapel gave him his only respite from the libertine pleasures of the city.

Returning to England by way of his native town, he formed the second passionate attachment of his life, this time for Lavater's niece. Her name was Anna; he called her Nanna and addressed several insipid poems to her. He was still penniless; she came from a solid bourgeois family and did not even care for him very much, so that he had no hope at all of winning her hand; but he managed to pose as the distraught and determined lover. At the same time he found consolation of sorts with at least two other young women: Martha Hess, who was dying of consumption, and her married sister Madeleine Schweitzer, who was to become Mary's friend much later. All three girls were nicely brought up and inaccessible for anything more than a flirtation: Martha ill, Anna on the point of accepting another suitor, Maddy the bride of one of Fuseli's friends. This last proved the smallest impediment of the three, and Herr Schweitzer had reason to be annoyed.

On leaving Zürich Fuseli launched into a new series of melodramatic and erotic letters. One was addressed to a married woman friend of Anna's:

> Each earthly night since I left her, I have lain in her bed – when she perceived me, a voice from her bed always asked me, 'How is Fr— Schw—?' O how I would answer that dainty-de-

mure languishing of yours, if once you were in my arms! And for your sake, you slanting eye of love, you creature of roses, lilies and violets, you womanly virginity, you precious coaxer of tears, you who make me wring my hands so desperately – for your sake Italy and my native land are become foreign countries for me and the spring sunshine darkens. But go and take another – for I have belonged to another, and perhaps I still do.[5]

In June he wrote to Lavater from London, reaching a *fortissimo* of passionate utterance:

Is she in Zurich now? Last night I had her in bed with me – tossed my bedclothes hugger-mugger – wound my hot and tight-clasped hands about her – fused my body and her *soul* together with my own – poured into her my spirit, breath and strength. Anyone who touches her now commits adultery and incest! She is *mine*, and I am *hers*. And have her I will – I will toil and sweat for her, and lie alone, until I have won her. And woe to him, who dares to desire her; church and altar are but stone and wood –[6]

and so on; it was a 'state of phrenzy', but for whose benefit it is hard to say. In any case, Fuseli soon calmed down. In August he wrote to Lavater asking coolly for news of the Swiss girls: 'Lots about Nanna and Maddy, and so you will save me from Polly and Nancy and Peggy' (i.e., London prostitutes). He ended the letter characteristically with the word *Basciami* – not sending a kiss, but asking for one.

The next ten years of Fuseli's life were the ones that turned him into something approximating to a respectable English painter, licensed to show eccentricities but not overstepping the bounds into anything too openly scandalous. Mary was his last indiscretion. No doubt she saw herself as an Héloïse; her curiosity about the world she had scarcely seen, the grandiose emotions she had scarcely experienced, the art she had not sufficiently studied or appreciated – all could be satisfied by him. He had only to talk, and she to listen and worship. The prospect was irresistible to them both. Their meetings multiplied, at Johnson's, at George Street where Fuseli took to dropping in, then at his studio where he invited her. She made Sophia's acquaintance too, writing her off mentally, no doubt with Fuseli's encouragement, as a nothing. Presently Mary wrote a review of Rousseau's *Confessions* in the *Analytical* in which she excused the writer's adulteries and abandonment of his children on the grounds of Thérèse's 'negative' character. There must have been some smiles.

Sophia bore no children, and as far as we know Fuseli fathered none. What his sexual eccentricities amounted to must be left to guesswork. Mary told Godwin specifically that there was nothing improper in her relationship with Fuseli; she enjoyed 'the endearments of personal intercourse and a reciprocation of kindness, without departing in the smallest degree from the rules she prescribed to herself'.[7] But Fuseli enjoyed talking and writing about sex; he liked drawing it; whatever was solemn and serious about Mary he probably took pleasure in shocking, whatever was ardent he inflamed further. He lived at the very opposite pole of experience from the idealistic and rather childlike Dissenters. From him Mary learnt much about the seamy side of life – who else would have told her about the unnatural vices of the Romans and the Portuguese? – as well as about the painful and driving force of obsessive love. Obviously there was a time when they were in love with one another, and playing with fire; the increase of Mary's love to the point where it became torture to her is hard to explain if it remained at all times entirely platonic. (The subsequent destruction of her letters by her grandson suggests that he thought them incriminating.)

Whatever happened or did not happen between them, Fuseli certainly continued the process started by the Kingsboroughs, of arousing her erotic imagination. But then, tormentingly, she found she could progress nowhere. It may be that Johnson warned either or both of them. There was no question of a public scandal; things had to remain static. For Fuseli, it was flattering to be known as the object of Mary's passion, to be seen about with her and give rise to discreet conjecture and gossip; and there was always Sophia at home. There is a story of his behaviour at a Covent Garden masquerade, to which he escorted Sophia, Mary and Lavater's son who was visiting London, which suggests just how quickly he could retreat when he felt threatened. A man dressed as the devil (Fuseli's familiar of course) hung about and annoyed his party, at which Fuseli suggested, in his jocular, offensive way, that he should go to hell:

> ... but the dull devil, instead of answering in character, 'Then I will drag you down with me,' or making some bitter retort, put himself into a real passion, and began to abuse me roundly. So I, to avoid him, retired from the place, and left the others of the party to battle it out.[8]

As time went by Mary, like the devil, grew more intense and demanding; she said there was nothing 'criminal' in her love, but still it proved too much for Fuseli to cope with. He had taught her his scorn of convention, he was teaching her willy-nilly to be more honest with herself about what she really wanted; he himself was learning the skill of retreat. As she became increasingly frantic in her feelings and dissatisfied with their relationship, he slipped quietly back into the protection afforded by his marriage. Convention had its uses after all.

In August 1790, Mary was given the opportunity of meeting another domesticated wife, when Henry Gabell, her flirt from the Irish packetboat, invited her to stay with him and his bride in their home near Salisbury. Mary reported to Everina that the household was efficiently run, and Ann herself 'a Doric pillar for proportion without beauty. I am never disgusted by their frequent *bodily* displays of fondness' she continued, likening them to Adam and Eve and making an arch reference to Darwin's *Loves of the Plants* for good measure. A week later she had grown less kind:

> Whenever I read Milton's description of Paradise – the happiness which he so poetically describes, fills me with benevolent satisfaction – yet, I cannot help viewing them, I mean the first pair, as if they were my inferiors – inferior because they could find happiness in a world like this – a feeling of the same kind frequently intrudes on me here.

and

> I think I could form an idea of more *elegant* felicity – where mind chastens sensation, and rational converse gave a little dignity to fondness.[9]

It was impossible for Mary to admit that she was jealous; such an acknowledgement cost too much in humiliation, cut across what she believed about her own independence and self-sufficiency, and might even seem to threaten the status of her platonic attachment to Fuseli. But the spectacle of women who were her inferiors achieving marriage and, in Ann Gabell's case, winning love even from a sensible, educated man, simply because she was pretty, aroused in Mary a pain and rage she could not overcome.

[8]

The Amazon

THE Fuseli affair dragged on, less and less satisfactorily for all concerned. Sophia seems to have adopted the classic tactic of the ignorant and amiable wife, though she may have bitten her lip on occasion. He, confident that she adored him, knew how to keep her in order if she ever appeared on the point of complaining: 'Why don't you swear, my dear? You have no idea how much it would ease your mind.' With Mary, who was perfectly capable of criticizing and wrangling even where she loved, that tone could not be used.

Politics became a saving distraction for her. Long before the Bastille was stormed in July 1789, her Dissenting friends were keenly following the preliminary rumbles of revolution in France, and when the explosion came they were beside themselves with joy. 'Hurrah! Liberty, Reason, brotherly love for ever! Down with kingcraft and priestcraft! The majesty of the people for ever!' shouted young Harry Priestley, waving his hat in the air as he brought the news to his father.[1] Few of the English expressed their pleasure in quite these terms, but there was general admiration for the way in which France, held to be a nation of servile, superstitious and cowardly creatures, had thrown off 'the iron yoke of slavery ... Ill betide the degenerate English heart that does not wish her prosperity' wrote Anna Seward to Thomas Christie as he dashed across to Paris to inspect the situation.[2]

He came back with a glowing account. So did many more. Before the end of the month the Wedgwoods, good businessmen as well as staunch Unitarian Dissenters and friends of Priestley, had planned special celebratory medallions depicting 'the figure of Public faith on an altar and France embracing Liberty on the front', and snuffbox tops with the head of the Duke of Orleans upon them.[3] These were to satisfy the general enthusiasm, but the Dissenters naturally enough saw the successful Revolution on the other side of the channel as a signal for pressing for an improvement in their own status at home. It was all part of the irresistible process of amelioration. Unfortunately there was a stubborn resistance to such improvements in England. Even Pitt, who had supported the Dissenters until now, turned against their cause in 1789.

Mary's fervour for the principles of the Revolution developed rapidly and was unmixed with any doubts; having learnt her politics from the Dissenters she continued to adopt their attitudes and followed their particular struggles sympathetically. In October Priestley was writing to friends predicting the spread of revolution to other countries than France. On 4 November, the anniversary of the 1688 Revolution in England, Dr Price delivered a sermon at the Old Jewry meeting house which was attended by some at least who went in expectation of a political rather than a religious discourse (Godwin, for instance, was there). It took the form of a Nunc Dimitis at the end:

> And now methinks I see the ardour for liberty catching and spreading; a general amendment beginning in human affairs; the dominion of kings changed for the dominion of laws, and the dominion of priest giving way to the dominion of reason and conscience.

Price then suggested that a congratulatory message be sent to the National Assembly in Paris; this was done, and the text published with the sermon.

This speech and action of Price's set off a chain reaction of events in England. Burke was so infuriated by it that he started work on his *Reflections on the Revolution in France*. During the year in which he was writing it the old English hatred of Dissenters began to appear again amongst the people, encouraged by the government, quick to see how things might move if ordinary citizens were invited to admire those who had overthrown their rulers. In Birmingham, Priestley held himself braced for violence; almost febrile with anticipation, he bombarded Johnson with requests for books and pamphlets.[4] No violence came for the moment, however, but in March 1790 Fox again proposed relief for the Dissenters in the House and again was outvoted. In July Dr Price spoke once more, this time a toast at a Bastille Day dinner at the Crown and Anchor tavern in London. He expressed his hope that a United States of the World might be established, and praised France for its intention of abandoning war as an instrument of policy. To the government, this may have seemed so much naive nonsense from an old and feeble man, but privately he was meditating worse things: the possibility that 'a scheme of government may be imagined that shall by annihilating property and reducing mankind to their natural equality, remove most of the causes of contention and wickedness'.[5] Levelling ideas were in the air once more after all, even if their exponents were exasperatingly saintly and gentle old theorists.

Priestley wrote to congratulate Price on his Bastille Day toast, saying:

> I do not wonder at the hatred and dread of this spirit of revolution in kings and courtiers. Their power is generally usurpation, and I hope the time is approaching when an end will be put to all usurpation, in things civil and religious.[6]

And Price wrote in October,

> The majesty of the people is the only sacred majesty ... all civic authority is a *trust* from them ... the governing power in every nation ought to be, not the will of any man or classes of men pretending to hereditary rights, but the collected wisdom of the nation drawn from the general mass.[7]

If, as was perfectly possible, letters like this were intercepted and read by government spies they would fully confirm

Burke's suspicions of the Dissenters; and whether he saw their letters or not, he became absolutely convinced that their presence was dangerous for England.

In November his *Reflections* appeared. Mary read them at once, and seeing the principles she had so unhesitatingly taken up as her own under attack, and a smear set upon the good name of her beloved benefactor and teacher Dr Price, she was in a fury of indignation. 'It is impossible to read half a dozen pages of your book without admiring your ingenuity or indignantly spurning your sophisms' she wrote.[8] It was a fair comment; Burke's *Reflections* became the Bible of reaction, and even his opponents had to concede that he had made a good job of it. Half a dozen people, amongst them Mary, set out to refute it. Johnson, who knew the value of quick publication in such circumstances, encouraged her to set to work at once and had the sheets printed as she wrote. Her pamphlet was to be called *A Vindication of the Rights of Men* (*vindication* was a fashionable title, amongst the quarrelsome tribes of non-conformists especially).

In the middle of composing – her pamphlet ran to several scores of pages – she began to flag. This is Godwin's account of what happened next:

> When Mary had arrived at about the middle of her work, she was seized with a temporary fit of torpor and indolence, and began to repent of her undertaking. In this state of mind, she called, one evening, as she was in the practice of doing, upon her publisher, for the purpose of relieving herself by an hour or two's conversation. Here, the habitual ingenuousness of her nature, led her to describe what had just past in her thoughts. Mr Johnson immediately, in a kind and friendly way, intreated her not to put any constraint upon her inclination, and to give herself no uneasiness about the sheets already printed, which he would cheerfully throw aside, if it would contribute to her happiness. Mary had wanted stimulus. She had not expected to be encouraged, in what she well knew to be an unreasonable access of idleness. Her friend's so readily falling in with her ill-humour, and seeming to expect that she would lay aside her undertaking,

piqued her pride. She immediately went home; and proceeded to the end of her work, with no other interruption but what were absolutely indispensible.[9]

A Vindication of the Rights of Men was a ragbag into which Mary stuffed the ideas she had picked up over the past few years in her reading and conversation, without any attempt to sort them out or reason with Burke at the level he required. The tone was impatient, the arguments sketchy. But it was redeemed by its dominating emotion, a humanitarian sympathy for the poor, and by a passionate contempt for the wilful blindness of the privileged to what kept their system going. If anything held the writing in shape, it was this, from the early pages where she exclaimed 'Security of property! Behold, in a few words, the definition of English liberty,' to the end, where she suggested that waste land should be reclaimed and large estates divided into small farms as a cure for urban poverty.

When she came to theorize about the good society, she imagined one in which 'talents and industry' should be encouraged and enabled to win just rewards, in which younger children should not be sacrificed to eldest sons, in which women should aspire to something more than the wish only to be loved, in which press gang and game law and slavery should be abolished, and the poor succoured as of right, not for charity's sake. All this was admirable no doubt, but so rapidly and allusively set down that it cannot have been expected to do more than dazzle readers already in agreement with her point of view. It could not make converts; the impression was of a mind darting to and fro over its own experience, so sure of its conclusions that it dispensed with discussion.

She leapt over logical hurdles and indulged all her personal obsessions: feckless parents, noble ladies who neglected their children, tutors ignominiously treated by their aristocratic employers. There was even a reference to the consoling power of religion in the lives of those who had lost their youthful friends. It may have been this personal emphasis and wild indulgence in anger and enthusiasm that made Priestley ignore Mary's book rather pointedly, although he expressed a keen interest in seeing all the answers to Burke. Fuseli too was unimpressed, but the general public was easier to please than either of these gentlemen, and much more interested in the tone of the work than the detail of the argument.

Mary's was the first reply to Burke to be printed, and it was manifestly written out of a good heart and generous indignation. It proved so popular that Johnson brought out a second edition in January, this time with her name upon it – the first edition had been anonymous. She was famous suddenly. Johnson was delighted: when Paine's *Rights of Man* appeared shortly afterwards, the names of Wollstonecraft and Paine were bracketed together as revolutionaries. (Johnson had planned to publish Paine too but been warned off; the whole crew of perfectibilists, from Priestley to Holcroft, held their breath while another publisher was found, and rejoiced when the book appeared uncut: 'It will be read the more on account of the stoppage' commented Priestley wisely.)[10]

Tributes were in order for Mary from the less precise. Johnson and Fuseli's Liverpool friend, William Roscoe, visited London and was so impressed by Mary that he commissioned a portrait of her. She took the trouble to have her hair powdered and curled for the occasion – a most unrevolutionary gesture – but was not very pleased with the painter's work.*

Roscoe was something of a poet as well as a patron of the arts; he had already hailed the Revolution in several verses, and presently he produced a satirical ballad, *The Life, Death and Wonderful Atchievements of Edmund Burke,*

* Until 1950 this unattributed painting remained in the possession of the Roscoe family; it is now in the Walker Art Gallery, Liverpool.

in which Mary was again honoured. Burke was depicted in a mad mood:

And wild he roam'd the country round,
  And angry scours the streets
And tweaks the nose, or kicks the breech
  Of every whig he meets.

The neighbours first were all surpriz'd,
  Then sorry as he past,
Then laugh'd his antic freaks to see,
  But angry grew at last.

An lo! an Amazon stept out,
  One WOLLSTONECRAFT her name,
Resolv'd to stop his mad career,
  Whatever chance became.

An oaken sapling in her hand,
  Full on the foe she fell,
Nor could his coat of rusty steel
  Her vig'rous strokes repel.

When strange to see, her conq'ring staff,
  Returning leaves o'erspread,
Of which a verdant wreath was wove,
  And bound around her head.[11]

It was flattering to be offered a verdant wreath, even by Roscoe's less than sublime pen. Mary began a friendly correspondence with him, unburdening her cares about her brother Charles, who was still not settled, and some of her feelings for Fuseli.

Dr Price may just have had time to be touched by Mary's loyalty in springing to his defence, but in April he died. It was as well for one who had said his Nunc Dimittis to the French Revolution to depart before the backlash grew too fierce; he was mourned by his friends, and by the political clubs in France, and remained the bane of the English reactionaries. Burke's abuse was continued after Price lay in Bunhill Fields, and by the same token the radical Skirving hung his portrait in his prison cell as he awaited transportation.[12]

A month after Price's death Burke quarrelled with Fox in the House of Commons: the friendship and political alliance of years was broken by the Revolution. This was the signal for everyone to rush to extremes. In June Priestley formed a Constitutional Society in Birmingham. Almost at once rioting broke out; the houses of the Dissenters were now attacked and burnt as he had feared they might be a year before. Priestley's papers were stolen and handed over to the Secretary of State, Dundas, who never returned them, and his laboratory, probably the finest in the world, was smashed to bits. Citizens who wished to keep the 'Church and King' mobs at bay hastily wrote 'No philosophers' on their doors. 'Philosopher' and still worse 'philosophess' became dirty words with the English public for several decades.

Priestley came to London. His wife was anxious to emigrate at once, before anything worse happened to them, but he was reluctant. Sheridan invited Priestley to meet Fox to discuss their future policy; Fox failed to turn up and Priestley was wary of becoming involved too far in party politics; nevertheless, he was promised more support. At Hackney, where Dr Price's place was vacant, there was wrangling amongst the congregation as to whether to appoint Priestley. Some of the old women were nervous; a young coal merchant, John Hurford Stone, already a keen revolutionary, was amongst those who pressed Priestley's claim.[13] After a few months the congregation agreed to have him and he settled there with his family. He and Stone became good friends, and presently Stone decided to move himself and his wife and children to Paris, where Harry Priestley had also been sent. Mary's old friend the poet Samuel Rogers, also intimate with Stone and Priestley, made a trip to France too, not with any intention of settling but in order to taste the pleasure of the revolutionary way of life: he danced with peasant girls to the tune of *Ça ira*, and joined in intellectual parlour games with Madame de Condorcet.[14] Anna Barbauld dashingly attended a Revolutionary dinner at the Crown and Anchor.

In France, the king's attempted flight and interception at Varennes made the establishment of a republic increasingly likely. Thomas Christie, in Paris again, reported that everything was calm and that he had been amused to read English newspaper accounts of the streets running with blood even while he was enjoying his coffee at a table on the pavement.[15] Perhaps he had missed the fifty-two deaths in the Champ de Mars.

American acquaintances of Christie's did however choose this moment to leave Paris for London. They were Joel Barlow, a poet turned businessman, and his wife Ruth (he called her Ruthy) who trailed along gamely in the wake of her footloose and mercurial husband. Barlow and Ruthy were friends of Paine's and carried introductions from Jefferson to Priestley and Johnson too; almost at once they were on easy terms with all the London democrats, whose ideas they entered into enthusiastically. As soon as they met Mary, they struck up a warm friendship with her.

Barlow was a man of some talent and more energy and charm, an intellectual adventurer of the kind who flourishes in a revolutionary climate and where there is a wide area to move about in. Born on a Connecticut farm, he was convinced of the superiority of American institutions over all others, but was still eager to visit Europe and spread the good news. He had fought in the battle of Long Island during a college vacation, and since then taken up teaching, the law, poetry: not lyrics but large-scale stuff, no less than the first American epic, *The Vision of Columbus*, which had brought him a certain fame. In 1788 he found an opportunity in business, acting as agent for a land company, and set off for Europe, leaving Ruthy behind for the moment. After a brief visit to London he settled in France, working in Le Havre and Paris, where he lived over a gambling club.

In 1790 the company he worked for failed, but he brought his wife over just the same and found odd bits of business; he was never much at a loss.

The Barlows' rearrival in England may have been due to a desire to escape from France in a troubled moment, but once in London he was perfectly happy to settle in Litchfield Street, talking poetry with fellow-writers, lending support to the English democrats, and still doing a little business at the same time. He told Mary about the pleasantness of life in America, offered jokingly to adopt her brother Charles since he himself was childless, and set about writing pamphlets along the same fervently republican lines as hers and Paine's. He even went so far as to predict a general and irresistible revolution that would give power to the class of men 'that cannot write, and in a great measure ... cannot read ... men who reason better without books than we do with all the books in the world'. In spite of this phophecy, books still seemed appropriate for the moment, and Johnson promised to publish what Barlow wrote.[16]

Like most of Mary's friends at this time, he was a theorist who enjoyed juggling with new ideas but had little sense of what practical politics might require in the way of manoeuvre, discretion and compromise. The contrast between their personal mildness and the easy way in which they talked of overturning the institutions of centuries baffled both English moderates, who grew terrified of them, and French extremists, who expected more action of them than they ever saw. But Mary was equally delighted by their ideas and by the comradeship she found amongst them. 'I never saw joy comparable in its intensity to that occasioned by the early promise of the French Revolution' another lady who had known some of the believers said later.[17] For three years this joy continued to bind them together in a certainty that they knew the truth and that it was bound to prevail. It was still possible to imagine the imminence of a brave new world, whatever Burke had to say on the subject.

[9]

A Vindication

In September 1791 Mary moved across the river to a larger house in Store Street, behind the British Museum.[1] Immediately to the north lay fields, farms and nursery gardens stretching away to the distant heights of Hampstead. The streets around the Tottenham Court Road were not particularly salubrious, but writers, artists and theatrical people found the area cheap and convenient. The first faint whiff of the north London bohemian intelligentsia seems to rise in the air at about this time, to thicken, and remain hanging over the place ever after.

Soon after her move, she must have heard news of her old pupil, Margaret King, who was married on 12 November, thus achieving the rank of Countess at the age of nineteen. It may have struck her ex-governess as a disappointingly conventional and undemocratic piece of behaviour, but she was too busy in her own world now to waste time grieving over the apparent defection. The next day she dined at Johnson's, and amongst her fellow guests were her friend Paine and William Godwin, whom she knew well by reputation but had not actually met before. Godwin records that he had not read any of her work, and that he found her insistence on talking when he wanted to listen to Paine irritating: Mary's refusal to hold her tongue, and Godwin's annoyance, made an apt starting point for their relationship.

Godwin had just started work on his own *Political Justice*; he was living meagrely on a publisher's advance – not Johnson's – and had given up his journalistic work entirely to devote himself to slow and concentrated composition, at the rate of a few paragraphs a day. Paine was also absorbed in writing the second part of his *Rights of Man*. Mary may have talked more because she had less on her mind. At all events the gathering, which should have been a remarkable one, failed to come to life and the guests found themselves resorting to ill-natured gossip. They parted company none too pleased with one another.*

But it is possible that Paine dropped into Mary's mind at about this moment the idea of a book on women's rights. In Paris, where he spent half his time, he was on terms of intimacy with Condorcet, and must have known something of the *philosophe*'s vehement advocacy of the idea of equal education and civil status for women. The subject was in the air and needed an outspoken champion in England; why should Mary not produce a second *Vindication* for her own sex?

Ever since Montesquieu French writers had been nibbling at the question from a theoretical viewpoint, but Condorcet had given unequivocal support for a programme of immediate advancement of women to equal rights in his *Lettres d'un bourgeois de Newhaven*, published in 1787.[2] The arguments advanced in this essay were clearly an extension of the arguments used by English political writers of the Seventies in their demand for universal suffrage: the same current of thought that had impelled the Dissenters and their associates to advocate political reform had arrived at its next perfectly logical objective. However, it had needed the mind of a man freed from all religious fetters to reach it; Condorcet, who loathed his Jesuit schoolmasters and had been charmed, soothed and re-educated in the *salons*, had no fear of women. The situation was different in England.

English Dissenters were still held to the concept of a patriarchal system with a male God at its head; the Unitarians denied the divinity of Jesus but not (of course) the masculinity of his father. God was responsible, they thought,

* Godwin lists a man called 'Shovet' as one of the company. A barrister called Shove advised Priestley about the theft of his papers in Birmingham: possibly this was the same man.

for inflicting various physical penalties and humiliations on women which no amount of goodwill could overcome. (Condorcet dismissed menstruation as of no more account than fluctuations in the general health of men.) It was almost impossible to approach the question of sexual feelings without guilt in England or Scotland, amongst the thinking classes at any rate; even freethinkers were troubled by it. Hume, for instance, had categorized the sexual appetite as obviously the most gross and vulgar of all. From such a perspective, women, who aroused (as a rule) the gross appetite, were all too easily held to blame for it and consigned to the role of temptresses and distractions from the serious business of life. The Dissenting love of domesticity and early marriage was one way of dealing with the problem, since a woman placed in the context of family life was less disturbing than one removed from it, standing alone as a claimant to an individual voice amongst the individual voices of men. The hold of *Paradise Lost* over the Dissenting imagination was very powerful.

So that while Mary had been encouraged to think adventurously by the Dissenters, they were not prepared to put forward any directly feminist claims themselves or (on the whole) support her when she came to do so.* The subject

* But see George Dyer's comments, below, p. 143. Coleridge was also of course an ardent feminist during his Unitarian phase; his plans for the Pantisocracy included releasing women and servants from domestic drudgery by the following means:

'Let the married Women do only what is absolutely convenient and customary for pregnant Women or nurses – Let the husbands do *all* the rest – and what will that all be –? Washing with a Machine and cleaning the House. One Hour's addition to our daily labour – and *Pantisocracy* in its most perfect Sense is practicable. – That the greater part of our Female Companions should have the task of Maternal exertion at the same time, is very improbable – but tho' it were to happen, An Infant is almost always sleeping – and during its Slumbers the Mother may in the same room perform the little offices of ironing Cloaths or making Shirts.'

It is certainly a charming picture Coleridge paints.

had in fact been raised once and allowed to lapse. John Cartwright, one of the reformers associated with Price, Burgh, Priestley and Jebb, had actually discussed the question of female suffrage in the Seventies, though only in response to a joke made by one of his opponents. He regarded the idea as preposterous, and claimed that women themselves found the suggestion absurd. His remarks led to no further discussion at the time.* More recently, in the winter of 1788, Jeremy Bentham had also turned his independent and systematic mind to the subject of suffrage and prepared a series of notes intended for the use of Mirabeau. In them he set out all his objections to women's suffrage. He listed five: their involvement in necessarily absorbing occupations that must distract them from political thought; their inevitable economic dependence on the male sex which might make it hard for them to express disagreement; the difficulty of pursuing their education when they were obliged to lead domestic lives; the small need they had of a vote when they were already so powerful through man's sexual dependence on them; and the domestic strife that might arise as a result.

It was a curious list, and Bentham was too logical not to find answers to all the objections; by suggesting a secret ballot and a literacy test, and by pointing out that the distractions to which women were subject were no greater than those of the labouring classes in general, he demolished the case against female suffrage. He did not however choose

* See Appendix I, p. 341. The Dissenting women apparently agreed with him; their ablest political writer, Ann Jebb (1735–1812), wife of the reformer and herself an ardent advocate of universal male suffrage, never broached the question of female. 'She had a nice and even scrupulous sense of honour and propriety, and a delicacy of mind which admitted no compromise with masculine boldness in which some females, of a highly cultivated intellect, have at times indulged', according to her obituarist. She corresponded with Cartwright, and may have been his authority for saying that women themselves did not want the vote.

to publish either his queries or his conclusions, and it seems unlikely that they ever reached Mirabeau either.*

Condorcet returned to the subject in his essay *Sur l'admission des femmes au droit de Cité* in 1790: 'Either no member of the human race has real rights, or else all have the same; he who votes against the rights of another, whatever his religion, colour or sex, thereby abjures his own.'[3] And if women tended to put personal considerations before general social justice, this was the result of their deficient education and social conditioning, he said. He invited serious replies to his claims on their behalf: he had had enough of the jokes and ranting that were the usual response.

Condorcet's arguments remain the classic feminist ones. But they did not reach England, and Mary herself was either wholly ignorant of his work (in spite of Paine) or preferred not to mention it. She could scarcely have known of Bentham's, and in any case the suffrage issue was not in the forefront of her mind. She thought of herself as a philosopher, and to some extent as a political theorist, no doubt; but her most effective claim to a hearing was one that neither Cartwright, nor Condorcet, nor Bentham, could make: she knew the subject from inside.

Johnson, perceiving that she had the perfect theme, urged her to set to, and she began immediately. The speed at which she worked may have owed something to pressure from him. She made no attempt to study the history of the subject or do any special reading or research. In fact she spent somethink like six weeks in all upon *Vindication of the Rights of Woman*; 'would she had blotted a thousand' is a phrase that haunts the air as one reads. There is no doubt that Condorcet's ten pages pack more logic than Mary's three

* Halévy listed Bentham's objections in an appendix to his *Formation du radicalisme philosophique* (1901) but curiously omitted the marginal annotations which answered them. They can be seen in the Bentham MS. at University College, London, Portfolio 170, p. 115, folder 5.

hundred; but on the other hand she hit the exact tone of righteous indignation that is still effective – indeed it has become the staple tone of much successful journalism. Her book is still read, his essay has never been reprinted.

She intended to take her work up again and produce a more leisurely second volume, well aware herself of the deficiencies of the first, but the final sheet of this first, and as it turned out only, volume was handed to the printer on 3 January 1792. She sat down and wrote to Roscoe:

> I am dissatisfied with myself for not having done justice to the subject. – Do not suspect me of false modesty – I mean to say, that had I allowed myself more time I could have written a better book, in every sense of the word . . . I intend to finish the next volume before I begin to print, for it is not pleasant to have the Devil coming for the conclusion of the sheet before it is written. Well, I have said enough of this said book – more than is civil, and not sufficient to carry off the fumes of ill humour which make me quarrel with myself.[4]

The *Vindication* is a book without any logical structure: it is more in the nature of an extravaganza. What it lacks in method it makes up for in *élan*, and it is better to dip into than read through at a sitting. The theme is this: that women are human beings before they are sexual beings, that mind has no sex, and that society is wasting its assets if it retains women in the role of convenient domestic slaves and 'alluring mistresses', denies them economic independence and encourages them to be docile and attentive to their looks to the exclusion of all else.

Mary declared her allegiance to the doctrines of social equality: society must rid itself of kings, armies, navies and church hierarchies; and of perfectibility: God meant us to be happy, and 'all would be right' in the future. She drew the classic comparison between women and a subject class of men, such as slaves: they were property, and 'from the respect paid to property flow, as from a poisoned fountain, most of the evils and vices which render this world such a dreary scene to the contemplative mind'. Her feminism was presented not as an adornment or improvement upon the existing structure of society so much as an aspect of an ideal future society. Woman's perfectibility was to go hand in hand with man's; the rights of man and the rights of woman were one and the same thing. It was as bad for men to be domestic tyrants as to be kings; 'all power inebriates weak men'. Women 'may be convenient slaves, but slavery will have its constant effect, degrading the master and the abject dependent'.

Total financial dependence by one sex on another robbed both of dignity and made it almost impossible for women to act as free moral agents. Mary was the first person to apply the phrase 'legal prostitution' to marriage. She also discussed straightforward prostitution, which was a major problem in the society she lived in. Magistrates were obsessed with it as they are with delinquency today; they were constantly suggesting ways of clearing the streets of women, both by rigorous punishment and offers of re-education in institutions. In the face of this Mary bravely stated her view that prostitutes were ignorant and underprivileged rather than wicked, and made a classic attack on the attitude of well-intentioned reformers: 'Asylums and Magdalenes are not the proper remedies for these abuses. It is justice, not charity, that is wanting in the world!'

But at this point she went off into a discussion of chastity that reads a little oddly. If prostitutes could be said to save the virtue of good women (a point of view much favoured and advanced with complete confidence by Lecky in the middle of the nineteenth century) they were also, said Mary, responsible for undermining the chastity of good women, because they put into their heads the idea that they should attempt to hold their husbands' affections by sexual means. And to Mary this was a bad thing; she adopted the view, shared later by many suffragettes, that sexuality was wrong in itself, redeemed only by parenthood, and largely imposed on women by men. She even went so far as to speak disapprovingly of husbands who 'seduce' their wives, and expressed the view that it was better for marriage to exclude passionate love.

Her view may have been based in part on ignorance of the sexual nature of women, though it seems unlikely: Fuseli's conversation alone should have enlightened her. More probably it was something she felt she ought to say, an accepted view amongst her more innocent and respectable friends. Or again, it may have been what the vast majority of women really felt in an age when there was no effective birth-control.* After the first excitement and flattery of young love, sex was indeed something imposed by men upon women, which they chiefly wished to avoid because of its likely consequences. The greater sexual enthusiasm of French women and English prostitutes probably rested on their command of a simple birth-control device: the sponge.†

* A survey of the views of Italian married women on sex, taken in 1973, showed that most of them regarded it as a trial rather than a pleasure.

† According to Peter Fryer's *The Birth Controllers* (1965), eighteenth-century prostitutes were the repositories of female wisdom on the subject of birth-control in England, and it was not practised by decent women. In France however the bourgeoisie contrived to have very small families and there were reproaches from the church aimed at the successful efforts of married people to avoid conception from the 1770s onwards. The sponge was mentioned directly in a book called *Le Rideau levé, ou l'éducation de Laure* in 1786. In 1797 Bentham made the first English reference to the sponge, and in 1823 the radical Francis Place tried to start a campaign to popularize its use in England amongst married people of all classes. Coming from those concerned with human rights and feminism (the young J. S. Mill was a distributor of Place's pamphlets), the campaign had little success (and was furiously suppressed by the authorities). The sponge was not wholly reliable, but had the great advantage of simplicity – French women were reputed to wear one attached to a ribbon tied round the waist – and of course control by the woman herself.

In 1798 the doctor Thomas Beddoes referred to 'the means [the

But Mary was certainly ignorant of any means of birth-control other than the one referred to in the *Vindication*, which is the suckling of one baby to prevent the conception of another. It was not reliable, but it was time-honoured and carried the extra appeal of seeming to be a self-rewarding procedure: the baby's benefit was also the mother's. (Suckling was the fashion amongst radicals, and Mary's friend Roscoe had enormous success with his translation of *The Nurse,* a long Italian poem in its praise.)

Mary's opinions on sexual matters were to be wholly altered by her subsequent experiences, though whether to a more or less realistic point of view is open to some doubt. But it is certain that, had she stuck to the prim attitude expressed in the *Vindication*, she would have been much more acceptable to the British public than she became.

Her views on education were shaped, probably indirectly, by the psychological theories of the *philosophe* Helvétius, who preached the supreme importance of environment and expectation. If girls were encouraged from their earliest years to develop their minds, nourish ambitions and exercise their bodies exactly as boys were, said Mary, they would develop equal capacities and talents: 'speaking of men, women, or professions, it will be found that the employment of the thoughts shapes the character both generally and individually'. Let women therefore be trained for professions and careers: medicine (not just nursing), midwifery, business, farming, shopkeeping. This would free unmarried women from the 'bitter bread of dependence' and enable mothers and widows to plan their lives and manage their

poor] use to prevent increase of family', but without specifying what the means was; he was of course a feminist and a radical. And, again in the mid-1820s, William Thompson, the most outspoken of feminists, appeared to take for granted that birth-control was easily practicable in planning his ideal communities.

affairs more rationally. Rousseau's contention that educated women would lose their power over men enraged her particularly: 'This is the very point I aim at. I do not wish them to have power over men; but over themselves.'

Mary favoured coeducational day-schools, lessons given by informal conversational methods, with lots of physical exercise, both free and organized. Coeducation would lead to early marriage: preferable, she pointed out briskly, to a system that encouraged boys to sow wild oats amongst girls of a lower class whilst respectable girls were kept segregated and ignorant until they were offered in the marriage market. Her picture of an ideal family was undeniably attractive: the babies nourished by an intelligent mother, not sent away first to nurses and then to boarding school; and the fathers friends rather than tyrants to their children, who should have the right to judge their parents like anyone else. Mary understood instinctively that the emotional balance of the adult was formed in early childhood. 'Few I believe have had much affection for mankind who did not first love their parents, their brothers, sisters and even the domestic brutes, whom they first played with.' Sexual reproduction should be explained 'gravely' by the parents, to prevent their heads being filled with nonsense on the subject.

To the accepted view that women should be delicate and dependent, Mary pointed out the actual conditions in which the vast majority of her sex were forced to struggle:

> ... with respect to virtue, to use the word in a comprehensive sense, I have seen most in low life. Many poor women maintain their children by the sweat of their brow, and keep together families that the vices of the father would have scattered abroad; but gentlewomen are too indolent to be actively virtuous, and are softened rather than refined by civilization. The good sense which I have met with, among poor women who have acted heroically, strongly confirmed me in the opinion that trifling employments have rendered woman a trifler.

And she did in fact raise briefly the question of women's legal position, saying it should be revised and suggesting they should take an interest in politics with a view to parliamentary representation:

> I may excite laughter, by dropping an hint, which I mean to pursue, some future time, for I really think that women ought to have representatives, instead of being arbitrarily governed without having any direct share allowed them in the deliberations of government.
>
> But, as the whole system of representation is now, in this country, only a convenient handle for despotism, they need not complain, for they are as well represented as a numerous class of hard working mechanics, who pay for the support of royalty when they can scarcely stop their children's mouths with bread.

A long section of the book was given over to attacks on earlier writers who either made light of women's capacities or praised them for the very qualities Mary distrusted: pliancy, docility, cunning, timidity. Characteristically, Mary lashed out at anyone who had offended, sparing neither her friend Anna Barbauld nor her learned French contemporaries Mesdames de Genlis and de Staël, any more than Rousseau or the fatuous Chesterfield. She was not writing to please.

The book ended abruptly, as though her indignation had boiled itself out of steam for the moment anyway. She had associated feminism firmly with radicalism and an anger directed at social conditions and assumptions, but avoided a vengeful approach to the male sex. She was prim and ignorant on the subject of the sexual relationship, but knew and insisted on the importance of the family. There is in the *Vindication* an absence of sourness, falsity or hysteria which has not always characterized feminist writing; her book remains remarkable both in its scope and its tone.

[10]

London 1792

At the beginning of 1792 Mary stood at the peak of her success as a writer: she had produced an original and deeply felt book, thirty years' rage distilled in six weeks' hard labour. It was a best-seller at once and established her name before the world; according to Godwin she became for a while the most famous woman in Europe. There were certainly those who scoffed at it, notably Horace Walpole, who classed Mary as a 'philosophizing serpent', along with Paine and Horne Tooke: it was her politics rather than her feminism he objected to. Hannah More encouraged him in his scorn, boasting that the title of the *Vindication* alone was enough to prevent her from reading it, and Walpole coined another, probably the most famous, description of Mary: 'hyena in petticoats'.[1]

There were others who discussed the *Vindication* without ever seeing a copy, as jokes about its authorship reveal;* but it was reviewed in respectful tones and circulated merrily all over the British Isles. Roscoe pressed copies on the ladies of Liverpool.[2] Lady Palmerston, the meekest of

*A Wolverhampton pamphleteer seems to be referring to Paine in a rather laboured joke in answer to a scurrilous right-wing suggestion that Paine was sexually inadequate as a husband: 'Well, if that really be Thomas Paine's way, I would advise him to study the *Rights of Woman*, which may be the title of his next book; which, as he seems to be a sharp fellow, will, no doubt, teach a good lesson to our wives and daughters.' (*A Letter from Timothy Sobersides, Extinguisher Maker*, 1792, published, curiously enough, by Johnson.) Another satirical pamphlet, this time hostile to Mary, on the *Rights of Boys and Girls*, linked her ideas with those of Paine, Barlow, Priestley and Price, and referred to her (rather pleasantly) as 'Mrs Mary with the hard German name'.

wives, warned her husband that 'I have been reading the Rights of Woman, so you must in future expect me to be very tenacious of my rights and privileges'.[3] Mary Hays, a young Dissenter living in south London, wrote enthusiastically expressing her belief that the book was 'a work full of truth and genius';[4] she had feminist views of her own, but she laid aside for the moment a half-finished attempt to cover the same subject and instead persuaded Johnson to introduce her to her rival author at a breakfast party. She became Mary's most fervent female disciple, and presently she and her youngest sister Elizabeth produced together a volume of *Letters and Essays* larded with respectful references to Miss Wollstonecraft and urging other women to 'unite in intention' now that they had been shown the way to claim their rights. The Hays sisters were on friendly terms with many prominent Dissenting ministers and scholars, notably Disney and Priestley in London, and William Frend and George Dyer in Cambridge, who appear to have encouraged them in their feminist ideas.*

She was not the only active disciple. In 1792 Thomas Beddoes printed a poetical *Letter to a Lady on the Subject of Education* that was judged too free in its sentiments to be distributed. Such was his concern for the condition of women that he used a woman compositor to set up his work:

* In fact Dyer was distinctly feminist in his sympathies. In a footnote to his *Poems*, published in 1792 by Johnson, he wrote:

'I have observed, that the most sensible females, when they turn their attention to political subjects, are more uniformly on the side of liberty than the other sex ... The truth is, that the modes of education and the customs of society are degrading to the female character; and the tyranny of custom is sometimes worse than the tyranny of government. When a sensible woman rises above the tyranny of custom, she feels a generous indignation; which, when turned against the exclusive claims of the other sex, is favourable to female pretensions; when turned against the tyranny of government, it is commonly favourable to the rights of both sexes. Most governments are partial, and more injurious to women than men.'

'employment for females is among the greatest *desiderata* of society,' he wrote.[5]

'Have you read that wonderful book, The Rights of Woman?' Anna Seward was asking her correspondents in February;[6] her accolade in itself was probably worth some sales, the equivalent of a favourable review in a weekly today. French, German and Italian translations were planned, and American editions soon appeared. The sensible thing for Mary to do now was to work hard on the second volume; instead, she dithered and dissipated her energies in writing reviews. 'Her exertions were palsied, you know the cause' said Johnson;[7] she was still obsessed with Fuseli, and he was more inclined to laugh at her for her great book than admire her for it: 'the assertrix of female rights' is not quite the phrase of a devotee.[8]

Her feelings were a torment to her, and the more insistently she expressed them the more Fuseli withdrew from her into mockery, indifference, the protection of his marriage. Mary claimed to respect the institution, but the time she spent with other friends did little to increase this respect. Paine had found marriage an impossible state to endure, Johnson was never even tempted by it; John Opie and his wife Mary, whom she saw a good deal of, were heading for disaster, for she was a flirt and he was indifferent to her.[9] Ruth Barlow, abandoned in London while Joel went off to pay visits here and there, in the country and later abroad to see Lafayette, comforted herself by calling constantly on Mary and reading aloud Joel's love letters; Mary was not impressed.[10] She herself boasted of a proposal of marriage from a 'proper man' with a fine house at this period, but only to say she had turned it down.[11] In the same letter to her sister she mentioned that Fuseli had given Charles a present of £10; evidently it was understood in her family how Fuseli dominated her life and excluded all other possibilities for her.

She may even have hoped that society's attitude to marriage would change; in France an easy divorce law was talked of, and she must have known that Thomas Christie, Johnson's partner, had brought over a French mistress, Catherine Claudine Lavaux, a married woman, to await the birth of his child in London; no doubt Catherine Claudine hoped to marry Christie once she had obtained a divorce.[12] The folly of indissoluble marriage was a subject much discussed amongst her radical friends. Thomas Holcroft's novel *Anna St Ives* was published, and reviewed by Mary; it contained a portrait of a spirited radical heiress who managed to reconcile her duty to society with her sexual inclinations, and was entertained by her lover's meditations on a future state of society in which marriage should have ceased to exist altogether:

> Of all the regulations which were ever suggested to the mistaken tyranny of selfishness, none perhaps to this day have surpassed the despotism of those which undertake to bind not only body to body but soul to soul, to all futurity, in despite of every possible change which our vices and our virtues might effect.

Holcroft was careful to explain that women would be well advised to retain the protection of the law until the world had arrived at a state in which men had ceased to be libertines, and in fact he ended the story with Anna's marriage. But this book was certainly interpreted as an attack on established morality.

Anna St Ives's lover was the son of a steward who managed to better himself even in the current state of society, and only dreamed of a different future for mankind. But in January a group of London working men, led by a cobbler called Thomas Hardy, decided dreaming was not enough. They founded a club on the French pattern with the avowed intention of pressing for parliamentary reform, annual parliaments and votes for all men (women of course were not mentioned): it was called the London Corresponding Society. Hardy's inspiration had come, he said later, from a

Dissenting Minister who lent him books by Price, Cartwright and Jebb. The government was alarmed at this rousing of a class of men who had been silent for so long, especially when other clubs began to be formed all over England and Scotland; and what they particularly disliked was the link between working men and educated Dissenters. In the middle of February the second and more inflammatory part of Paine's *Rights of Man* appeared; it was distributed all over the country and passed eagerly from hand to hand. In the same month Johnson brought out Barlow's *Advice to the Privileged Orders*, which adopted the same stance as Paine and was received with ill grace by those for whom it was intended. Only Fox teased the House of Commons by making flattering references to it. Barlow followed up his prose suggestions with a poem entitled *The Conspiracy of Kings* in which he held up his native country for admiration and issued some solemn warnings both to 'Burke, degenerate slave ... the sordid sov'reign of the letter'd world' and to the monarchs of Europe (Louis XVI was rumoured to be working on a translation of Burke):

> The hour is come, the world's unclosing eyes
> Discern with rapture where its wisdom lies;
> From western heav'ns th'inverted Orient springs,
> The morn of man, the dreadful night of kings.
> Dim, like the day-struck owl, ye grope in light,
> No arm for combat, no resource in flight;
> If on your guards your lingering hopes repose,
> Your guards are men, and men you've made
> your foes ... &c.[13]

Mary naturally applauded both Paine and Barlow. At the same time her own book brought her a distinguished visitor in February: Talleyrand, Bishop of Autun, an aristocratic revolutionary who had come to England to win support to his cause. His mission was semi-official – he was supposed to be buying horses for the French army – and he was travelling with a party of friends with similar backgrounds and allegiances.

Talleyrand was as cynical and corrupt a man as ever rode the course of a revolution, but to Mary at this moment he appeared in the welcome guise of a progressive bishop, a figure dear to left-wing idealists for his ability to attach a normally conservative God to the radical programme. The *Vindication* was actually dedicated to the Bishop of Autun, partly out of respect for what he stood for and had already written on the subject of education, and partly in the hope that he would be instrumental in improving the education of girls in France. Thus complimented, and always prepared to inspect a bluestocking, Talleyrand made an appointment to call at Store Street.

He may have been amused at what he found: wine offered in teacups by a high-minded, intense and talkative spinster. The conversation was in English, as Mary's spoken French was not fluent, and unfortunately neither party recorded it. Talleyrand considered virtuous women a little ridiculous, and he was a snob, but he knew how to be charming to anybody.* And at least the welcome accorded at Store Street made a change from the reception given him at the English court, where the King froze and the Queen simply turned her back and walked away. Nor indeed were Pitt and his fellow government officials in the least disposed to be swayed from unsympathetic neutrality by anything Talleyrand had to say.[14] The only other warm reception he had was from Mary's Dissenting friends, who gave a dinner for him in Hackney, to which Fox and Sheridan were also invited.[15] Talleyrand was accompanied on this occasion by his friend Madame de Genlis and her adopted daughter Pamela; Pamela's beauty was toasted, and Stéphanie de Genlis wore

* Madame de Staël's transvestite portrait of Talleyrand as 'Madame de Vernon' in *Delphine* is worth looking up to see how slippery, treacherous but irresistibly charming he seemed to his contemporaries.

a real stone from the Bastille, polished and set in gold, around her neck.[16] Had the term radical chic been invented it would have done duty that evening.*

In March the French party dispersed. In their wake another political club was formed in London, the Friends of the People, with a membership derived largely from the middle classes and the aristocracy; many of the Hackney diners joined. The old Society for Constitutional Information of 1780 was revived and began to cooperate with the London Corresponding Society. Barlow joined the SCI and became a leading spirit. In May the King issued a proclamation against seditious meetings and writings, which put political clubs, publishers and writers all into a potentially dangerous position. Priestley, still protesting that his concern was not with politics but religion, nevertheless encouraged his eldest son to take up French citizenship: he himself was awaiting the result of Fox's new appeal for the Dissenters in the House before making up his mind whether to leave for America. On 11 May Fox did propose yet again the repeal of the acts barring Dissenters from civil rights; Burke seized the opportunity to make one of his more violent speeches.

He accused the Unitarians of being a political faction, bent on subverting the state and rebuilding it on the French model; he referred to 'the Constitutional, the Revolutional

* Madame de Genlis, at this time in her mid-forties, was born into the minor aristocracy and started her career as a lady-in-waiting to the family of Philippe, the royal duke who became known as Égalité during the Revolution. She became his mistress, and when the official post of tutor to his children fell vacant, she had the wit to propose herself for the job, becoming the first woman to invade this masculine preserve. She was a prolific writer and her educational ideas were similar to Mary's; politically she was of course liberal and supported the early stages of the Revolution. Mary was not polite about her in the *Vindication* and there is no record of direct contact between the two women. English society, which had taken no notice of Madame de Genlis's sexual indiscretions before the Revolution, used them as a pretext to shun her later: a familiar pattern.

and the Unitarian Societies' in one breath, likening them to loathsome insects that might, if they were allowed, grow into giant spiders as large as oxen, building cables in which to catch everyone who opposed them. Even this grisly image did not exhaust Burke's vituperative powers; he named Priestley and Price (although he was dead) as hot and dangerous men; he said the Dissenters formed one fifth of the nation and made no attempt to dissociate themselves from their dangerous leaders, who were prepared to call in foreign forces to help them in their plots; and he added that, like Hannibal, they swore their very children at the altar. The implication, of course, was that they swore them to treachery.[17] After such oratory the House not surprisingly voted against any relief for Dissenters.

Meanwhile Paine took a trip into his native East Anglia, alarming the gentry and encouraging gatherings of the many flourishing Revolution Societies: at this time there was said to be one in every village. While he was there, he was served with a summons for sedition. He returned to London to appear in court in June, only to find his trial postponed. And still the membership of the clubs increased: in London, in the industrial centres of the north, in Scotland where Christie's friend Thomas Palmer was active in assisting the working men of Dundee. The government sent out spies and opened the mail of those they suspected of plotting its overthrow: Paine, Talleyrand, Johnson's old friend and author Horne Tooke, whose after-dinner toasts and singing of *Ça ira* were a noted feature of the SCI meetings. But the mood of the English radicals remained earnestly optimistic, and the singing of *Ça ira* continued.

In midsummer Mary, Johnson and Fuseli agreed to make a trip to France together, as so many of their friends had already done. The plan was to set off in August for a stay of about six weeks, and whatever private qualms Johnson may have entertained about the effects of such an expedition on the mutual relationships of the group, he did not express them; in any case, Sophia was to be of the party. In preparation for the adventure, Mary decided to send her foster-child Ann to Ireland, where Everina was willing to take charge of her; later she went to Ruth Barlow, and after that Mary seems to have lost touch and interest.

Success had brought other changes in her. Her brother Charles remarked on how handsome she had suddenly become: she had not bloomed with youth, but with success she began to. She gave up her insistence on the essential virtue of dowdiness; perhaps the sight of her own cross and hungry-looking schoolmarm's face in the Roscoe portrait had been enough to change her mind. She also had some money to spend on herself for the first time in 1792, and in spite of her self-appointed role as spiritual mate to Fuseli she must have noticed the sort of women he liked to draw. As it happened a general change of fashion, towards an informal and even childlike look, was taking place; it suited Mary as the stiff and elaborate styles of the Eighties had never done, and if she could not approach the appearance of an Emma Hamilton in her deliciously negligent clothes, she could at least let her hair take on its natural wisps and curls, cut it in a fringe like a girl's and adopt a plain, wrapped dress.* It did her no good with Fuseli, but allowed

* In one respect Mary resisted the new fashion: she did not abandon her stays. Dress reform interested some of her contemporaries, but not her: Erasmus Darwin expressed satisfaction on medical and aesthetic grounds that women were leaving off stays in the Nineties, but the care with which Mary looked after hers is evident from the fact that her daughter Fanny was wearing a pair marked M. W. when she died in 1816!

In 1789 Alexander Jardine, an army officer friendly with Godwin, published a book (*Letters from Barbary, France, Spain, etc.*) in which he advocated shorter skirts to be worn over drawers for women: drawers were still the prerogative of men at that time. 'The sex would certainly gain by shewing a little more of their legs' said Jardine; 'such things though apparently trifling, may have great influence over female character'. He also considered women should be given 'more her to appear in a new light to those less determined to keep alive the memory of her beaver hat and bedraggled days. Amelia Opie's description says Mary was regarded as plain by her own sex, but attractive to men: tall, with a good figure, irregular features, a pleasant expression, soft, light hair curling over her cheeks; hazel eyes, long lashes and fair skin.[18]

The Paris party set off as planned and got as far as Dover, but there they paused. There was news of trouble from France; Paris was in confusion and probably dangerous. It was no time for foreigners to be visiting and, although Mary would gladly have gone on, the others were less inclined to be bold. Presently they all returned to London.

It was in the disappointment and *désœuvrement* of this moment in a dusty, half-empty London in August that Mary made her final bid to link herself with Fuseli. She called on Sophia, who had so far taken the line of deliberate, dignified ignorance demanded by the situation, and amazed her by asking to be admitted to the household on a permanent basis. Her wish, she explained, was to be his spiritual partner; she was not trying to supplant Sophia's position as the legal wife of the flesh, but she felt herself truly united to Fuseli by a mental affinity. She could no longer bear to live separately. She must see him every day.

Whether she had warned Fuseli that she intended to spring such a proposal on Sophia we do not know; he had a habit of carrying her letters about in his pockets unopened, or so he told a friend later, so that he may have received a warning without heeding it. Perhaps he would not have bothered to intervene in any case, but trusted Sophia to cope. As it was, she broke into understandable fury as soon as Mary had finished her absurd and innocent

influence in the councils of taste and learning; and it might be as well if they were not entirely excluded from other councils'. Unfortunately neither Mary nor anyone else took up his recommendations.

request; she sent her packing and told her on no account ever to return to the house again.

It was a simple enough solution to the situation that had caused Mary so much anguish, and she retreated at once, shrinking into herself as though she had been sprinkled with acid. Fuseli did nothing at all; doubtless he was a little nervous of a scandal. Somebody – Johnson probably – persuaded Mary to leave town for a while. Despondent and humiliated, she did so.

She told herself that what she had wanted was quite reasonable, but whether she believed it in her heart is another matter. She felt that Fuseli had treated her badly: what had begun in pleasure and excitement had become a power struggle in which she had become increasingly exposed and vulnerable as he grew stronger and more ruthless. Perhaps that was the essence of any sexual relationship. When she arrived back in September, she found a parallel drama taking place amongst her friends. Thomas Christie's mistress had borne him a daughter at the end of July; the parents had named her Julie. There can scarcely have been a more perfectly endowed revolutionary baby than this Julie Christie, child of free love, born to a Unitarian radical Scotsman and a Parisian adulteress, in the heat of the London summer of 1792, and named for the sublime and sentimental heroine of the *Nouvelle Héloïse*. But now Christie proceeded to behave less like Saint-Preux than the author of the *Confessions*. When little Julie was six weeks old and the divorce laws were on the point of being passed in France, enabling Catherine Claudine to be legally rid of her husband at last, he announced that he himself was to be married to an English carpet heiress, Rebecca Thomson of Finsbury Square. Whether she knew about Catherine Claudine and the baby at this stage is uncertain; probably not. But Christie was confident that he could bring everyone round. He was also strongly motivated by a chronic shortage of money. Somewhat tactlessly perhaps he carried Rebecca off to Paris for a wedding trip, taking his sister too, in spite of the news of massacres and the refugees pouring into England.

In October there was new sadness for Mary when her brother Charles travelled north to Liverpool to sail for America at last. She was bitterly upset at the parting – Charles was her favourite in the family, and she never saw him again – but she had to swallow this 'bitter pill of life' too.[19]

Paine had now decided to return to Paris rather than linger in England to face his trial. Johnson was busier than ever, distributing unprecedented numbers of pamphlets with titles calculated to provoke the government: 'Is all we Want, Worth a Civil War?' was one. The clubs were pressing hard for a National Convention to be called in England, and the *Analytical* gave its support to this idea and deplored the folly of the parliamentary parties in refusing to entertain it. Barlow, shuttling between Paris and London, produced another pamphlet, this time addressed ostensibly to the French Convention (albeit in English), urging them to establish a truly democratic republic on humane and elevated principles: public education for all, no death penalty, no standing army, no colonies. Mary told Roscoe how much she approved of Barlow's ideas, but it must have become increasingly clear that there was no immediate prospect of their being adopted in England at any rate.

The news of massacres of priests and prisoners in Paris produced faltering and revulsion amongst many English sympathizers. Cowper despaired of the revolutionary cause now, Blake laid aside his red cap of liberty and Anna Seward, the perfect barometer of middle-class opinion, announced that she found Burke more persuasive than she had done at first reading and was 'sick of mischievous oratory'. Soon she was in full cry against Priestley and wishing he would leave the country. But he too was experiencing some doubts about the French; he wrote to Stone lamenting their public debates,[20] and declined an invitation to become a member of the new Convention, pleading poor French and the old excuse that theology was his field, not politics.

Mary adopted a brisk tone on the massacres; she wrote to Roscoe,

> let me beg you not to mix with the shallow herd who throw an odium on immutable principles, because some of the mere instrument of the revolution were too sharp. – Children of any growth will do mischief when they meddle with edged tools. It is to be lamented that *as yet* the billows of public opinion are only to be moved forward by the strong wind, the squally gusts of passion.[21]

And there were still some who shared her optimism; in November a dinner given by the Friends of the Revolution drank forty toasts, including one to the patriot women of Great Britain.

But the position of the English democrats was becoming more dangerous. A Dissenting minister called Winterbotham was sentenced to two years' imprisonment for preaching against the monarchy. Roscoe found himself ostracized in Liverpool. Johnson fell ill in November, his asthma no doubt affected as much by the political situation as the weather. Barlow left for Paris yet again, leaving poor Ruth alone to face the unpopularity his writings had brought. The coffee houses and taverns began to refuse radical clubs permission to meet on their premises, intimidated by threats of having their licences withdrawn. A magistrate newly returned from a spell of duty in Newfoundland, John Reeves, was so outraged by the tone of the London democrats that he founded an Association for Preserving Liberty and Property against Levellers and Republicans; the government lent its support and the forces of the right were soon stronger than ever. Even Jeremy Bentham, who had been prepared to advise the revolutionary theorists in France, set out one morning to join John Reeve's' association, though he was deflected on the way by a friend and later thought better of it.[22] News came from Manchester that another Church and King mob had attacked the house of a well-known radical, Thomas Walker.

Rather than stay in London and be miserable both about her personal life and the political situation, Mary decided to set off for France once again, alone and determined not to falter. There she believed she might forget her private sorrows under the sheltering wing of an exaltedly virtuous government, and in the company of fellow idealists of all nations who made their headquarters in Paris.

[11]

Paris: Expatriates and Politicians

On 12 November Mary had written to Roscoe, warning him that he should not visit London in the near future if he hoped to see her:

> I intend no longer to struggle with a rational desire, so have determined to set out for Paris in the course of a fortnight or three weeks, and I shall not now halt at Dover I promise you, for as I go alone neck or nothing is the word.[1]

The 'desire' was of course her wish to live with Fuseli, the 'rational' no more than a claim set up in defiance of whatever disapproval or dismay her friends might express or even feel. Otherwise her unhappiness broke out in facetiousness; she could not resist mentioning that gossip had married her to Johnson, an idea patently absurd to Roscoe or any of their personal friends. 'I am still a Spinster on the wing' she added, superfluously. 'At Paris, indeed, I might take a husband for the time being, and get divorced when my truant heart longed again to nestle with old friends.'

The joke covered her anxieties about her continuing state as a spinster, something that brought not only pain but ridicule too as she grew older. William Hayley, a popular writer whom Barlow had been visiting, had lately published a three-volume study of old maids, weighted with pseudo-learned references and a scattering of *doubles-entendres*, which attributed to them an almost automatic development of malice, envy and meanness as a direct result of their biological failure. Bluestockings married and unmarried had turned on Hayley and scoffed at him for his 'batter'd theme'[2] but the very fact that it *was* battered pointed to a generally accepted attitude; indeed it was hard not to grow sour, prim and envious if the circumstances of life excluded you from knowledge and affection. Mary knew it; she could be all these things on occasion.

Her reference to divorce, imagined as a freedom to be used by the aggressive and inconstant woman, not a rejection or humiliation, said something else about her state of mind. Fuseli had allowed Sophia's patience to triumph over Mary's pursuit, but Mary could not imagine herself in Sophia's position; she must always be the agent, and she obviously took some pleasure in her little picture of herself choosing and rejecting men lightheartedly.*

As good as her word, she set off on 8 December, not bothering to store her furniture since she intended to be home again in about six weeks. Johnson, even if he was not her husband, could at least keep an eye on Store Street while she was away. The trip to the coast took twelve hours, almost as much in darkness as light, a mournful seasonal reminder of the difference between the false start of the summer and her present lonely journey. But she was always a good traveller, and had the enthusiasm of the political pilgrim to buoy her up. It was needed; Channel crossings were unpredictable and usually meant delays and discomforts at all stages. Inns were draughty, boats dirty; a good wind might blow you from Dover to Calais in five hours, a calm could mean hammocks slung across the cabins and two days aboard. Mary's boat seems to have made reasonable time and presently her feet were set down by French sailors on French shingle. Here was the new society she had wanted to see so much.

Other travellers to France during this period complained of the delays occasioned by filling in detailed passports, the

* A French jurist had already asked whether the new divorce laws might not lead to the abandonment of ageing and helpless wives, but they were generally regarded as a liberation rather than a threat to women: see Ph. Sagnac, *La Législation civile de la Révolution française* (1898).

instructions that they must be kept handy for inspection on the road at all times, the emphatically proffered advice on showing solidarity with the regime by wearing (and paying a good price for) tricolour cockades. Mary can have had no objection to putting a red, white and blue ribbon in her hat but it was no charm against the fatigue of the rest of the journey. Another two days by coach had to be endured, over the wet and potholed roads, through St Omer, Arras and Péronne, and so to Paris. Tired out, and beginning to catch cold, she arrived during the first days of the trial of the king, which had opened on 11 December. The beauty of the city, mud-grey under its soft and changeable sky, did not appear to her for the moment.

Paris struck most Londoners as a nasty place, with its narrow, filthy, ill-lit streets, its lack of pavements, its furious drivers spattering dirt with their coaches and fiacres, its mannerless pedestrians democratically and mercilessly shoving their way along. The English judged the French as conceited and contemptuous people on the whole; they found the beggars, with their hands in muffs and their huge revolutionary rosettes, cheeky; and the women, who went rouged and hatless in the streets, shocking. A year before Mary's visit there had been an atmosphere of general euphoria to redeem this, and the crowds in the cafés and the *places* had been good-tempered; but since August there had been a change. Just before the massacres in September, Lady Palmerston was struck by the 'total absence of everything like a person of fashion, or a carriage better than a fiacre ... there's an air of ferocity and self-created consequence in the common people very uncomfortable.'[3] To Mary, the absence of fashionable society and the confident air of the common people were welcome enough, but she was bewildered and a little nervous all the same. Things were not quite as she had imagined or as Christie had described them.

She had arranged to lodge with a family; the wife, Aline, was the daughter of Madame Bregantz who ran the Putney school at which Eliza and Everina had taught. As at Newington Green, one has the sense of a network of industrious, educated and careful women who helped one another with modest but efficiently planned arrangements. It was necessary in any case for Mary to take private lodgings of this sort; a room in a hotel was far beyond her means. Aline was quite newly married, to Monsieur Fillietaz, a merchant. The rue Meslée, where his house stood, was north of the river, in the Marais, an ancient district where the buildings turn tall blank faces to the narrow streets, looking inwards instead over private courtyards. Close by was the Temple, the square-towered medieval building in which the royal family was held; the first thing Mary must have noticed as she arrived was that the streets were full of soldiers and knots of people gathering to catch a glimpse of the king as he travelled to and from his prison, or of his wife and children taking their daily walk in the gardens. Sympathizers collected discreetly at the closed windows of the houses overlooking the gardens; the hostile stood in the streets to jeer.

This was unpleasant, whatever view one took of the monarchy. And there was another shock to be faced on arrival: neither Aline nor her husband was at home. Perhaps for them it was not the best time to be receiving an English guest, even one with connections in high places, whose occupants changed after all so quickly. Merchants, whose clients were largely aristocratic, were already in difficulties and frightened of attracting attention in any way. Monsieur and Madame Fillietaz remained out of town for some weeks, whilst Mary struggled to take her bearings as best she could.

In London she was used to walking almost everywhere, but it seemed impossible to go about Paris on foot, and the cost of a hired carriage was more than she liked to spend. So at first she stayed indoors in the Fillietaz mansion, empty except for its band of chattering servants, curious and not perfectly polite to the English lady. They pretended to understand her requests but failed to carry them out: when she asked for something, 'dust was thrown up with a self-sufficient air'[4] but nothing was done. Mary was annoyed to find she could not manage even simple matters in the spoken language; after all, she had translated Necker some years before. So she wandered about the vast house, 'one folding door after another', feeling increasingly exasperated and forlorn. She was used to being snug; her cold deteriorated into a cough; no doubt she felt a simple, painful home-sickness for Store Street, St Paul's Churchyard and the attentions of her familiar maid.

On 26 December, while she was still waiting for the Fillietazes to come back, she saw Louis being driven through the silent streets lined with guards, and wrote an account of the scene to Johnson. It impressed and frightened her:

> I have been alone ever since; and, though my mind is calm, I cannot dismiss the lively images that have filled my imagination all the day. – Nay, do not smile, but pity me; for, once or twice, lifting my eyes from the paper, I have seen eyes glare through a glass-door opposite my chair, and bloody hands shook at me. Not the distant sound of a footstep can I hear. – My apartments are remote from those of the servants, the only persons who sleep with me in an immense hotel ... I wish I had even kept the cat with me! – I want to see something alive; death in so many frightful shapes has taken hold of my fancy. – I am going to bed – and, for the first time in my life, I cannot put out the candle.[5]

This is a very different tone from her brisk dismissal of violence to Roscoe in November. Now she felt horror, and her nightmare fantasy – it cannot have been literal truth – of the bloody hands and glaring, peeping eyes, reads like a forecast of the Terror.

What she had witnessed was merely Louis's journey to attend his trial on the day of the opening of the defence, and yet she seemed quite certain he was going to die. The only possible explanation for this is that she had already discussed the outcome of the trial with people who knew the king as good as dead once he appeared before his judges: possibly Christie, who was a friend of Danton[6] and may have repeated his opinion to her. It was through Christie that Mary received money orders from Johnson, so he must have called on her in the rue Meslée early in her stay in Paris.

Soon after this the Fillietazes did turn up at last; they proved polite and friendly, but disappear from Mary's letters again almost as soon as she has commended their good manners. And although she seems to have stayed in the rue Meslée for some months, it was no more than a convenient lodging; she began to go out more and more, spending her time with friends from London, with other foreign groups and with various French politicians.

The life of the expatriate community in Paris during that winter and spring, tied as it was to the shifting fortunes of the French leaders, is difficult to piece together; it disintegrated rapidly and was overtaken by a holocaust. Many witnesses died. Survivors were often frightened or ashamed to recall the part they had played, and fell into the carefully guarded silence of those who have put away childish things and regret they ever had truck with them. Snatches of reminiscence, letters and legal documents build up a picture of sorts, but it remains fragmentary: a few facts, a few guesses, a blurring of gossip.

White's Hotel was the centre of the English and American activities; here both Paine and Barlow lodged, and a series of dinners was held during the autumn and winter, attended by most of the expatriates. The dinners engaged the attentions of the English government spy and, of course, of French observers, who formed some exaggerated notions of the extent of English support for the Revolution. Those who attended them were united by a hope that revolution would occur in the British Isles, but were not in a position to do very much to bring it about; looking back, it is easy to be wise about the vanity of their hopes, but impossible not to admire some of them. Paine was one, the lawyer John Frost another; he had been a reformer since 1780, when Pitt had been his friend and associate. In September 1792 Frost, as delegate for the Society of Constitutional Information, had accompanied Paine across the Channel (he reported back that Paine's only complaint about his reception was the intolerable amount of kissing French politicians inflicted on him).[7] Frost returned to England at once, but came back in November with Barlow, whose expenses he paid on this occasion; he also carried a letter from the SCI offering support to the French government and promising a gift of one thousand pairs of shoes for the French army. Opinions are divided as to whether the shoes were delivered to Dunkirk or intercepted by the English authorities; what is certain is that they annoyed Pitt. Citizen Frost knew by now that he would find a cold reception when he returned to England.

Christie's activities also impressed the French and worried the English government, who watched his correspondence and held him in deep suspicion as an 'associate of Condorcet, Horne Tooke and Thomas Payne'.[8] Riots in Forfarshire were attributed to his influence, and the same troubles were noted with satisfaction in France:

> Déjà l'Écosse parait imbue de nos principes. Voyez à Dundee M. Dundas brulé en effigie; voyez-y l'arbre de la liberté planté par le peuple; voyez-le abattu dans la nuit par deux aristocrates, et voyez enfin le lendemain leurs maisons rasées par le peuple.[9]

Christie, like most of his friends, seems to have hoped the people of Great Britain might rise up against their rulers in effective local protests without any more encouragement than the peaceful attempts of the corresponding societies to organize a convention. In a sense, they were counting on the government to make things intolerable in order that the revolution should be brought about. They wished to remain unimpeachable themselves, and were not prepared to organize violence, though prepared to overlook a little in France.

Other young men in Paris that winter were Henry Redhead Yorke, a fiery boy from the West Indies 'madly in love with ideal liberty', and Jeremiah Joyce, the Dissenting tutor of the sons of the great Lord Stanhope. Then there was James Watt, son of the great engineer, and Thomas Cooper from Manchester, who said the four months he spent in Paris were the happiest of his life, and worth any other four years. Watt's friend Wordsworth was also lingering to hear of the birth of his child in Orleans, where he had left Annette Vallon with friends, promising to return and marry her. A daughter was born on 15 December; once the news arrived he set off for London to try to earn some money and promote the revolution in England. He made straight for St Paul's Churchyard and Joseph Johnson, and began work on a political pamphlet.*

Christie and Barlow were both in business as well as politics. Another businessman with a streak of opportunism was Priestley's friend from Hackney, John Hurford Stone.

* The famous lines in *The Prelude* describe Wordsworth's euphoria; others from *The Excursion* look back at the same period:

> For rights,
> Widely – inveterately usurped upon,
> I spake with vehemence; and promptly seized
> All that Abstraction furnished for my needs
> Or purposes; nor scrupled to proclaim,
> And propagate, by liberty of life,
> Those new persuasions ...
> Here nature was my guide
> The Nature of the dissolute.

Goethe had something similar to say:

> Alle Freiheitsapostel, sie waren mir immer zuwider;
> Willkur suchte doch nur jeder am Ende für sich.

(I always disliked them, all those apostles of freedom; in the last resort each of them was merely seeking licence for himself.)

Stone's wife and children were settled in Paris, but his affections were now engaged quite openly by the poet Helen Williams. She welcomed Mary warmly to her salon in the rue Helvétius, and must have carried her off to dinners at White's, where songs of her own composition were sometimes sung after the toasts. Helen was irresistible, a plump, fervent and ringleted creature who had long been famous in London for her cultural tea-parties and her enthusiasm for liberal causes; her books were subscribed by bishops, Wordsworth addressed one of his earliest sonnets to her when he was an undergraduate.* Fanny Burney noticed how pretty she was, 'but so excessively affected that I could not talk to her'.[10] When the Revolution came, Helen had begun to alarm her friends with something more than affectation: Walpole bracketed her with Anna Barbauld ('Jael and Deborah') as a revolutionary fiend, and she was thought to be 'sacrificing her Reputation to her Spirit of Politics' when she crossed the Channel in the company of Stone.[11] Later she defended her behaviour by accusing Rachel Stone of being a notorious adulteress; whether this was true or not, Helen took Stone's name some time before he obtained a French divorce.

Mary was unruffled by these irregularities. She wrote to Everina that:

> Miss Williams has behaved very civilly to me, and I shall visit her frequently, because I *rather* like her, and I meet French company at her house. Her manners are affected, yet her simple goodness of her heart continually breaks through the varnish, so that one would be more inclined, at least I should, to love

* She wept. – Life's purple tide began to flow
In languid streams through every thrilling vein;
Dim were my swimming eyes – my pulse beat slow
And my full heart was swell'd with dear delicious pain.

Helen also supplied Wordsworth with part of the subject for *Vaudracour and Julia* (Annette providing the rest); but the poet claimed that he did not actually meet Helen until much later in life.

than admire her. Authorship is a heavy weight for female shoulders, especially in the sunshine of prosperity.[12]

Mary could be tactful when she chose; Miss Williams was not her ideal of womanhood, but she was doing her best, attending classes in Roman history and mathematics at a *lycée* in order to improve her education although she, like Mary, was over thirty. She was intimate with Madame de Genlis; she cultivated the society of French politicians and she habitually went to the Jacobin club with Madame Roland to hear the speakers. What she particularly admired about the atmosphere of Paris, she said, was that the old-style gallantry in which women sought only to please and men to flatter had given way to something better: 'une estime mutuelle, un intérêt commun pour les grandes questions du jour'.[13] The questions of the day were certainly great, but they did not entirely stand in the way of old-style gallantries, either between Helen and Stone or amongst other members of their circle. They could even be said to have acted as a stimulant to some.*

* Stone was concerned in a piece of matrimonial fixing that culminated in a wedding at the end of December between the United Irishman, Lord Edward Fitzgerald, and Pamela, Madame de Genlis's charge. The affair drew together almost every thread in the world Mary now inhabited: expatriates, educationists, revolutionaries, bluestockings and idealistic adulterers. Lord Edward had already been cashiered for his political opinions. He had served in America, where he had spent some months in the wilderness, making so favourable an impression on the Indians that he was offered honorary tribal status: thus he could claim to be a Bear as well as a United Irishman. He had refused to meet Pamela when she was in London in the spring, explaining that he had disapproved of bluestockings; but when he came to Paris at the end of October he saw Madame de Genlis and Pamela at the theatre and was instantly struck by the girl's appearance. Stone was called on to arrange a meeting. It took place at White's, and within weeks the couple were married. They departed at once for Ireland, where Pamela became the intimate friend of yet another radical lady, Margaret Mountcashel.

The other household Mary visited most often was that of the Christies. They were lavish in their hospitality, and liked to arrange outings to the theatre, the ballet and the opera as well as evening parties and, when the weather allowed, excursions into the country around Paris in which Mary was usually included. Here again she could not avoid witnessing several emotional entanglements which suggested that marriage was indeed changing its nature in revolutionary society. Catherine Claudine had returned to Paris with Thomas's baby daughter Julie, and he seems to have persuaded her to hand the child over, either to his wife or some other person in his employ. He was also intent on diverting his sister Jane from her engagement to one of Lafayette's adjutants, now in exile and no longer a suitable potential brother-in-law for a supporter of the French government. The German naturalist Georg Forster, who was in Paris in 1793, has left a good picture of the Christies; he met them soon after making friends with Mary, whom he described as 'a very pleasant woman and very forthcoming, more so than other Englishwomen'.

> Apart from Miss Wollstonecraft I have made the acquaintance of Mr Christie, a clever Scotsman ... His wife and sister are with him; their manner, unlike that of most Englishwomen, is pleasant and affable. The sister in particular is graceful and gay, intelligent and well educated ... Christie has invited me to spend the evenings at his house whenever I wish and I confess I find it refreshing to be among English people and enjoy their quiet love of freedom rather than the exaggerated fanaticism that is current here. Warm feelings and cool thinking are the attribute of these happy people, while with most Frenchmen the heart is ice and only the head glows.[14]

Forster coached Jane Christie in French, and her brother suggested he might consider learning the printing trade and settle in England later. It became quite clear to Forster that Christie was trying to make a match between him and Jane, and though he liked her very much he had absolutely no wish to marry her; quite apart from her engagement, he was already married himself and deeply devoted to his wife.

Christie may have heard that Mrs Forster was living with another man in Forster's absence, and assumed there would be a divorce; but in fact his letters to his faithless wife express his love and understanding and his hope that he might be reunited with her and her lover and children. A gentle and brilliant man, he saw none of his hopes fulfilled, but died suddenly the following winter in Paris; had illness not carried him off, he would almost certainly have gone to the guillotine.*

Jane did indeed jilt her French officer after a time, not for Forster but for another foreign philanthropist with better prospects, Gustav von Schlabrendorf, a Swede. He was not married; and he became a close friend and admirer of Mary's too. It is possible that she met him through the Schweitzers, to whom Fuseli must have given her an introduction; Johann Carl Schweitzer was a Swiss banker with an unbankerly enthusiasm for the Revolution and his wife Madeleine was Fuseli's old flame, Maddy. Mary and Maddy eyed one another with interest and sympathy, tinged in Maddy's case with a certain amount of malice, since they had both burned their wings at the same candle. Still, they became good friends and Herr Schweitzer always regarded Mary with the greatest respect; it was said that he had been seriously annoyed by his wife's flirtation with Fuseli, so he may have been prepared to listen sympathetically to Mary's troubles, of which she seems to have made no secret. After her death he wrote some lines to Fuseli accusing him of hardheartedness:

* Though German by birth, Forster, born in 1754, had spent his boyhood at Warrington Dissenting Academy (where his father taught), like so many of Mary's circle, and he may have learnt his French from Marat, who was teaching there in the early Seventies.

Ich meld es zum Elysium
Wollstonecraft und Lavatern, es sei
Das hart'ste Erz zu deinem Bild – dein Hertz! *[15]

It seems unlikely that sexual and marital complications were any commoner at this period than at all others, but there was at least a sudden outburst of candour about them in Paris that Mary had not come across before. In her world it had been understood that the aristocracy and the lowest classes indulged themselves in vices of all sorts, but the middle classes professed on the whole to support strict virtue. Mary's Dissenting friends insisted on the importance of chastity for both sexes, and even in freethinking France, Manon Roland's bourgeois self-respect would not allow her to follow her own sexual inclinations. But now for a while there was a definite movement to release sexuality from its Christian straitjacket: nuns and priests were urged to marry on the grounds of the unhealthiness of celibacy; unmarried mothers were to be assisted and not shamed, and divorce, as we have seen, easily and sensibly arranged, whether by mutual consent or unilateral demand. In Paris, though not in the rest of the country, it flourished.[16]

Diderot's attack on traditional Christian attitudes to sexual behaviour in his *Supplément au voyage de Bougainville* suggested an approach to sex involving nothing but simple enjoyment; the value of chastity and the institution of marriage were both brought into question by the philosopher. Diderot's fable confronted a flustered missionary with some cheerful South Sea Islanders who pressed their daughters on him and were grievously insulted by his attempts to fend them off. Since the act itself is both natural and pleasurable, why should it not be enjoyed without regard to other considerations? asked Diderot. And since children are a blessing to society, why should society not love them

* 'I announce to Wollstonecraft and Lavater in Elysium that in any portrait of you the hardest element must be your heart!'

all, asking no questions about their parentage, and rearing them in common?*

Diderot's attitude to children and society in the *Supplément* was very close to the one Godwin was working out in *Political Justice*, with the difference that the Englishman, reared in the Dissenting tradition, could not dissociate sexual pleasure from guilt as Diderot could. Godwin tried to deal with it by suggesting that the human race might outgrow the need for sex altogether as things improved. Mary had also adopted a largely censorious attitude to sexual activity in the *Vindication*; but in France she began to learn an attitude closer to Diderot's. Von Schlabrendorf reported an exchange between her and a Frenchwoman who boasted of her complete lack of sexual desire: 'Pour moi, je n'ai pas de tempérament'(*tempérament* means libido or sexual appetite). To which Mary answered at once, 'Tant pis pour vous, madame, c'est un défaut de la nature.'[17] This no longer sounds like the author of the *Vindication*. Under the combined pressures of a different intellectual approach and the flagrant examples of so many of her friends, that severe and somewhat innocent lady was disappearing.

Important as this particular change of attitude was to Mary, she was living through a frightening political crisis which still absorbed most of her attention. At the end of December came the news of Paine's sentence in the English courts; he was outlawed. This was not much of a surprise or worry, but reports that the people of England were now burning him in effigy were more alarming. There was some talk of burning Miss Wollstonecraft too, according to Eliza, but the project was put aside, in her county at any rate, with a 'Damn all politics' from her stout neighbours.[18]

* The *Supplément* was written in 1776 and although not published until 1796 circulated in manuscript in Paris and was certainly much discussed. The abbé Bourlet said that Diderot, through his '*joyeuseté de philosophe*' was '*le vértable initiateur de la sans-culotterie*'.

The next blow to the expatriates was the passing of the death sentence upon Louis XVI. Paine tried his utmost to persuade his French friends to vote for mercy, but was hampered by his ignorance of the language. Miss Williams also did her best with her political friends. Thomas Muir, the Scots radical on a sedition charge, skipped his bail in order to come to Paris to plead for Louis's life but, arriving a day too late – the execution took place on 21 January – returned sorrowfully and honourably home to face his trial, only stopping at Dublin on the way to visit the United Irishmen. And now Frost also decided to leave; the fire went out of the dinners and Monro, the government spy, decided there was little point in remaining on the wrong side of the channel. He went home too.

Only Barlow the irrepressible greeted the guillotining with a verse of his own composition, intended to be sung to the tune of *God Save the King*:

> Fame, let thy trumpet sound
> Tell all the world around –
>   How Capet fell.*
> And when great George's poll
> Shall in the basket roll
> Let mercy then control
>   The Guillotine.[19]

For an avowed opponent of capital punishment, this was less than tactful; it was also the clearest possible indication that he had thrown in his lot irrevocably with the French. His Ruthy was still in London, patiently awaiting a summons and listening to Johnson's warnings that her husband's pamphlets were making no money. She complained that she had been pointedly dropped on her husband's account, and that Burke was denouncing him sarcastically as 'the prophet Joel'.[20] Soon she would pack her bags too and join him; they were never to return to England.

* 'Carpet' was the revolutionaries' name for Louis.

Mary did not spend all her time with her fellow-expatriates. According to Godwin, she knew 'the majority' of the French leaders and as she had crossed the channel with the intention of writing about the political scene for the English public she made an effort to understand it. France had been a republic since September, ruled by the National Convention, a body of deputies elected by what was called universal suffrage, though in fact it excluded all women, and most men were reluctant to vote, since the ballot was not secret.* There were no such things as political parties in the English sense, and loyalties in the Convention shifted from issue to issue and week to week in a manner that confused contemporaries and still confuses posterity. But by the winter of 1792 two loosely formed groups had emerged and were increasingly opposed, each trying to bring about the downfall of the other. The Montagne was accused of aiming at dictatorial powers, the Girondins (or Brissotins) of conspiring with the king and the monarchists.†

The Montagne was prepared to adopt ruthless tactics in order to 'safeguard' the Revolution; they were the men with the glowing heads and hearts of ice noted by Forster. Robespierre emerged gradually as their leader; Mary detested him. Her friends were mostly amongst the Girondins; we have Godwin's authority for her intimacy with Madame Roland, whose salon was a meeting place for many of them; her husband remained a minister until the end of January 1793. French historians of this century have dealt harshly with the Girondins and preferred to extol Robespierre for his economic policies and his singlemindedness, but Mary, during her brief acquaintance with them, found the Giron-

* Cobban estimates that only about seven per cent of the population actually voted.

† M. Sydenham's *The Girondins* (1961) demonstrates how difficult it is to use the term Girondin with any strict accuracy, but it is used here in the usual broad sense and applied to those *conventionnels* who were proscribed in the summer of 1793.

dins congenial and admired them for their idealism and courage. The majority of them came from backgrounds similar to her own; they were the same generation (few of them were over forty), lawyers and writers for the most part, believers in religious toleration, sympathetic towards women's advancement, deeply concerned with social questions. If they were inclined to political romanticism and susceptible to the pleasures offered by the salons of Paris, these were things she could sympathize with easily enough. They vacillated, but they did not murder; they failed to control the mob, but did not use its worst instincts to serve their ends.

Paine, Christie and Helen Williams were all in a position to introduce Mary amongst the Girondins. They included Brissot, the best known, who had made his way from an obscure background (he was a pastrycook's son) as a radical pamphleteer; he had tried to organize resistance to the despotic government of France from abroad during the Eighties and been imprisoned and released through the efforts of Madame de Genlis, one of whose protégées he married. He was prominent in the anti-slavery movement, and this had brought him into contact with Condorcet, whom he revered, saying: 'The most durable monument to our Revolution is philosophy. The patriot *par excellence* is a philosopher.'[21] Condorcet and Brissot were often allies in the Convention.

Another of this circle was the lawyer Pétion, who became Mayor of Paris, a childhood friend of Brissot; he and his wife were particularly friendly with Helen Williams. Other lawyers were Gensonné, Guadet, Vergniaud, the great orator from Bordeaux, Lanjuinais from Brittany, Buzot, and the young Barbaroux from Marseilles who denounced Robespierre and Marat with particular ferocity. Louvet was another writer who had been a bookseller's clerk.

As a group they were anglophile; it was their intellectual heritage from the *philosophes* – Voltaire, d'Alembert, Rousseau had all helped to create this admiration for England and its institutions – but it was one of the things that was held against them by the Montagne, with its passion for closing the French ranks against the outside world: *La Révolution, Une et Indivisible.* Paine, though officially American, was suspect to Robespierre because he advocated the plan of a federal republic for France, on American lines, and he was influential with the Girondins. Two of Paine's close friends, who spoke English well and translated his speeches and writing for him, were also of Madame Roland's inner circle: the doctor François Lanthenas,* and Bancal des Issarts, a brave and thoughtful man but an ineffectual politician. Most of his colleagues objected to the death penalty in theory, but he was almost alone in voting against the execution of the king on these grounds. Bancal had published a book called *Le Nouvel Ordre social* in which he set forth his ideas about the state's obligation to provide work and sustenance for all its subjects; he had known Christie and Catherine Macaulay as well as Paine in London in 1791, and he was also close to Condorcet. His ideas were certainly congenial to Mary.

This group probably made up her chief acquaintances, but she managed to meet some obscurer figures too. François-Noël Babeuf, a young surveyor from Picardy who arrived in Paris in January 1793 (he was on the run from a prison sentence for a Robin-Hood-style fraud), had written a book advocating common ownership of land and other measures to raise the countryside above its present misery; he found a job in Paris as a civil servant, working in food distribution, and began to see the problems of urban misery too. He is chiefly remembered for his later 'conspiracy of

* Lanthenas saved his own skin by abandoning the Rolands, and survived the Terror, despised by Robespierre. Evidence of Mary's friendship with him is found in the fact that her brother James Wollstonecraft had Lanthenas as his sponsor when he applied for French citizenship; see below, p. 256.

equals' in 1796, an unsuccessful plot inspired by communistic ideals which led to his execution; but clearly he made a great impression on Mary in person long before that. She said that 'she had never seen anyone of greater ability or strength of character' than Babeuf.* They seem to have indulged in some utopian dreaming together, foreseeing the disappearance of urban life and the spread of small farms and villages all over the land; it was a prospect that appealed to Bancal too.[22]

While the Girondins were still in the ascendant, during the winter of 1792–3, the Convention was occupied with organizing armies to face the increasing threats of foreign invasion, trying the king and pursuing its internecine strife. It was also at work on something more directly interesting to Mary, no less than an attempt to re-create the whole fabric of French civil life. Committees of various kinds were set up, their task to examine existing institutions and propose reforms. Paine was at work on the constitution with Condorcet. The legal committee was preparing the machinery to break the power of the patriarchal family and give a much greater degree of independence to wives and children. The education committee, on which Condorcet and Bancal both served, was also very active, and this body invited Mary to present a paper. She was working on it in December and January, but in the end it was not delivered.[23] The declining influence of those who had invited her contribution, and the ascendancy of the chauvinist and (one might add) male chauvinist Montagne, prevented it.

On the matter of women's rights the Gironde was mark-

* The history of this remark is as follows: Mary must have made it to Southey when she was seeing a good deal of him in 1797; he stored it up for over thirty years, during which his own political views changed, and used it in his ferocious (and anonymous) attack on Babeuf in the *Quarterly Review* in 1831 (lxlv 177). The article and its sequel were pretexts for attacking Robert Owen and the co-operative movement too. Owen told Mary's daughter Fanny how much he admired her mother: see Dowden's *Life of Shelley*.

edly more progressive than the Montagne: if no one else went as far as Condorcet, and Madame Roland rejected the idea of equality in theory, in practice she was too obvious an example of ability in her sex to be ignored. Women with feminist ideas tended to associate themselves with the Gironde; the divorce laws were enacted during their period in power, and as late as the spring of 1793 Lanjuinais spoke in the Convention about the possibility of granting civil rights to women once their education had caught up with that of men.[24] But the Jacobins and the *sans-culotte* journalists waged a ferocious war on the role and pretensions of the women connected with the Gironde.*

The friendship between Mary and Manon Roland can have lasted only a few months, but must have given both women cause to think furiously. Manon had spent her life in conscious devotion to the duties of daughter, wife and mother, opposed to any idea of emancipation for women. She had published nothing, and her power had come to her almost by chance, through her husband, but by the time she met Mary she was deeply dissatisfied and resentful of that husband, and her insistence on mixing political and personal considerations was helping to bring his cause to grief. She was a woman who subscribed to the idea that her sex should find its fulfilment entirely through service to others, but in practice she was unable to contain herself within such a framework.

She came, like Mary, from a modest background. She was born Manon Phlipon, her father being a Parisian engraver with a workshop full of apprentices; but, as the single surviving child of her parents, endowed with beauty and precocious intelligence, she was encouraged to enjoy life to the full and allowed in particular to read what she liked. She became a worshipper of Rosseau, formed a passionate

* See below, p. 192 et seq.

attachment to a convent school friend, and lost her faith discreetly. She suffered agonies when her mother died and her father took a mistress he felt he could not introduce to his daughter. Manon disguised herself and called on the woman to size her up, then retired to a lodging in a convent, continuing to visit her father once a week to make sure his darning was properly done. Her self-control was as great as her ability to project herself into dramatic roles: perfect daughter, perfect friend, perfect wife.

She was attractive enough to subjugate many men and thoughtful enough to ask herself how she could use this particular power, but she never came up with any very satisfactory answer. Marriage should mean the total subordination of wife to husband, she said, but she also wrote to her confidante: 'Qu'il est triste de se dire: Je connais assez les hommes pour ne plus pouvoir les estimer beaucoup désormais.'[25] She was in a classic dilemma, wanting to adore a higher species but face to face with creatures who struck her as dismally unsatisfactory. When she was twenty-six she married Roland, whom she had known for some years, in a spirit of filial respect (and possibly to get away from her convent lodging); and whatever her principles, in practice her marriage took on the aspect of a remodelling of Roland in the mould required by Manon. She seems constantly to have imagined how much better she would have handled things if she had been the man in any given situation. In her *Memoirs* she speaks of the pain and disappointment of her wedding night not once but twice, adding for good measure that it was not due to any lack of sensuality on her own part: 'Je doute que jamais personne ne fut plus faite pour la volupté et l'ait moins goûtée.' (The revelation was spared to Roland, who was dead by the time the *Memoirs* appeared, though not at the time they were written.)

Whatever her proclaimed aversion to the emancipation of her sex, then, she herself was not a docile or satisfied woman. She bore one child, a daughter who was breast-fed dutifully but painfully and was a disappointment to her. There were no more babies; instead, in her position as ideal but dissatisfied wife, she began to collect young men. For a time there was a plan to found a rural community, a French Pantisocracy of sorts, with Brissot and Bancal and Lanthenas, but Manon's energies found a wider field through her husband's membership of the Jacobin club. They went to Paris in 1791. He was appointed Minister of the Interior in March 1792, dismissed for his hostility to the king (it was probably Manon who drafted the offending document), and recalled after the proclamation of the Republic. His subservience to his wife was common knowledge, not just a matter for jokes in the gutter press but something to be referred to in the Convention itself.

By the winter of 1792 Manon was endangering herself by her political meddling; she was also in love with the *conventionnel* Buzot. Her principles were such that she rejected the '*impulsions brutales des sens*' and did not become his mistress (he was married too) but told Roland of her love and was bewildered and angry when he reacted to her high-minded behaviour with indignant jealousy. In December Roland was still minister, Madame had her dinners, her salon and her influence. But she knew the situation was moving against her in the Convention, and she sent her daughter to the country for safety.

Whatever contact there was between Madame Roland and Mary occurred between this moment and the end of May 1793, when the Girondins were arrested. Manon was prejudiced in favour of clever Englishwomen – like Mary, she revered the republican historian Catherine Macaulay – and there were obvious similarities in their backgrounds and ideas in spite of the difference over feminism. Manon may have influenced her English friend away from any incipient sympathy for the revolutionary leaders to the left of her own position. Certainly she painted such a delightful picture of her habitual way of life before the dark days of 1793 that

Mary was carried away with enthusiasm for it, and wrote this account of its pleasures and virtues:

> It is a mistake to suppose that there was no such thing as domestic happiness in France, or even in Paris. For many French families, on the contrary, exhibited an affectionate urbanity of behaviour to each other, seldom to be met with where a certain easy gaiety does not soften the difference of age and condition. The husband and wife, if not lovers, were the civilest friends and tenderest parents in the world – the only parents, perhaps, who really treated their children like friends; and the most affable masters and mistresses. Mothers were also to be found, who after suckling their children, paid a degree of attention to their education, not thought compatible with the levity of character attributed to them; whilst they acquired a portion of taste and knowledge rarely to be found in the women of other countries. Their hospitable boards were constantly open to relations and acquaintances, who, without the formality of an invitation, enjoyed their cheerfulness free from restraint; whilst more select circles closed the evening, by discussing literary subjects. In the summer, when they retired to their mansion houses, they spread gladness around, and partook of the amusements of the peasantry, whom they visited with paternal solicitude. These were, it is true, the rational few, not numerous in any country – and where is led a more useful or rational life?
>
> ... Besides, in France, the women have not those factitious, supercilious manners, common to the English; and acting more freely, they have more decision of character, and even more generosity. Rousseau has taught them also a scrupulous attention to their personal cleanliness, not generally to be seen elsewhere: their coquetry is not only more agreeable, but more natural: and not left a prey to unsatisfied sensations, they were less romantic indeed than the English; yet many of them possessed delicacy of sentiment.[26]

There is no mistaking the envy in Mary's voice. Still, it is as well to remember that in England and Ireland she had seen an equivalent way of life only from the standpoint of governess or paid companion, whereas in France she felt herself a social equal of Madame Roland. Nor would Madame Roland's servants have endorsed the account of the attractions of her way of life; indeed, some of them testified against her at her trial.

There is one other curious and tenuous link between Manon and Mary, forged by the fact that they shared an admirer in the *conventionnel* from Clermont-Ferrand, Paine's friend and translator, Bancal des Issarts. In 1790 he had carried on a sentimental flirtation with Manon which had culminated in his rather rapid departure for London, but they remained on good terms and corresponded regularly thereafter. Her last letters to him were written early in 1793 and concerned his sudden passion for another woman, which he decided to confide to her. Manon offered to assist him in his wooing; the lady in question, an Englishwoman, was referred to only by her initials, as M. W.

It has always been assumed that these letters stood for Helen Maria Williams, because Bancal did in fact propose to her nearly four years later, in 1796, and he certainly knew her in 1792.[27] But if it was Helen, we have to explain away not only the dropping of the initial of the name by which she was always known, but other things too: M. W. is afflicted with a deep melancholy which Madame Roland urges Bancal to turn to his advantage by comforting her:

> M. W. vous accorde estime, intérêt, amitié, sympathie; meritès sa reconnaissance et son attendrissement; gemissès avec elle du sujet melancolique de ses regrets; que votre passion généreuse devienne pour elle le premier, le plus doux des consolateurs; aimès-la assés pour désirer véritablement d'adoucir sa tristesse; songès qu'elle ne peut encore parfaitement vous connaître et vous apprécier.[28]

Mary's distress over Fuseli was known to many of her friends, and she was new to Bancal's circle ('elle ne peut parfaitement vous connaître'), whereas Helen had been in

Paris for some time. Mary was intending to leave again soon, Helen was installed; and surely Madame Roland, who knew Helen well, must have heard a whisper of her public liaison with Stone, and would have hesitated to urge Bancal on with the words:

> Ou j'entends absolument rien au cœur humain, ou vous devez devenir le mari de Mlle ... si vous conduisez bien et qu'elle demeure ici trois mois. Constance et générosité peuvent tout sur un cœur honnête et sensible qui n'a point d'engagements.[29]

But Bancal was not a successful wooer. In March he had to leave Paris under orders from the Convention to talk to Dumouriez, and the departure saved his life even if it lost him his chance with Mary. Dumouriez handed him over to the Austrians, who kept him in prison, and he did not return until after the Terror. By the time he proposed to Helen in 1796, unavailingly of course, Mary had long since left France. Bancal proceeded to become very pious and later conducted a furious campaign against the divorce laws: he said they were undermining Christian marriage. He gave up the attempt to find himself an intellectual wife, married a French provincial girl and fathered a large, dull family in perfect respectability. If he ever thought back to the *Nouvel Ordre social*, Manon, Tom Paine and *les anglaises*, he was too discreet to mention them.

Mary was also given the chance to leave France in February 1793, perhaps by Stone, who made a mysterious trip to England just then. She turned it down. War had been declared on 1 February; it was seriously suggested in the Convention that a separate address should be delivered to the people of England, explaining that the war was against King George and his government and not against them, but Marat, who knew England, exploded into cynical laughter at the idea and it was scotched. He was right: the overwhelming majority of the English rallied as usual to the prospect of fighting the French.

A few sympathizers with the Revolution remained in England. There were educated Dissenters, the members of the political clubs, scattered provincial ladies and gentlemen such as Roscoe, the radical novelist Bage, Thomas Poole in Somerset and Eliza Fletcher in Edinburgh. Some were threatened with knocking down, some merely cut. Mrs Fletcher was accused of practising with a small home guillotine on her backyard hens against the day when larger victims should become available.[30] The boys of Winchester staged a rebellion of their own in February, planting the red cap on the Founder's Tower, and there was a handful of young literary idealists at large who were all ardent for liberty: Southey at Oxford, Coleridge at Cambridge and Wordsworth in London, kept in check from publishing his violent republican propaganda only by Johnson's paternal vigilance.

Correspondence between the two capitals grew more difficult. Letters were liable to be seized by the police on either side of the Channel, and the mail boats ceased to ply in March. Mary's letters to Roscoe for this period have disappeared, and many to her sisters; but she continued to receive money from Johnson, cashing the orders as they arrived through Christie.[31]

In London one of her acquaintances entered into a mildly conspiratorial activity: William Godwin entrusted to a revolutionary friend John Fenwick, who went over to Paris at the end of February, a copy of his newly published *Political Justice*. A little later Godwin himself called boldly on the departing French ambassador Chauvelin with a letter addressed to the Convention. Chauvelin described the incident in a letter of his own:

> Au moment où je quittais Londres William Godwin vint me prier d'offrir en son nom à la convention nationale un ouvrage qu'il venait de composer sur les institutions politiques. Il joignit

à cet ouvrage qui ne m'a été remis que depuis peu de jours, une lettre à la convention qui lui sera une nouvelle preuve, qu'en devenant l'effroy des tyrans et des esclaves, la nation française n'a pas cessé d'être l'espoir et la consolation des hommes vertueux et libres de tous les pays.

Paris le 26 avril, l'an 2 de la R.[32]

To Godwin, France still appeared as the hope and comfort of the virtuous and the free, but in Paris itself nobody was quite sure any longer who was virtuous and who free. On 15 February Condorcet submitted his finished plan for the new constitution and found it opposed by Robespierre and the Jacobins on the grounds that it was not democratic enough and gave too much power to the provinces. The Girondins rallied to Condorcet, and the rift grew more dangerous. By the end of the month there was rioting in the streets, something Mary had never experienced before. Soon she was to see not only shops plundered but the presses of unpopular journalists destroyed: it was scarcely the freedom she or Godwin had in mind when they praised the Revolution.

[12]

Imlay

FROM the time war was declared on England, life in Paris had been growing more difficult. There was inflation, less food was coming in from the countryside, and people were short of sugar, soap and candles. At night they waited in long lines outside the bakers' shops: the modern use of the word 'queue' was invented in Paris in 1793. Foreigners, as long as they had foreign currency, were not too badly off, but they began to be regarded with more suspicion. On 24 February they were ordered to renew their passports, and inn-keepers were warned to look out for them and report on their movements. Mary was not in any difficulties as long as she remained in the Marais with the Fillietazes, but she could not help being aware that she was an object of suspicion, carefully observed by a hostile bureaucracy. New committees were set up to control goods and people; in March a special body was established for watching aliens, who had to declare all their sources of income and produce six witnesses apiece to their respectability before being issued with a certificate of residence. She now thought of leaving for Switzerland, where life would be easier, but she could not get the appropriate passport, so she stayed on.

At the end of March a decree was passed obliging every citizen to inscribe the names of all residents in his house on the door; the citoyenne Marie Wollstonecraft saw herself emblazoned in the rue Meslée. She was not pleased by the terminology of the Revolution, and dismissed '*sans-culotte*', '*citoyen*' and '*égalité*' as inventions fit only to cajole the minds of the vulgar, who were now certainly in the ascendant in Paris.[1] Things grew still worse: in the north

General Dumouriez defected, in the Vendée there were uprisings of great ferocity. The Comité de salut public was set up. Rumours circulated that the English were planning to invade Brittany and that Pitt was paying women to attempt political assassinations. On 12 April all foreigners were prohibited formally from leaving the country. The expatriates who remained, trapped in this uncomfortable situation, drew together anxiously.

While public affairs were menacing and unpredictable, Mary retreated from any attempt to comment on them. And almost immediately something happened to transform her life and turn her energies in a new direction. In itself the adventure was banal: she met an American army captain who seduced her.

His name was Gilbert Imlay; on first meeting him at the Christies early in the year she took a dislike to him and avoided his company. Probably she formed a fairly true estimate of his character and intelligence at the start. In any case, with her views, she would be inclined to look askance at a man who boasted of being a captain in the army (even the American army) and was now engaged in business.[2] But he was able to present other facets: he was a writer, and he told Mary he was keen to return to the American wilderness and establish himself as a farmer once he had made enough money to buy a decent piece of land. What he did not mention, naturally enough, was that he had left a pile of debts behind him when he quitted America in 1786, and that he would be greeted by a lawsuit or two if he did return. He did not tell her either that he was actively planning, throughout April and May, to join in a proposed French expedition against the Spanish colonies in Louisiana.

Where he had lived and how he had supported himself during the last six years was a mystery, but he had found time to write two books. His *Topographical Description of the Western Territory of North America* had been published in London in 1792 and was admired by prospective emigrants for its useful and entertaining picture of life in the Kentucky backwoods. It is still readable enough. It was on the basis of his high opinion of this book that Thomas Cooper introduced Imlay to Brissot in March 1793 and the Louisiana plot was hatched. Imlay's other book, about to be published in London when Mary met him, was a novel called *The Emigrants.* Cast in a series of letters and intended to contrast the liberty of the new world with the degeneracy and artificial manners of the old, it was a wholly atrocious piece of work. If it appealed to Mary at all it must have been because it advocated divorce and contained a portrait of a brutal and tyrannical husband.

Imlay was on good terms with Barlow and Christie. There may even have been some innocent plotting amongst them to bring the affair with Mary about: she was thirty-four in April and Gilbert a bachelor of thirty-nine. He was a handsome man, tall, thin and easy in his manner, 'a most natural, unaffected creature';[3] and he knew how to apply the flattery of the wooer who is held back in his pursuit by no scruples at all, unlike other men who had been interested in Mary. It gave him a considerable advantage. Imlay boasted of his zest for life, of having roamed in the wilderness. He told Mary that he had lived with other women before and that he considered marriage a corrupt institution; and she had not a glimmering of worldly wisdom to suggest that this meant he held himself free to deceive and leave her too in due course. Evidently he mentioned a previous mistress who had been a 'cunning woman', enabling Mary to think tenderly of him as the victim of other women's wiles: it is old seducer's talk.

Once she began to fall in love, she constructed a mental image of him which bore little relation to his true character. In her very last letters to him she refers to his image, clinging to it as some sort of justification for having involved herself with him in the first place; and probably

Imlay too for a while imagined himself into the flattering new role in which he could perform to a new audience. His business troubles could be half forgotten; his American background allowed him to play the noble savage and critic of corrupt European manners; at times the dream of returning to a life of arcadian simplicity could be evoked too. When he described a backwoods farmhouse and a family of six children, it fitted in wonderfully with an old Wollstonecraft family dream: Mary's mother had spoken of a cabin in the New World.

He had intellectual pretensions; he was handsome, confident, liked by her friends and able to offer a perfect solution for the future. Perhaps the humiliation of Fuseli's rejection could be wiped out. Imlay's behaviour, the freedom she saw around her in Paris, and her sense that she was growing old, must all have played their parts in allowing her to respond to his advances. He was probably attracted by her fame; perhaps he enjoyed cheering her up, seeing this woman who was not used to sexual flattery grow animated as he applied it. He was good-natured, he was at a loose end, and he did not think ahead much, a traveller with a built-in sense that he could always move on if things became difficult. Probably he intended to be good to Mary as far as he intended anything definite, but he had no idea of what he was taking on. In Virginia Woolf's phrase, 'tickling minnows he had hooked a dolphin'.[4]

By mid-April his attentions to Mary were marked enough to be noticed by Barlow, who mentioned the matter to his wife in a letter, and by one of Paine's friends, who saw them together often at the Christies' evening gatherings, which were growing increasingly gloomy with the deteriorating political situation. But whatever Mary felt on behalf of her French friends, she had moved into a different mental world. 'Her confidence was entire; her love was unbounded. Now, for the first time in her life, she gave a loose to all the sensibilities of her nature,' says Godwin, writing of this love of his wife's as though it were the source of all his knowledge of the emotion:

> ... her whole character seemed to change with a change of fortune. Her sorrows, the depression of her spirits, were forgotten, and she assumed all the simplicity and vivacity of a youthful mind. She was like a serpent upon a rock, that casts its slough, and appears again with the brilliancy, the sleekness, and the elastic activity of its happiest age. She was playful, full of confidence, kindness and sympathy. Her eyes assumed new lustre, and her cheeks new colour and smoothness. Her voice became cheerful; her temper overflowing with universal kindness: and that smile of bewitching tenderness from day to day illuminated her countenance, which all who knew her will so well recollect.[5]

Godwin must have been transposing something of what he witnessed in 1796 to 1793. No matter; it has the ring of absolute truth about it.

Mary boasted of her freedom from formal marriage ties to Ruth Barlow; but in her heart she regarded her relationship with Imlay as involving 'sacred' principles and emotions.[6] The same Mary who had written off Rousseau's adulteries so breezily, excusing them on the grounds of his wife's negative character, could not imagine that her lover might treat her in the same way without the same justification. Women who have gone to great lengths to raise themselves above the ordinary level of their sex are likely to believe, for a while at any rate, that they will be loved the more ardently and faithfully for their pains.

'I slept at St Germain's, in the very room (if you have not forgot) in which you pressed me very tenderly to your heart,' she wrote to Imlay later. Perhaps it was in an hotel room on the left bank she first allowed herself the happiness of those 'sensations that are almost too sacred to be alluded to'.[7] The use of the word *sacred* is charming: lacking a religious sanction, the relationship took on a holy nature of its own.

But if her private dream was beginning to seem the most important thing in the world, the course of the Revolution still determined much of what happened to her and Imlay. On 30 May the streets of Paris filled with soldiers once again, the tocsin began to ring and the Girondins, no longer able to fight off their accusers, went into hiding, fled, or stayed to be arrested. Paine's letters to Danton and Marat, begging them to try and stem the 'mania for denouncing' and suggesting that the Convention might move out of Paris, did no good at all. Madame Roland visited the Convention, dramatically veiled and clothed in black, to see what was happening. Her husband and child were in the country, but she made no effort to join them, and on 1 June she was arrested.

The Convention had moved the guillotine to the Place de la Révolution, beside the Tuileries gardens; the trees were in leaf, not yet whitened by the summer dust of the city. The Fillietazes were now anxious to shut up their house and leave town, and Mary, helpless and perhaps unwilling to witness more in Paris for the moment, decided to do likewise. She was offered the use of a small house at Neuilly, not far beyond the new Longchamps toll-gate. The northwest has always been the prettiest way out of Paris; Neuilly then was a tiny country village; the Bois de Boulogne, a wild tangle of trees, stretched away to meet more belts of forest around St Cloud and Versailles. The house lent to Mary stood in a garden, and an old gardener acted as part-host and part-servant. He took a fatherly interest in her, and warned her against going into the woods of an evening on account of the robberies and murders that were supposed to take place. She took no notice and one day walked as far as the palace of Versailles itself, wandering alone through the empty rooms and vast gardens. Like most visitors she found the place slightly eerie, a deserted stage awaiting its actors; but she encountered no ghosts.

All through June, July and August Imlay visited his mis-

1

Sober clothes and powdered hair: this earliest known portrait of Mary, painted by an unknown artist in 1791 when she was thirty-two, shows her very much as the governess and frequenter of Dissenting circles. It was commissioned by William Roscoe, the Liverpool radical, who hailed her as an 'Amazon'.

2
Left Richard Price (1723–91) had only a few years to live when he befriended Mary. From early poverty he had become a leader of Dissent; he advised British statesmen and corresponded with French and American political theorists. Mary adopted many of his views on reform and revolution and shared his hopes for a utopian future.

3
Below Newington Green, a north-eastern suburb of London where Mary ran her school with her sisters. Here she met Price, whose chapel can be seen in the centre; together with a couple of the eighteenth-century houses, it is still standing today, though the sheep have gone.

4 and 5
Caroline and Robert, Lord and Lady Kingsborough, young Anglo-Irish aristocrats who employed Mary as governess to their elder daughters. She fell out with them in less than a year, and within another year they had separated; the family was later involved in a series of scandals which were attributed to Mary's influence.

6

A second portrait of Mary, again by an unknown artist. She looks still fiercer than in the Roscoe one, though younger and more attractive; but the haircut, the dress and the hat, which resembles hats worn by French revolutionary women, suggest a later date, probably after 1795.

7

Joseph Johnson (1738–1809), Mary's chief benefactor, patron and adviser. He was the second son of a Dissenting Liverpool farmer, a lifelong bachelor, asthmatic and secretive. His shrewdness made him one of the most eminent publishers of his time; his concern for the oppressed led him to publish radical books and finally earned him a spell in prison.

8

Right Self-portrait of Henry Fuseli (1741–1825), born Johann Heinrich Fuessli in Zurich, writer turned artist, friend of Johnson, Blake and Mary. She had the bad luck to fall in love with him at the time when he was casting off an extravagantly unconventional role in order to become a correct Royal Academician.

10

Above Lawrence's pencil drawing of Thomas Holcroft (*left*) and William Godwin at the Treason Trials of 1794. Their posture, clothing and spectacles give them a Robespierrean air, but they never sought anything more than moral influence, and achieved little enough of that.

9

Left In St Paul's Churchyard stood Joseph Johnson's shop. He lived in rooms above, and entertained 'a Menagerie of Live Authors' here, including Mary, who dined several times a week with him during the years 1787–92.

11
One of the engravings made by William Blake for Mary's *Original Stories* in 1791.

12
Manon Roland (1754–93), republican and heroine of the Girondins. She befriended Mary in the winter of 1792–3, and helped to form her views on French life and politics; like Mary, she was born into the petty bourgeoisie, unlike her she did not care about the condition of her sex. She was imprisoned in June 1793 and guillotined in November.

13
Helen Maria Williams (1762–1827), the radical poet who inspired Wordsworth in his youth. She sacrificed 'her Reputation to her Spirit of Politics' by crossing the channel with a married English revolutionary, John Hurford Stone. Stone, Helen, Mary and Mary's American lover Gilbert Imlay talked of establishing a farming community together in the States.

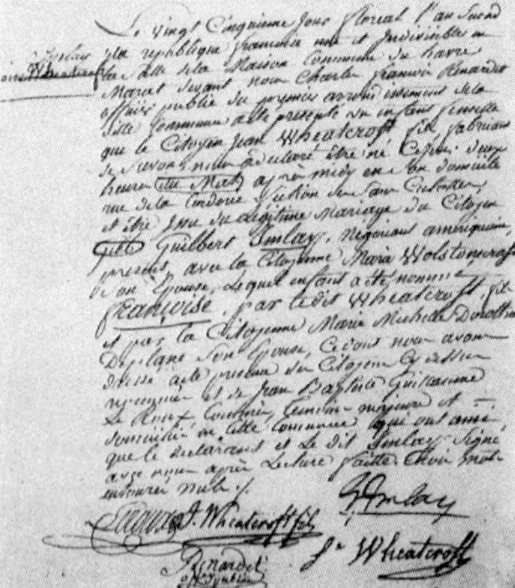

14
Above A gouache by Le Sueur showing a Frenchwoman wearing the striped trousers of the revolutionary soldiers, and another dancing *Ça Ira* in more conventional dress.

15
Left Fanny Imlay's birth certificate issued in Floréal, l'an II, and preserved at Le Havre ever since. Gilbert Imlay signed and testified to his 'légitime mariage' to the 'Citoyenne Marie Wolstonecraft'.

17
Opposite bottom left Amelia Alderson (1769–1853), daughter of a Dissenting doctor in Norwich. Godwin proposed to her shortly before becoming Mary's lover, and though Amelia had turned him down the friendship between the women did not survive Mary's marriage to Godwin.

16
Above Le Sueur's view of a women's club in Revolutionary France; they are reading improving literature and donating their jewelry to the Cause.

18
Below right Elizabeth Inchbald (1753–1821), actress and writer, another lady admired by Godwin. Mary was jealous of her and called her 'Mrs Perfection'; she dropped Mary and Godwin on their marriage. Coleridge said he would run away through 'worlds of wildernesses' to avoid her 'heart-picking look'.

19
Title page of Godwin's *Memoirs* of Mary. The prettified portrait did nothing to quell the storm of abuse that greeted the book in 1798.

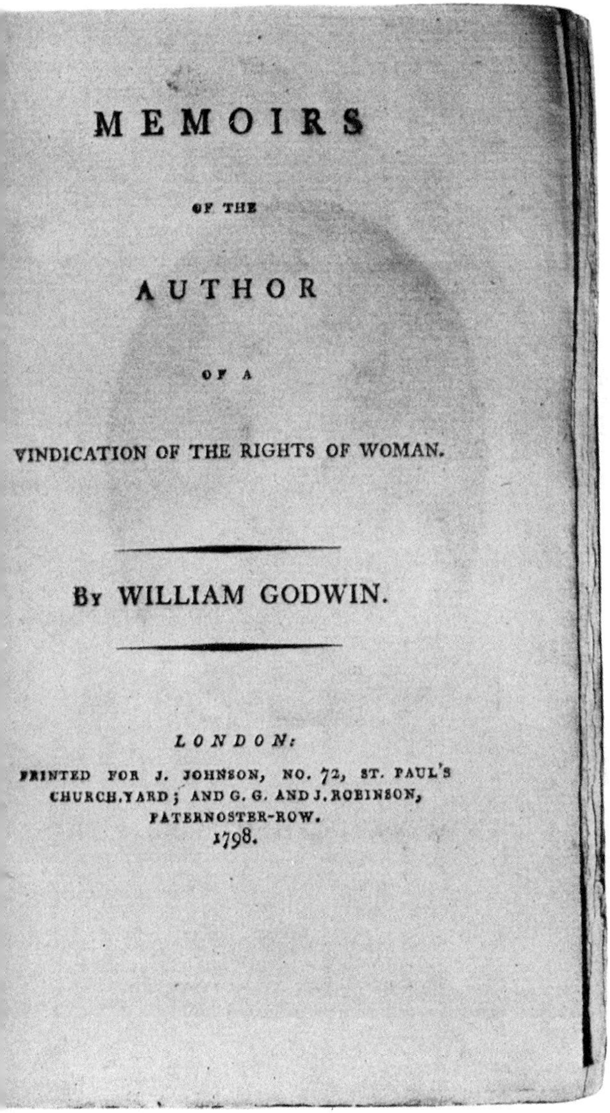

MEMOIRS

OF THE

AUTHOR

OF A

VINDICATION OF THE RIGHTS OF WOMAN.

By WILLIAM GODWIN.

LONDON:

PRINTED FOR J. JOHNSON, NO. 72, ST. PAUL'S CHURCH-YARD; AND G. G. AND J. ROBINSON, PATERNOSTER-ROW.

1798.

20
Opie's famous portrait of Mary, looking plump and rather sad. It was probably painted when she was pregnant with her second child.

21
Another version of Mary, brought much closer to conventional standards of beauty.

No 594 } William Godwin of this Pariſh Bachelor &
Mary Wollstonecraft of the same Parish Spinster were
Married in this Church by Licence
this Twenty Ninth Day of March in the Year One Thouſand Seven Hundred
and Ninety Seven By me [illegible]

This Marriage was ſolemnized between Us { W Godwin
Mary Wollstonecraft

in the Preſence of { Jas Marshal
[illegible]

22
The marriage licence of Mary and Godwin at old St Pancras Church. She set herself down firmly as 'spinster'.

23
Old St Pancras Churchyard, still quite rural when Mary was married and buried there, with the Fleet River running at the foot of the hill. It was soon encroached on by Somers Town slums, railway lines and gas works. Mary's body was removed to Bournemouth in 1851, but the gravestone put up by Godwin remains.

tress at Neuilly, and they enjoyed a delicious secret happiness. The old gardener brought Mary grapes when she entertained; he also made her bed for her, she told Godwin innocently when she recalled this time. She and Gilbert had a lovers' joke about the toll-gate through which he had to pass every time he came to see her: *la barrière* was its French name, and Mary was to call her baby 'the barrier girl' and Imlay's good moods his 'barrier-face'.

The three months provided a honeymoon for which she had prepared with years of curiosity, expectation, disappointed hopes and – probably – fantasies of ideal happiness. From the way in which she had spoken of other couples in her earlier letters she obviously envied their experience, and from her way of writing afterwards it is clear that she was intensely happy with Gilbert, so happy indeed that it became almost impossible for her to write him off later when she should have done. If you believe, as she did, that love derives first of all from a mental and spiritual sympathy, it becomes very difficult to acknowledge to yourself that you have been wrong in your estimate of your partner. Mary could not say to herself that although Gilbert was physically attractive and delightful to her, he was not really very clever, congenial or interesting once the excitement of hearing his stock of ideas and experiences was complete. He had to be idealized into a worthy recipient for her love.

The pressure of circumstances helped her to do this for a while. Cut off from most of her friends, living alone in a hidden spot in a foreign country and suffering the strain of hearing frightening accounts of what was happening in Paris, the temptation to adore and cling to him was even greater than it would have been otherwise. In any case, a woman brought up as Mary had been would have found it difficult not to be serious about her feelings. She knew that depravity could exist in women, but found it hard to believe that it might be enjoyable, or that she might be capable of anything like it herself; and it certainly never occurred to her that what she felt for Gilbert was the simplest of physical yearnings.

For him too the pleasure was considerable at first: there was a feeling of triumph about transforming a clever and strong-willed woman who did not normally suffer fools gladly into a creature eager, dependent and trembling. Even the most cynical of men may be touched by effecting a change of this kind; it is a powerful form of flattery, the sensation that in procuring his own pleasure he is doing a supreme favour too. Mary, charming and loving and deferential, with her serious plans for the future, probably did for a while win him over to a genuine disposition to regard her as his 'best friend and wife'. Only the role of wife was to be docile, not imperious; to await love eagerly, not to attempt to command it; and Mary, though tender, was not meek. Charming as their stolen meetings were, she began to long to live with him permanently.

Soon there was a reason for insisting on setting up house together. Mary must have considered the possibility that she might become pregnant, even though she may have regarded her age as a certain protection. But in August she did conceive her first child. When she began to suspect it might be so, she refused to stay in Neuilly and moved determinedly back to Paris. The idyll had not lasted long.

[13]

La Liberté des Femmes

WHILST Mary remained at Neuilly, life inside the gates of Paris took on the inconsequence of a feverish dream. Festivities and arrests succeeded one another faster and faster. By day there might be parades under the brilliant sky (it was a hot summer), doves released in the air to symbolize freedom, *fleurs-de-lys* ceremonially burned, fountains in the form of breasts gushing republican nourishment; by night the police tramped, rapped on suspect doors and searched from cellar to attic for the republic's enemies. There were *repas républicains* for enthusiasts who liked to picnic in the streets, and the theatre did huge business. Other gatherings took place at the foot of the guillotine. It was as though adrenalin were pumping fear and excitement through the bloodstream of the entire city, its clubs and committees, its packed prisons, the Convention chamber, the very streets in which each house now bore the required inscription: *Liberté, Égalité, République Une et Indivisible.*

In June Robespierre proposed that all foreigners should be expelled from France in the interests of this *indivisibilité*: the idea was obviously impractical, but things grew nastier for foreign businessmen who did not know how to efface themselves or lacked connections with the new men in power. Both Christie and Stone were denounced.[1] Imlay must have had his anxious moments too. The collapse of the Louisiana plan had left him dependent on what he could pick up through commercial dealings. As an American he was at least less suspect than the British, and it may have been now that he began to be useful to Christie; early in August the whole Christie family was arrested and imprisoned, and though they were released after a few days, Thomas was scared and took them all off to Geneva. Stone felt secure enough to remain in the rue Jacob, and Helen Williams continued to brave it out too, but more and more of their French friends escaped if they could, Madame de Genlis amongst them.

On 24 June the new constitution was proclaimed, a hurriedly revised version of the one Condorcet and Paine had worked on so painstakingly together. It lacked the balances and safeguards they had devised, and Condorcet at once protested; he was denounced, police were sent to arrest him at his summer house in Auteuil, and he just had time to escape into Paris, though it was generally assumed that he had managed to make his way to safety abroad.

The proscription of Condorcet meant the end of any publicly proclaimed support for feminism in France. A few days after his disappearance, Charlotte Corday dealt it a further blow by stabbing Marat to death. She was hoping to produce a reaction in favour of the Girondins by this piece of heroism (she had been brought up on the works of her ancestor Corneille), but the effect of the killing was the exact reverse of what she had intended, and it also gave impetus to the anti-feminism that already existed amongst the Jacobin deputies and *sans-culotte* journalists. Now that one woman had appeared as an assassin, they could claim that this was the logical outcome of allowing any woman to leave their proper sphere between cradle and *pot-au-feu*, and meddle in the affairs of men. Charlotte was sent precipitately to the guillotine, and the news sheet *Répertoire du Tribunal révolutionnaire* printed the following account of her:

Cette femme, qu'on a dite forte jolie, n'était point jolie; c'était une *virago* plus charnue que fraîche, sans grâce, malpropre, comme le sont presque tous les philosophes et beaux esprits femelles. Sa figure était dure, insolente, érysipelateuse et sanguine. De l'embonpoint, de la jeunesse et une évidence fameuse:

voilà de quoi être belle dans un interrogatoire. Au surplus, cette remarque serait inutile, sans cette observation généralement vraie, que toute femme jolie et qui se complaît à l'être tient à la vie et craint la mort.

Charlotte Corday avait vingt-cinq ans; c'est être, dans nos mœurs, presque vieille fille, et surtout avec un maintien homasse et une stature garçonierre . . . Sa tête était farcie de livres de toute espèce; elle a déclaré, ou plutôt elle avouait, avec une affectation qui tenait de la ridicule, qu'elle avait tout lu . . . cette femme s'était jetée absolument hors de son sexe; quand le nature l'y rappelait, elle n'éprouvait que dégoût et ennui; l'amour sentimental et ses douces émotions n'approchent plus du cœur de la femme qui a de la prétention au savoir, au bel esprit, à l'esprit fort, à la politique des nations, qui a la manie philosophique et qui brule de se mettre en evidence. Les hommes bien pensants et aimables n'aiment pas les femmes de cette espèce; alors celles-ci s'efforcent de parvenir à mépriser le sexe qui les méprise; elle prennent leur dédain pour du caractère, leur dépit pour de la force, et leurs goûts, leurs habitudes ne tardent point a dégénérer en extravagance et en licence prétendue philosophique.*

* 'This woman, described by some observers as very pretty, was not pretty at all; she was a fleshy virago, grubby and graceless like most female wits and philosophers. Her expression was hard and arrogant, her face red and scabby. True, she was well-built, young and confident, which was enough to let her pass as a beauty during interrogation. None of this would be worth insisting on were it not that beautiful women who care for their appearance usually want to live, and fear death.

Charlotte Corday was twenty-five; in our society that means she was almost an old maid, especially when her mannish behaviour and build are taken into consideration . . . Her head was stuffed with booklearning; she said, or rather confessed with ridiculous affectation, that she had read everything there was to be read . . . she was a woman who simply cast off her sex; when nature recalled it to her, she experienced only disgust and annoyance; romantic love and other tender emotions cease to touch the heart of a woman who aspires to knowledge, wit, learning, politics and philosophy, and who wants to make a name for herself. Decent men do not care for such women, and because of this they in turn profess to despise men; they come to regard their own scorn as a sign of character, and their

The course of the feminist movement in France during the Revolution was confused and, though it began hopefully enough, tragic in its outcome. Much of the theoretical discussion of women's rights had come from men initially, in their capacity as legislators. Even apart from Condorcet, the early work of the Comité de législation had been inspired by a wish to give women equality before the law. The patriarchal family, emblem of the monarchical system, was to be recast, and women were to have the same property rights as men, and an equal voice in family matters. There was talk of their 'natural' rights being restored to them, from men such as Danton, Desmoulins and Couthon as well as Condorcet.[3]

Amongst the women themselves feminist activities had taken place outside any official framework.[4] Early in 1790 a Dutch baroness, Etta d'Aelders, who had come to Paris to report on conditions to her government, became an enthusiast for various aspects of the Revolution. She addressed a mixed debating club (the Cercle social, in which Condorcet and Bancal were both active) on the subject of women's rights, and though her French was halting her sentiments were applauded. In July 1791 she published an *Appel aux françaises sur la régénération des mœurs et nécessité de l'influence des femmes dans un gouvernement*, suggesting that clubs for women should be established in each section of Paris, and a system of correspondence set in motion between all the Parisian clubs and such provincial clubs as were already in existence.*

The initial aim of all these clubs seems to have been to offer services to the community rather than exert political pressure. Hospital inspection, school supervision, the making of bandages for the army and the organization of welfare

bitterness as energy; and their tastes and habits soon degenerate into foolishness and licence, which they label philosophic behaviour.'[2]

* Etta d'Aelders, or Etta Palm as she became, was later accused of spying; her name disappeared after 1792, like so many others.

projects (such as the protection of young girls newly arrived in cities) all suggest the sort of non-political activities that bourgeois women traditionally go in for when their men depart for the wars. They were supporting, not demanding; responding to a crisis, not aggravating it by asking for more education or political power. There are indications however that some of them felt they might be rewarded when times grew easier again. Etta d'Aelders's idea of correspondence amongst the clubs suggests that she may have been thinking of forming a pressure group; and in September 1791 the Dijon club also suggested that all eighty-three *départements* of France should organize similar societies so that they could collectively play a real part in the events of the post-emergency period when it arrived. But of course they did not achieve any of this. It would have been a marvel if they had: their failure can be compared with that of the (masculine) English corresponding societies in the face of persecution.

At first the women's clubs were not disapproved by the authorities. True, a rumble of anti-feminist protest was heard after the publication in September 1791 of the *Déclaration des droits de la femme et de la citoyenne*, modelled on the declaration of the Rights of Man, by a pamphleteer called Olympe de Gouges: there is more to be told of her in a moment. A paper called *Révolution de Paris* took the opportunity to state its view that:

> La liberté civile et politique est, pour ainsi dire, inutile aux femmes et par conséquent doit leur être étrangère. Destinées à passer toute leur vie renfermées sous le toit paternel, ou dans la maison maritale, nées pour une dépendance perpétuelle depuis le premier instant de leur existence jusqu'à celui de leur trépas, elles n'ont été douées que de vertus privées ... Une femme n'est bien, n'est à sa place que dans sa famille ou dans son ménage. De tout ce qui se passe hors de chez elle, elle ne doit savoir que ce que ses parents ou son mari jugent à propos de lui apprendre.*

* 'Civil and political liberty is of no use to women and should therefore be kept from them. Since they are destined to spend their

But this was not the official view; in the spring of 1792, about the time the *Vindication* appeared in French, both Etta d'Aelders and Olympe de Gouges were given the opportunity of addressing the Assemblée. Olympe spoke on a political matter unconnected with feminism, and the Baroness asked for divorce laws, equal educational opportunities and the same majority age for both sexes. During this same spring the Jacobin club gave an admiring reception to a notorious young woman called Théroigne de Méricourt who had decided to lend her support to the Revolution. She was attractive, and had a flair for publicizing herself; her lovers had made her rich, and now she took to going about Paris in a riding habit and making speeches to other women:

> It is time at last that women should throw aside their shameful inactivity in which ignorance, pride, and the injustice of men have kept them for so long. Let us return to the times when our mothers, the Gauls and proud Germans, spoke in the public Assemblies, and fought beside their husbands.[6]

For a while things did indeed seem to move in the right direction. In September 1792 the age of marriage without parental consent was lowered from thirty to twenty-one for both sexes, and the divorce laws that interested Mary so much were passed.*

---

entire lives under their fathers' or husbands' protection, and are born to be dependent from the cradle to the grave, they have been endowed only with private virtues ... A woman is acceptable only in the context of her father's or her husband's household. She needs to know nothing of what goes on outside beyond what they may see fit to tell her.'[5]

* Divorce was by mutual consent or on the petition of one party; the grounds then could be absence or abandonment, political migration, notorious infidelity, a prison sentence, madness or incompatibility of temper. The procedure involved a gathering of friends before a municipal officer, a discussion and an attempt at reconciliation. In the absence of mutual consent there must be three reconciliation attempts, and failing reconciliation divorce was granted in from one to six months. Both spouses were free to marry

The Convention even seems to have planned to appoint women as civil servants; in June 1793 there was a woman amongst the employees of the Comité de salut public, according to Michelet. Lanjuinais, a Girondin deputy, gave his backing for the granting of civil rights to women once their education had been raised to the level of men's. Another *conventionnel*, Silvain Codet, proposed in the Comité d'instruction publique that girls should be educated to take up farming, banking, business and teaching.[7]

But the majority of the deputies were too busy with more pressing matters to devote much thought to feminist ideas, and by 1793 some who had been a little shamefaced about opposing part of an ideal philosophical programme were beginning to find ammunition for their belief that it was dangerous to encourage women to participate in public life. Madame Roland was an easy target, Charlotte Corday another; there were also much rougher ones to contend with. The Société des républicaines révolutionnaires, a Parisian women's club of the extreme left, began to patrol the streets clad in red and white striped trousers and bits of military uniform, seeking entry to the Convention and the Jacobin club. In the latter they were at first well received, and the names of the *citoyennes* Lacombe, Lecointre and Léon are all in its minutes, but soon their unruliness made them generally unpopular. They attacked, physically, anyone they did not like the look of, and frightened a good many people, including Mary.*

---

again a year after the divorce; children under seven went to the mother, older boys to the father; both parents had to contribute to the upbringing of the children according to their means, and each spouse kept the property brought to the marriage. As divorce laws go, they are remarkably humane and sensible. One of the propaganda purposes of Mary's novel *Maria* was to point out the need for similar legislation in England, where divorce was still extremely expensive, complicated and difficult to obtain.

* A passage in her book on the French Revolution, in which she condemns the behaviour of the women who marched to Versailles in

The *citoyennes* certainly dealt a blow to the cause of their own sex, helping to build up male resistance to any idea of women's rights and giving pause even to better-educated women (a pattern that repeats itself in feminism whenever there is unruly behaviour from its adherents). Probably most men did want women to remain as they had always seemed, peaceful embodiments of continuity, during the period of confusion and rapid change they were living through. In the provinces as well as Paris, attacks on women's clubs and the behaviour of women in mixed clubs revealed some of the anxieties of the men: women were accused of talking too much, of immoral behaviour, of getting themselves up like actresses and (a really basic threat) of putting pins on the chair of the club president – a man.[8]

In January 1793 an article in *Révolution de Paris* alleged that the women's clubs had become the bane of domestic happiness. A Madame Blandin-Demoulin of Dijon was so angered by this that she sat down and composed an answer, which the editor had the grace to print. It was thoughtful and articulate; she was a republican, and well-read, and she quoted Montesquieu and called on her countrymen to renounce despotism towards women, since no virtue could be expected of slaves. Some of her expressions suggest that she had been reading Wollstonecraft as well as Montesquieu.[9]

Unfortunately her voice was an isolated one. It may have been she who had urged that the women's clubs should work together (in September 1791), but she was barred from leadership geographically: any provincial who wanted to make a real mark had to go to Paris. In Paris, the aristocratic and bourgeois women lacked the will (Madame

---

1789, is inexplicably ferocious in its condemnation of them unless it is read in the light of the behaviour of the *citoyennes* in 1793. I think she equated the two groups in her mind.

Roland) or the stamina (Madame de Condorcet) to lead a feminist movement. Most of them also despised their social and intellectual inferiors. Madame de Staël believed in the rights of the exceptional individual but was quite uninterested in the condition of the majority. Madame de Genlis went so far as to ridicule the spectacle of women joining in debates at the Société fraternelle (a mixed club with a petty-bourgeois membership):

> Curiosity carried me once only to a public sitting of the Société fraternelle. As a scene it was odd, frightening and ridiculous. The women of the people spoke there, although they did not actually go up to the platform, but they frequently interrupted the speakers, and uttered long speeches from their places.[10]

To Madame de Genlis the absurdity was self-evident; to us it suggests something more hopeful, a concern with public affairs and self-education to be encouraged rather than scorned. But the class rift was not to be bridged, and when royalist satirists linked the names of the great ladies of the revolution with the plebeian Olympe and Théroigne it probably exacerbated their dislike of the pretensions of all uneducated women. They were unable to reflect that each of them was struggling equally against a sense of confinement, and that society offered few forms of advancement to women beyond selling themselves in one way or another, so that it was scarcely surprising if some of the women who made feminist claims had started life at a lower social level than de Genlis or de Staël.

Both Théroigne and Olympe showed a vehement desire to be taken seriously for their ideas and to escape from their pasts, but in both cases it proved too difficult in the long run, and the strain of leaving behind a way of life and a reputation wore them down. Olympe was reviled by royalist and *sans-culotte* press alike: 'De quoi se mèle-t-elle? Qu'elle tricote plutôt des pantalons pour nos braves sans-culottes!' or 'Qu'on imagine, à la Convention, deux cents femmes de l'espèce d'Olympe de Gouges, assises à côté de l'évêque Fauchet ...'[11]

Well, we may ask, why not? Olympe's mixture of flamboyance and real courage might have made her a good politician, irritating and eccentric. Later militant feminists have shown similar traits and deployed them successfully.

Olympe was born Marie Gouze in 1748. Her mother was a butcher's wife in the Midi; she believed her father was a marquis and resented his failure to acknowledge her or give her any inheritance. (This personal grievance gave her a particular interest in the treatment of illegitimate children, a much debated subject during the Revolution.) Olympe married young, a cook called Aubry, bore two children and then ran away to Paris to live by her wits. She found men to keep her, and though she was only semi-literate she began to dictate plays and pamphlets. Big, handsome, high-spirited and full of ideas, she was soon on quarrelling terms with the whole of the Comédie française.

By 1789 Mirabeau had heard of her and complimented her on her pamphlets. She was indefatigable in composing appeals for good causes: the abolition of the slave trade, the setting up of public workshops for the unemployed, a national theatre for women. And she was not merely jumping on a revolutionary bandwagon; she prided herself with some justice on her individuality.

By the time the Revolution was under way Olympe had saved enough money to print her pamphlets at her own expense and have her plays put on, if only to be hissed from the stage. She was established as a Parisian personality: she challenged people to duels, regretting that she was not a man to bloody more noses. Marat she loathed but had not a good word for Corday either. She had a rough wit: she invited Robespierre to go swimming with her in the Seine, both parties to wear weights on their feet. A republican until she saw the king in danger of his life, she then at once published a plea for him. This, and her general nuisance value, cost her her own head. 'Le sang, même des coupables, souille éternellement les révolutions,' she said; and 'les échafauds, les bourreaux, seraient-ce donc là les résultats d'une révolution qui devait faire la gloire de la France, s'étendre indistinctement sur les deux sexes et servir de modèle à l'univers?'[12]

Michelet credits Olympe with founding more than one women's club during 1790 and 1791, but what these clubs involved and who their members were is now quite obscure; they kept no surviving records of their activities and aims. Accounts of street processions led by Olympe sound depressing: the women were dressed up, girls in white, matrons in pink and widows in black – evidently even Olympe felt obliged to divide her own sex in terms of their relationship with men. What she wore herself is not stated. But both sexes were keen on fancy dress during the Revolution.

Théroigne was also involved in founding a mixed club with Gilbert Romme, a Frenchman employed as tutor by a Russian prince who had travelled to Paris to enjoy the Revolution. Théroigne's club set about translating the *Rights of Man* declaration into the dialect of the Auvergne and, less interestingly, proposed to distribute civic crowns to the most patriotic members of the government; it seems to have had no serious political or feminist object, and did not last long. But later, after an episode in which she left Paris and was imprisoned by the Austrians, Théroigne returned full of ideas about women working as propagandists and being in charge of educational projects. In 1792 she sought to ally herself with the Girondins and was accused in the press of being one of a triumvirate of women – Théroigne, Roland and de Staël – who precipitated the break between the Gironde and the Montagne.

Today Théroigne's energies might well have gone into public relations or fund-raising activities, relatively harmless and safe pursuits, but she was in a more dangerous business, and she was attacked by a band of *citoyennes* in the Tuileries gardens in June 1793. They stripped her and beat her about the head with large stones, with the intention (presumably) of establishing that they were the true revolutionaries whilst she was only lukewarm, like the Girondins. After this she began to suffer from headaches and then to show symptoms of derangement; in the autumn she was arrested and her brother pleaded madness to save her life. The rest of that life was spent in confinement in stone-flagged asylum cells, scratching about in her straw and pouring cold water over her feet. At first she would sometimes ask to be released, but then she became withdrawn. She was very rarely violent, and sometimes talked of the Revolution.*

Olympe was already in prison by the time of the attack on Théroigne. She tried to escape the guillotine by pretending, at the age of forty-five, to be pregnant. Michelet could not resist a joke at her expense: 'un ami lui aurait rendu, en pleurant, le triste office, dont il prévoyait l'inutilité'. Doctors declared it impossible to diagnose so early a pregnancy and the public prosecutor, Fouquier-Tinville, claimed that prison conditions ruled out the possibility, a startling assertion given the actual state of the prisons. In spite of this farcical atmosphere Olympe died bravely when the time came. Her adult son wrote a careful letter to the Convention dissociating himself from his disreputable mother.

Both Olympe and Théroigne tend to be written off as something of a joke, allocated special little subsections in the history of the Revolution if they are mentioned at all,

* She died in 1817. An autopsy showed an 'abnormality' of the brain, but did not indicate whether it was congenital or acquired as the result of the stoning by her fellow-women. A profile drawing of her by Gabriel, taken in the Salpêtrière asylum a year before her death, is the only authentic portrait: her hair is cropped and it is the face of a middle-aged woman, but the line of nose, forehead and ear are beautiful, though the mouth and eye have caved in.

eulogized by the sentimental and scorned by the serious: unbalanced tarts who got above themselves and meddled with things they could neither understand nor cope with, and which finally and dramatically proved their undoing. Around Théroigne especially legends gathered; imaginary (and erotic) portraits were painted by nineteenth-century artists, and Carlyle devoted some fine writing to her brown-locked, fluttering figure in the madhouse. What has been forgotten is their genuine and legitimate excitement over the prospect of contributing directly to the world of action and ideas, even though they were women, and women of doubtful repute.

A streak of wildness and exhibitionism undoubtedly helped Théroigne to make a success as a *grande cocotte* in the first place; it also allowed her to speak well in public. But the description left by Mary's friend, the gentle and scrupulously observant Georg Forster, seems to be the best eye-witness account of her. It occurs in a letter to his wife, dated July 1793:

> Imagine a five or eight and twenty year old brown-haired maiden, with the most candid face, and features which were once beautiful, and are still partly so, and a simple steadfast character full of spirit and enthusiasm; particularly something gentle in eye and mouth. Her whole being is wrapped up in her love of liberty. She talked much about the Revolution; her opinions were without exception strikingly accurate and to the point. The ministry at Vienna she judged with a knowledge of facts which nothing but peculiar readiness of observation could have given.
>
> She speaks nothing but French, fluently and energetically, though not altogether correctly. But who speaks it correctly now? She has a strong thirst for instruction; says she wishes to go into the country and there study to supply the deficiencies of her education. She wishes for the company of a well-informed man, who can read and write well; and is ready to give him his board and two thousand livres a year. She is no more than a peasant girl, she said, but has a taste for learning.[13]

Forster may have been the dupe of his own idealism, but there is a truthful ring to his account of Théroigne; she appears as a recognizable human being rather than the picturesque harpy of legend, and her story is the sadder for it.

This sort of waste and abuse of talent and courage was calculated to interest Mary as well as Forster, but she remained entirely silent on the subject of Théroigne and indeed the whole feminist movement in France. It was not surprising that she found it confusing and dismaying. Probably she knew nothing of the provincial women's clubs, and she does not seem to have attended any of the reputable ones in Paris either. She hated violence and had no wish to see women in uniform or street gangs. Her most admired French woman friend, Manon Roland, had set herself against feminism. Corday's heroics probably appealed to Mary no more than the *Répertoire*'s remarks. There was also the question of her own position as a pioneer of high-minded sexual freedom; she was extremely sensitive in drawing a distinction between this and the positions of the merely disreputable. The reputations of women such as Olympe and Théroigne must have made her hostile.* But most important of all, by the summer of 1793 she was in no position, as an enemy alien under suspicion, to rally to the support of any man, woman or cause in any way whatsoever. France was by then a place in which courageous gestures or utterances exacted their utmost price.

A few absurdities were enacted in the later stages of the feminist struggle. In 1793 Chaumette, *procureur* of Paris and one of Condorcet's denouncers, was making a serious attempt to suppress prostitution on the grounds that it had become an unnecessary activity in regenerated France. Not

* Mary's intense dislike of accepting money from Imlay relates to this.

surprisingly, he brought down the rage of large numbers of self-supporting women on his head and failed in his mission. And in July he made his police suppress a play called *La Liberté des femmes*, with the remark that it would more aptly have been named *La Licence du vice*.[14]

In the same month Robespierre put forward a plan in the Convention which would have revolutionized the position of women as drastically as Plato's proposal in his *Republic*: he suggested setting up a system of state-run boarding schools for all children from the age of seven upwards, which would remove them entirely from the care of their parents. His aim appears to have been the formation of patriotic and virtuous citizens rather than the liberation of women, and it almost certainly looked to them as though he was threatening to deprive them of the very thing that made most of their lives most worthwhile. At all events, in the name of family happiness the men of the Convention threw out Robespierre's plan. It would be interesting to know whether there were any women at all who saw it as an opportunity rather than an affront, but the record is silent.

Before the end of 1793 the feminist movement was crushed. Only Condorcet, hidden in an upstairs room near the Sorbonne, continued to write on the subject of equal education and equal rights for women until the very last days of his life. His wife Sophie, who remained at Auteuil working on a translation of Adam Smith, visited him when she could and urged him to get on with the book he had been planning, a historical demonstration of the theory of perfectibility; and though he grew increasingly panic-stricken at the thought of what might happen to Sophie and his daughter as well as himself, he did complete his *Esquisse d'un tableau historique des progrès de l'esprit humain*. It owed a good deal to the influence of Price and Priestley, and described history in terms of a struggle between those who seek to control others by keeping them in superstitious ignorance, and those who wish to enlighten and thus set free the whole of humanity, including women and the supposedly inferior races. Condorcet did not think future improvements would solve all difficulties. He said man could hope to become 'only as happy as it is permitted him to be in the midst of sufferings, needs and losses, which are for him the necessary consequences of the general laws of the universe'. But both in the *Esquisse* and in another fragment in which he sketched a plan for an improved society, he reverted to the feminist cause. This is from the *Esquisse*:

> Parmi les progrès de l'espirit humain les plus importants pour le bonheur général, nous devons compter l'entière destruction des préjugés, qui ont établi entre les deux sexes, une inégalité de droits funeste à celui même qu'elle favorise. On chercherait en vain des motifs de la justifier, par les differences de leur organisation physique, par celle qu'on voudroit trouver dans la force de leur intelligence, dans leur sensibilité morale. Cette inégalité n'a eu d'autre origine que l'abus de la force, et c'est vainement qu'on a essayé depuis, de l'excuser par des sophismes.[15]*

In the *Atlantide ou projet de l'établissement d'une société perpétuelle pour le progrès des sciences* he stated once again that nobody would be in a position to make a proper judgement as to the relative capacities of the two sexes until there had been an actual experience of equality. (He also suggested, at a practical level, that women might devote themselves to making scientific studies of infant behaviour and child development.)

* 'As far as general happiness is concerned, one of the most important advances in human thinking must be the total destruction of the prejudices which have established differences in the rights of the two sexes (a difference which harms the favoured sex too). There is no justification for these differences, either in the physical nature of women, their intelligence or their moral sensibility. The only basis for inequality is the abuse of brute strength, and all the sophistry that has been brought to bear on the subject cannot alter this fact.'

None of this was published at the time; in September Condorcet was officially condemned to death. His wife no longer dared to visit him and he agreed with her that she should divorce him under the new law for the sake of their daughter's inheritance rights, which would otherwise be lost. He wrote directions that the child should be taught English (she was only three) and sent either to Lord Stanhope or to America in the event of the deaths of both her parents. He also wrote her a letter to be read when she was old enough, urging her never to feel bitterly about what had happened. Sophie, to make money, took a shop and sold her paintings. Condorcet wrote: 'Ja'i donné congé à la gloire; je ne veux qu'agiter doucement à des vents doux mon petit grain de poussière: folie d'aspirer aux siècles et de ne vivre rien de la vie présente et qui coule.'[16] Life that is lived from day to day and slips through your fingers; no one in Paris could now afford to forget how precarious it was.

Presently he lost his nerve, ran from the safety of his lodgings, was turned from the door of some nervous old friends and picked up by suspicious peasants. He poisoned himself on his first night in prison. Madame de Condorcet's divorce was granted when he was already dead, but she did not learn of his death until several months later. She had the *Esquisse* printed; Joseph Johnson published it in England; and little Eliza grew up to marry an exiled Irish revolutionary, Arthur O'Connor, nearly as old though nowhere near as wise as her father.*

Mary arrived back in Paris as the Terror was coming into full spate. From Lyons came reports of the frightful vengeance of the government upon its enemies there; from the Loire the *noyades*. On 9 October all the remaining English in Paris were arrested, including Helen Williams, Stone and

* O'Connor was born at Mitchelstown; he was imprisoned by the English, later found favour with Napoleon, and subsequently lived a tranquil life under successive French regimes.

his wife. Mary escaped only because Imlay had prudently registered her at the American embassy as his wife, to give her the protection of US citizenship.

Schlabrendorf, most inoffensive of men, had been in prison since 6 September. Mary visited him, and he found her more charming each time; later he decided he had been in love with her without realizing it. He released Jane Christie from their engagement.

On 16 October the Queen was guillotined; on the 31st Brissot and twenty other Girondins were executed, showing courage and grace to the end. Mary wept bitterly.

She might have spared a tear for the abolition of all the women's clubs on the same day; only one member of the Convention spoke in their favour. The red and white trousers of the *citoyennes* were seen no more, and the voices of the provincial ladies fell quite silent. On 3 November Olympe de Gouges followed the Girondins to the guillotine, and on the 8th Madame Roland, in a glow of conscious virtue and true bravery, went the same way.

The Convention rejected the civil code offered by the Comité de législation, which would have given married women a great measure of equality and independence; too many of the deputies were now ready to assert that the female sex was naturally inferior to the male, and incapable of administering its own affairs. This was the first real setback to the original philosophic ideal of the Revolution that all should be equal before the law.*

In 1792, a year before, a schoolmaster from Montpellier called Courdin had addressed the Comité d'instruction publique, expressing his support for the idea of equal educational opportunity and full political rights for women, but adding a caution: 'Je ne crois pourtant pas que l'exécution d'un tel projet puisse de long-temps être utile. La

* Within a few years moves to repeal the divorce laws were begun, not on the grounds that women were suffering by them but that they abused them. The laws were repealed in 1816.

culture de la raison n'a pas encore assez perfectionné la race humaine dans les deux sexes.'[17]

Courdin was right: having given the lead to the world in feminist practice, France crushed its own movement at birth. By 1795 the Comité d'instruction publique was receiving speeches suggesting that the proper activity of schoolgirls was washing their brothers' shirts. By 1822 Stendhal was complaining that the education of women was 'la plus plaisante absurdité de l'Europe moderne'.[18] Although the French produced a new translation of the *Vindication* in 1826, in the wave of enthusiasm for women's rights that preceded the 1830 revolution, the first state secondary schools for girls were not established until three more revolutions had taken place, in 1880. French women were not granted the vote until 1945.

On 10 November 1793, however, a use was found for some women: young girls of suitable appearance, spotless reputation and respectable background, were sought to impersonate the goddess of reason in every French city for the newly established Fête de la Raison. '*Chasté cérémonie, triste, sèche, ennuyeuse*' said Michelet, who took the trouble to look up one of these goddesses many years later. He observed with satisfaction that she had never been beautiful, '*et de plus elle louchait*'.

[14]

A Book and a Child

By the time the Festival of Reason was celebrated, Mary was alone again, this time in no idyllic garden but in a city full of soldiers. Almost as soon as she and Imlay had begun to live together (probably in the Faubourg St Germain where most of his friends were settled) he announced that he must leave. He had to go to Le Havre to attend to business matters there, but hoped to be back soon. Mary was left to her pregnancy, the book she had begun work on at Neuilly – *A Historical and Moral View of the French Revolution* – a round of prison visits and all too frequent news of the executions of her friends. One day she walked through the Place de la Révolution and, seeing the ground soaked in blood under the guillotine, exclaimed her horror and had to be warned to hold her tongue and depart quickly.[1]

With Gilbert in Le Havre, she took to letter writing again, though her comments on public affairs were necessarily guarded. She remarked that she expected the whole of Europe to be in a state of convulsion for the next fifty years, but it was not safe to go into any greater detail than this in writing. Robespierre was not mentioned until after his death, and none of the Girondins was named. When Helen Williams came out of prison in December she warned Mary it was dangerous even to be writing her book; she herself had destroyed the papers Madame Roland entrusted to her when she visited her in the Ste Pélagie prison. But Mary did not take this caution too seriously and was justly proud of the fact that she continued to work on her book through her pregnancy. The steady effort to keep thinking and writing was the more impressive when set beside her letters to Imlay, which show her as a creature almost entirely at the mercy of emotional impulse.

A few of her letters to her lover were relaxed and colloquial, with 'thees' and 'thous' and domestic jokes about his slippers, but most were written in a less easy mood; some characteristic Wollstonecraftiana put in its appearance early on: 'Life is but a labour of patience: it is always rolling a great stone up a hill; for, before a person can find a resting-place, imagining it is lodged, down it comes again, and all the work is to be done over anew!'[2]

Of course life in Paris was horrifying by any standards, and it is not surprising she grew depressed. Imlay did not shine as a correspondent, and his American friends were not inclined to burnish his reputation during his absence for Mary's benefit. Rather, they seem to have been disposed to tease her for her solemnity over the affair. One of them made a remark that upset her enough to make her despondent and ill (a disorder of the bowels, she very frankly informed her lover) for several days. She suffered, dashed off angry letters when he prolonged his absence, trembled before his replies, feared she had injured the baby by her emotion: 'the little twitcher' she called it, and was much alarmed by a pause in the twitchings. After this scare she determined to be calmer and take more exercise: 'my mind has always hitherto enabled my body to do whatever I wished' she announced firmly, in the manner of Holcroft.

The poor baby was to receive every sort of jolt, including a small ideological one; in October France established a new calendar and found itself in the middle of *Vendémiaire, l'an II de la république*. The week was stretched into a ten-day decade, and the months poetically renamed Brumaire, Nivôse, Germinal, Fructidor and so on; there were even plans to divide the day into ten-hour periods. A pregnancy thus became a matter of twenty-eight *décades* rather than forty weeks, and the little creature conceived in August 1793 was due not in May 1794 but in *Floréal, l'an II*.

Whatever the date and the calculation involved, she had presently to confess her condition to friends and acquaintances: 'Finding that I was observed, I told the good women, the two Mrs —'s, simply that I was with child: and let them stare! and —, and —, nay, all the world, may know it for aught I care! – Yet I wish to avoid —'s coarse jokes.' It is not hard to sense the nervousness under the defiant front here; her mind and her body can indeed do whatever she wills, but at a price. To hold oneself perpetually braced is not comfortable, and so there follows a stiff little lecture on the natural right of the mother to her child, 'considering the care and anxiety a woman must have about a child before it comes into the world'. The male bird protects the female, observes Mary, 'but it is sufficient for a man to condescend to get a child, in order to claim it. A man is a tyrant.'

Still the tyrant had to be placated with tender epilogues: 'I do not want to be loved like a goddess; but I wish to be necessary to you.' Or with explanations: 'When I am hurt by the person most dear to me, I must let out a whole torrent of emotions, in which tenderness would be uppermost, or stifle them altogether.'

But already these attempts to explain herself were meeting with a fairly blank reception. Her hints about how she might be mending her stockings whilst he read to her met with no invitation to join him in Le Havre: he simply said he could not leave. At Christmas she was still alone, except for visits to friends. Ruth Barlow and Madeleine Schweitzer had both become dear to her, and according to John Stone he spent his Christmas with 'the Barlows, Payne, Williams, Wollstonecraft and some others'.[3] Stone's next letter announced that 'Rights of Woman is writing a huge work, but it will be as dull as Dr Moore's Chronicle, and probably as inaccurate.'* His malice extended to reports on the Christie

* He was referring to Mary's book on the Revolution. Moore was a novelist who published a journal of his life in Paris.

scandal too: in December Catherine Claudine brought a successful court case against Thomas, suing for a pension and the return of Julie. Whether her child was ever returned is not known, and she is unlikely to have received a penny of her pension, since Christie was absent and in difficulties over money himself.

With Imlay gone Mary's financial situation had also become more difficult. Hitherto he had cashed her orders for her as Johnson managed to get them through, but now she was dependent on Imlay sending her something through his friends. She did not like taking his money, and did not care for his friends, but she was at the mercy of her situation. In difficulties, Mary usually opted for action, and in January, finding Imlay still not disposed to return, she took the coach for Le Havre. She was halfway through her pregnancy.

Le Havre was a strongly Jacobin town; in July it had renamed itself Havre-Marat. But it was tolerant of its old-established English trading community, and it was in the lodgings of an English soap merchant called John Wheatcroft that Imlay settled Mary to await the birth of the baby. Nobody knew her in Havre-Marat. The people were absorbed in politics and the problems of food supplies, chiefly interested in getting goods through the attempted blockade by the English fleet. She was an anonymous pregnant woman, honoured as women in her condition are in France, where the birthrate is low and new citizens are always welcome.

Imlay had many complaints to make about embargoes and the inefficiency of the French. Mary lamented only the lack of books and newspapers.[4] In March he had to make a short trip to Paris. Her letters flew lovingly after him:

We are such creatures of habit, my love, that, though I cannot say I was sorry, childishly so, for your going, when I knew that you were to stay such a short time, and I had a plan of employment; yet I could not sleep. I turned to your side of the bed, and tried to make the most of the comfort of the pillow, which you used to tell me I was churlish about; but all would not do.

She used the period of his absence to finish her book. The interest of the *Historical and Moral View of the French Revolution* is not in the factual element, since the narrative breaks off before the date of her arrival in France, and she gave no sources for her information; it is largely in its sidelong glances at her own experience, and in the passages where she tried to formulate her political faith. For instance, she resumed her quarrel with Burke: 'Prejudice renders a man's virtue his habit, and not a series of unconnected acts' he had written.[5] 'What is often termed virtue, is only want of courage to throw off prejudice'[6] answered Mary. She knew her opinion might appear 'daringly licentious, as well as presumptuous' but was not (of course) deterred by that: and as a woman who now felt very little bound to any class, religion or even national allegiance, she may have felt uniquely qualified to test her point of view in private life as well as becoming the apologist for its larger political application. What she had not yet grasped was the price exacted by the prejudiced from those who go in for moral pioneering.

In another wonderful, quite unexpected and prophetic passage she attacked the dehumanizing effect of industrialization:

The destructive influence of commerce is felt in a variety of ways. The most pernicious, perhaps, is its producing an aristocracy of wealth, which degrades mankind, by making them only exchange savageness for tame servility, instead of acquiring the urbanity of improved reason. Commerce also ... obliges the majority to become manufacturers rather than husbandmen; and then the division of labour, solely to enrich the proprietor, renders the mind entirely inactive. The time which ... is sauntered away in going from one part of an employment to another, is the very time that preserves the man from degenerating into a brute ... thus are whole knots of men turned into machines, to enable a keen speculator to become wealthy; and every noble principle of nature is eradicated by making a man pass his life in stretching wire, pointing a pin, heading a nail, or spreading a sheet of paper on a plain surface.[7]

Mary's feeling for what was feasible and right in human arrangements, and what was wrong and degraded, makes her sound here something like a founding mother of utopian socialism; we are only beginning to heed that particular message now. If she sometimes lacked moral sensitivity in her private dealings, it appeared much oftener in her political thinking.

She maintained that the great need of the age was for political scientists who could deal with the sort of questions she raised, and blamed the lack of them for the anarchic conditions prevailing in France. She no longer sought to extenuate violence at all, and considered it a primary duty of any government to control it. On the other hand, she had no regrets for the passing of the monarchy:

> The will of the people being supreme, it is not only the duty of their representatives to respect it, but their political existence ought to depend on their acting comformably to the will of the constituents. Their voice in enlightened countries, is always the voice of reason.[8]

The difficulty over what ought to be the voice of reason and whether it could be relied on in practice she glossed over rather quickly, and had the same trouble in considering the freedom of the press: she endorsed it passionately, but was distressed by its effects. In spite of problems like this, which better minds than hers have found no more tractable, she remained convinced that 'Frenchmen had reason to rejoice, and posterity will be grateful'; and that the critics of the Revolution had misunderstood it: 'malevolence has been gratified by the errors they have committed, attributing that imperfection to the theory they adopted, which was applicable only to the folly of their practice.'[9] And although she saw 'a race of monsters' rising to power as she wrote, she did not let her fear of them panic her into abandoning her belief in social justice.

Her credo was expressed in a way that is hard to improve on:

> That there is a superiority of natural genius among men does not admit of dispute; and that in countries the most free there will always be distinctions proceeding from superiority of judgement and the power of acquiring more delicacy of taste, which may be the effect of the peculiar organization, or whatever cause produces it, is an incontestable truth. But it is a palpable error to suppose, that men of every class are not equally susceptible of common improvement; if therefore it be the contrivance of any government to preclude from a chance of improvement the greater part of the citizens of the state, it can be considered in no other light than as monstrous tyranny, equally injurious to the two parties, though in different ways. For all the advantages of civilization cannot be felt, unless it pervades the whole mass, humanizing every description of men – and then it is the first of blessings, the true perfection of man.[10]

She also wrote to Everina during this time, a long letter in which she expressed her conflicting feelings about the French:

> My Dear Girl, It is extremely uncomfortable to write to you thus without expecting, or even daring to ask for an answer, lest I should involve others in my difficulties, or make them suffer for protecting me. The French are, at present, so full of suspicion that had a letter of James's imprudently sent to me, been opened, I would not have answered for the consequences. I have just sent off a great part of my MS. which Miss Williams would fain have had be burn [*sic*], following her example, and to tell you the truth, my life would not have been worth much, had it been found. It is impossible for you to have any idea of the impression the sad scenes I have been a witness to have left on my mind. The climate of France is uncommonly fine, the country pleasant, and there is a degree of ease, and even simplicity in the manners of the common people, which attaches me to

them – Still death and misery in every shape of terror haunts this devoted [meaning 'doomed' or 'cursed'] country – I certainly am glad I came to France because I never would have had else a just opinion of the most extraordinary event that has ever been recorded – AND I have met with some uncommon instances of friendship which my heart will ever gratefully store up, and call to mind when the remembrance is keen of the anguish it has endured for its fellow-creatures at large – for the unfortunate beings cut off around me and the still more unfortunate survivors.[11]

Another passage at the end of her book presented the ambiguities of her attitude towards the Revolution even more neatly:

It is, perhaps, in a state of comparative idleness – pursuing employments not absolutely necessary to support life, that the finest polish is given to the mind, and those personal graces, which are instantly felt, but cannot be described: and it is natural to hope, that the labour of acquiring the substantial virtues, necessary to maintain freedom, will not render the French less pleasing, when they become more respectable.[12]

The tone is prim, but the statement yearns towards a condition in which such a tone would never be heard, in which the imagination, the senses and the graces of life could be cultivated without a perpetual strenuous striving after virtue and shouldering of enormous burdens of social responsibility. Mary had felt the charm of French *mœurs*, and she was never able to forget it again; indeed, the narrow-minded censure of the English middle class made it seem all the more attractive.

And from now on she began to express a definite preference for life in France. She hoped her sisters might join her there once the war was over, and persistently said she wanted her child to be brought up in France. Remembering her belief that women lived below the level at which politics affect life, she seems all the same to have found things better for her sex in France. Maybe she felt too what Herzen expressed later, that there was more mental freedom even under the tyrannies of the continent than under the relatively liberal government of England, where the moral standards of provincial ladies could blast and wither a reputation and indeed a life. As far as the child about to be born was concerned she was fully justified in this belief.*

In April the Barlows visited Le Havre briefly. Mary discussed dresses and shirts and baby clothes with Ruth, and after she left wrote to say she had entirely finished her book and was now expecting the arrival of the 'lively animal' at any time. She had to wait until the twenty-fifth of Floréal (14 May); a French midwife attended her and her labour, though 'uphill work', was gone through with triumphant ease and rapidity. The baby, a girl, was born at two in the afternoon and judged an admirable creature. Apparently Gilbert and Wheatcroft carried her straight round to the Maison Commune du Havre-Marat to register her birth:

Le vingt cinquième jour Floréal l'an Second de la république française une et indivisible en la salle de la maison Commune du Havre Marat devant nous Charles François Renardet officier public du premier arrondissement de la ditte Commune a été présenté un enfant femelle que le Citoyen Jean Wheatcroft, fils, fabricant de savon, nous a déclaré être né Ce Jour deux heures

* At the same time as Mary was being enchanted by the French, Madame de Staël was forming the impressions of life in England which she set forth in *Corinne*, in which attitudes of the country ladies evoke the following reflections:

'Le devoir, la plus noble destination de l'homme, peut être dénaturé comme toute autre idée, et devenir une arme offensive dont les esprits étroits, les gens médiocres et contents de l'être, se servent pour imposer silence au talent, et se débarrasser de l'enthousiasme, du génie, enfin de leurs ennemis. On dirait, à les entendre, que le devoir consiste dans le sacrifice des facultés distinguées que l'on possède, et que l'esprit est un tort qu'il faut expier, en menant précisément la même vie que ceux qui en manquent.'

après midi en son domicile rue de Corderie section des Sans Culottes, et être issu du légitime mariage du citoyen Guilbert Imlay, négociant amériquain, présens, avec la Citoyenne Marie Wolstonecraft son Epouse, lequel enfant a été nommé Françoise, par le dit Wheatcroft fils, et par la citoyenne Marie Michelle Dorothée son Epouse.[13]

This was all the christening Fanny ever had. Her lay-godparents were of no more use to her in life than anyone else who might have taken responsibility for her welfare; after Mary left France they were heard of no more. It is clear from this document that Imlay found it convenient to say he was married, or embarrassing not to be, and although Mary boasted to Ruth Barlow about not having 'clogged her soul' by promising obedience she was not prepared to insist on her unmarried status amongst comparative strangers.

She wrote to Ruth about the baby now, how big her head was, how tenderly she and Gilbert loved her, how much milk she took, sucking so vigorously that her father said she would soon be writing the second part of the Rights of Woman: it was Gilbert's only recorded joke. Perhaps Mary seemed less formidable with a baby at her breast.

The French women who attended Mary were surprised at her determination to be up and about again so quickly. A month was the usual lying-in-time, but she went for a walk on the eighth day: 'my mind has always hitherto enabled my body to do whatever I wished'. (In this instance her instinct was of course correct, and far in advance of medical opinion.) Soon she was being urged to breed more children for the Republic, although some of the women of Le Havre had their doubts about her: she told Schlabrendorf that they called her 'the raven mother' and said she did not deserve her splendid child. Perhaps she expressed in their hearing the forebodings and gloominess that came so easily to her, which were certainly out of key with the resolute optimism required of good republicans.

Still, the three months that followed were largely happy.

They were also comparatively idle ones for Mary, with nothing to distract her from the enjoyment of the baby, whom she continued to feed herself, and the pleasure of Gilbert's presence. There was still talk of settling in America, accompanied perhaps by the Barlows and even the Stones: yet another ideal community in prospect; but the prospect came no closer.

In July – Thermidor – the Terror ended with the death of Robespierre and the prisons began to empty. Gilbert, unable to settle and eager to see what was happening in Paris, returned there in August and then announced he must go on to London; he told Mary he would send for her and the baby within a few months. There is no doubt he was in genuine difficulties over money, but equally he had already taken full measure of his unwillingness to live with his 'wife'. Whatever he had enjoyed in her company at first, he was now indifferent to, or even disliked. It takes a brutal man to announce such a fact; Imlay adopted the more usual course of disappearing and hoping something would happen to release him without the necessity of a display of cruelty on his part. He was in London throughout September. It was the same month Coleridge also lingered in town to avoid an unloved woman; the poet spent his evenings with a young man who tried to sell him land beside the Susquehanna, and naively assured him that 'literary characters make money there'.[14] He must have known Imlay.

But Imlay was failing to make money himself, either by literature, which he seems to have abandoned, or business. Instead he spent what he had on girls, or at any rate one girl who took a less lofty view of love and its sacred responsibilities than Mary (and did not allow herself to become pregnant either). Meanwhile Mary, having nursed Fanny through an attack of smallpox, decided to return to Paris. The journey was almost unbelievably unpleasant, as the coach overturned four times, and she had with her not only the baby but a young maid whom she had offered to take on in spite of (or perhaps even because of) the girl's pregnancy. The gesture was well meant but turned out more disastrously than the coach ride, since the girl had neither Mary's constitution nor her willpower and proved worse than useless. She had to be sacked, after Mary had discovered for herself what it was to be a 'slave' (her word) in charge of a small and active baby. By seven months Fanny was trying to stand, wanting to be danced, and cutting a tooth, which meant she would have to be weaned soon. Mary decided she needed two nurses, perhaps as a result of trying to manage on her own.

All the winters of the early Nineties were harsh, but the one that now set in was the coldest of the century; rivers and canals froze for weeks at a time, and in Paris particularly conditions were very bad. The harvest had again been poor, Robespierre's policy on prices had made the country people unwilling to sell to the towns while it lasted, and when it was reversed in December things grew even worse for a time because prices shot up. There was famine in Paris, wood and coal were almost unobtainable, and Mary was short of money and reduced to chopping her own wood for a fire. Still there were a few friends left to comfort her: the Schweitzers, Schlabrendorf and a new member of the expatriate group, Archibald Hamilton Rowan, a gentlemanly United Irishman in flight from British justice. After his first amusement at Mary's brazen appearance in public with a maid *en cortège* carrying the baby, he grew extremely fond of her.

Several men evidently found Mary attractive at this time. In spite of Imlay's neglect, the birth of her child had put a bloom on her. Schlabrendorf eulogized her face which, 'so full of expression, presented a style of beauty beyond that of merely regular features. There was enchantment in her glance, her voice, and her movement.' Hamilton Rowan, missing his wife and children, whom he saw no prospect of rejoining, was comforted by Mary's feminine presence and willingness to talk about his family. She did not mention Rowan in her letters to Imlay, but made a faint attempt to arouse his jealousy by telling him of flirtatious conversations with Rouget de l'Isle, the composer of the *Marseillaise*, and an anonymous French judge. But neither this, nor accounts of Fanny's playfulness, nor even her most heartfelt pleas made him show any signs of either wanting to leave London or sending for her to join him.

He had written to Eliza in November, in answer to a letter she sent via Johnson, saying that 'dear Mary' was unlikely to be coming to London for some while, and that he himself was on the point of leaving town. The lie was larded with assurances of vague good intentions, and followed by silence. Mary also received evasions and lies, and the letters that reached her were few and short. By Christmas she was certain that he had been unfaithful to her; her first assertion that she could never forgive such an action gave way to a miserable tolerance as long as it was merely physical infidelity. Soon her pride and ferocity were brought down to an abject readiness to endure every slight and humiliation he chose to inflict, partly for Fanny's sake and partly because she could not bear to acknowledge that she had been wrong about him.

It was impossible for her to accept that he was simply not interested in her sorrows. 'I have got a habit of restlessness at night ... I sink into reveries and trains of thinking, which agitate and fatigue me' she wrote; later she spoke of having a 'galloping consumption'. She expressed pity for Fanny for being a girl, since the world was run by men, 'systematic tyrants'; she still dreamt of the farm (in January); in February he dealt her another blow (a further confession of his affair perhaps) and she answered 'my soul is weary. – I am sick at heart ... I consider your requesting me to come to you, as merely dictated by honour.' She decided, once again, that she would support Fanny, but it was not so easy in a foreign country, with no Johnson to be her patron. She ended a letter: 'Perhaps this is the last letter you will ever receive from me.' The very next day she sent another, saying she was giving up the company of Americans and moving in with a German woman friend. Paris was still in a period of barbarity and misery, she said, while he could only think of eating, drinking and women. She felt deeply the humiliation of going to ask for money from his friends, and told him she had once set off and gone home six times without the courage to go in and ask the man she so much disliked for it.

Imlay now answered that she should come to London. Perhaps he thought she would have a better chance of earning money there; perhaps even he had a flickering wish to see her and his daughter again. She wrote back: 'England's a country, that has not merely lost all charms for me, but for which I feel repugnance that almost amounts to horror ... why is it so necessary that I should return? brought up here, my girl would be freer.' All the same, he did persuade her presently to come back to London; he had been seeing her brother James, who wrote to Eliza describing him as 'a fine handsome fellow'.[15]

Early in April she was in Le Havre again, preparing to return, but in no very hopeful spirit. From now on the idea of suicide recurred whenever the cycle of her emotions touched its low point. Fanny's helplessness and need were her chief deterrent, she said; however, she was becoming less necessary to Fanny. She had found an efficient and lively new maid, Marguerite, and Fanny was weaned. The absolute dependence of a nursling baby is tiring but also comforting, and the moment of weaning brings grief to the mother, leaving a sense of purposelessness and emptiness. 'I am nothing' wrote Mary to Imlay soon afterwards. All her life until now she had been actively pursuing some work, but now she was exhausted and everything seemed to be behind her.

He did not come to Brighton. She wrote to him to suggest a meeting at an hotel. A gap in the letters follows:

apparently she went to London and settled at his suggestion in some furnished lodgings at 26 Charlotte Street.* Her old home in Store Street was no longer available, since Johnson had put the furniture into storage. There is no indication of what he thought of Imlay and Mary's new status; perhaps Mary felt or imagined a certain coolness. In any case, he had political difficulties of his own. The Christies were also back in London, but short of money and low-spirited, living quietly in Finsbury Square and not in much of a position to help her; besides, he was Imlay's friend and in business with him. Apart from this, Imlay was thoroughly involved with his young woman and though he seems to have been nervous, apologetic, vacillating where details were concerned and even affectionate at moments, he was stubborn in his basic determination not to set up house as a husband and father.

Mary could never turn to her sisters for comfort; she, the dispenser of help and advice, could not bear to appear vulnerable in their eyes. Had she been able to unbend a little from this position, it might have been better for her, and would have spared them pain too; for two weeks after her arrival in London she made no attempt to communicate with them at all.

In her sense of loneliness and nothingness ('I am nothing') she made a half-hearted suicide attempt, swallowing enough laudanum to frighten her companions – probably Marguerite in the first instance, who may have called in Rebecca Christie. There was a bustle, Mary was roused, urged to think of her child, to look ahead; a woman of her capacities must have something to live for; and so on. Representations were probably made to Imlay too, and he came up with a curious half-solution to the situation. Would she be willing to undertake a business trip to Scandinavia on his behalf? There is an almost sublime effrontery about sending off a

* The numbers of Charlotte Street have been changed, and the house has gone.

discarded mistress, newly recovered from a suicide attempt and accompanied by a small baby, on a difficult journey into unknown territory, to recoup your financial disasters for you and leave you free to enjoy the company of her rival without reproach: in his own way, Imlay was a man of resource.

Mary recovered and expressed herself willing to fall in with Imlay's plan. Meanwhile, she began to see friends again. Mary Hays welcomed her very eagerly, and the painter John Opie, who was going through the long process of divorcing his wife, was pleased to renew his friendship with her. She did not see Fuseli, but Johnson gave her work for the *Analytical* and another task to take to Scandinavia.* He remarked, rather surprisingly, that he had never seen her looking better than she did in June that year, just before she sailed. She also wrote to her sisters, apologizing for her silence and promising them future financial assistance from herself and Imlay. She made no attempt to describe the true situation, and gave a stiff and awkward explanation of the fact that she did not wish to see them or invite them to live with her and Imlay because 'the presence of a third person interrupts or destroys domestic happiness'. In view of Mary's earlier opinions about wives and sisters, this did look like a shabby betrayal of her theories, and Eliza, bitterly hurt and indignant, returned the letter to 'Mrs Imlay' announcing to Everina that she would settle in her 'mother country', Ireland, and expect nothing more of the famous author of 'Rights of Women'. Had Eliza known the depths of Mary's distress she might have been able to forgive her; on the other hand, she must

* I suspect this may have been the job of correcting the first edition of Madame Roland's *Memoirs*; Johnson brought out two editions in two years, the second a marked improvement on the first, and supplied with a few footnotes that demonstrate a personal knowledge of French life. It would have been an obviously suitable piece of work for Mary to undertake.

have remembered the earlier occasions when she had been shunted here and there to suit Mary's ideas, and this latest dismissal off-stage, as though she were merely a prop in her sister's more important drama, was not to be borne meekly. Everina seems to have kept up some contact, though she did not approve of anything she heard of Mary's behaviour after her departure for France, but Eliza, after one more pathetic letter, severed all communication with her.

For a third time, now in the interests of his business affairs, Imlay committed himself to a sworn statement that Mary was his legal wife – 'my best friend and wife' – and dispatched her northwards to straighten out the affair of cargoes gone astray in Sweden and Norway. He remained in London, supposedly thinking up a solution to his personal problems.

In one respect he had judged Mary aright: she did enjoy travelling and was not in the least daunted by a prospect most women would have refused to contemplate. She set off for Hull with Marguerite and Fanny, and soon Fanny had learnt to imitate the sound of the post-horn. At Hull there was a tedious delay whilst cold north-east winds made the June days chilly and departure impossible. Mary brooded, wrote too many letters to Imlay, and received one in return in which he reproached her for having written disrespectfully about him to some common friends at the time of her suicide attempt. She apologized meekly:

> ... the regard which I have for you, is so unequivocal to myself, I imagine that it must be sufficiently obvious to everybody else. Besides, the only letter I intended for the public eye was to —, and that I destroyed from delicacy before you saw them, because it was only written (of course warmly in your praise) to prevent any odium being thrown on you.

Her only other distraction was a visit to Beverley, not far from Hull, which seemed to her adult eyes much scaled-down in size; and she noted the advance of Methodism and political reaction ('fanaticism and aristocracy') in Yorkshire with dismay.

Finally, on 21 June, the ship was able to sail. To go north at midsummer is exhilarating; and the facts behind Mary's Scandinavian journey show just how tough, businesslike and resilient she could be. They also put Imlay in a worse light than ever, as a man who would use a woman he was deceiving and preparing to abandon to sort out his slippery financial and legal problems. What he had done was this. In the summer of 1794, just after the birth of Fanny, he had bought a French cargo ship, *La Liberté*, at Le Havre. He renamed her the *Maria and Margaretha* – the allusion being presumably to Mary and her maid Marguerite – and appointed a Norwegian sailor, Peder Ellefson, as captain. He also reregistered the ship as a neutral vessel, describing her as a Norwegian cargo ship based in Kristiansand on the Norwegian coast, carrying ballast to Copenhagen; this was to deceive the British navy blockading the French ports.

The ship set sail in August 1794. Imlay was then told it had been sunk; but later he heard that Ellefson had turned up at his home town (Risør), and that the ship had been 'given' to its English first mate. Imlay applied to the Danish courts for justice. He had the strongest of motives for doing so, since the real cargo of the ship was not ballast but 32 bars of silver and 36 pieces of plate, some said to bear the Bourbon arms, and worth a fortune (they were valued at £3,500).

Mary must have known all this. During her trip she visited at least one of the judges looking into the case, and went to Risør, the home of Ellefson; and by the time she got back to England the ship had been reregistered at Gothenburg. So it looks as though she had some success in her negotiations. But the book she published later says nothing of these matters. All we can glean from *Letters Written during a Short Residence in Sweden, Norway and*

Denmark is that she was travelling on behalf of her lover on unstated business; that she was unhappy, and hoped to be reunited with him. The charm of the book lies in its melancholy tone, its fine, sometimes lyrical descriptive passages, mixed with acute observations of people and institutions. On the one hand she is a sensible and informative writer, on the other the book is personal in a way that is sometimes startling. Few travel writers and still fewer business investigators have taken a small child with them on their journey; the tenderness with which she writes of Fanny, 'my little frolicker', 'my little cherub', now 'hiding her face in my bosom', now running about on the seashore, 'the rosy down of health on her cheeks', and leaving her 'tiny footsteps on the sands', is the most touching feature of her narrative.

When Johnson published the *Letters* they found an enthusiastic public, not least among young poets. The wording of her description of the waterfalls she visited at Frederikstad and Trollhättan appears to have played a part in inspiring Coleridge's description of the sacred river Xanadu;[16] and the theme of the book – a solitary traveller wandering through wild, rugged and remote places, and suffering from the absence and indifference of a lover – helped to set a fashion for questing romantic journeys. Byron, Wordsworth, Shelley and Mary's as yet unborn daughter Mary, who sends her Frankenstein north at the end of his story, all read and followed in Mary Wollstonecraft's footsteps.

At the time of her journey, Scandinavia was hardly known even to the English traveller in search of the picturesque. Her first reaction to the rocky shores of Sweden was to fall in a faint upon them, but she found her physical health improving as she progressed, now by boat and now by coach, and often venturing on foot, amongst the small coastal towns of Norway and Sweden. She was observant, curious about the customs of the people, the relations between men, women and children, and also the status of servants, the educational institutions, and the organization of legal punishment and prisons. She found herself an object of curiosity and admiration too, as a woman traveller accompanied only by a baby and a maid, or even alone, for she left Marguerite and Fanny at Gothenburg for a few weeks while she travelled about, visiting Laurvig, Strömstad and Oslo (then called Christiania) and admiring the freedom of the Norwegians under their Danish monarch. She also met convinced republicans and found they were not disposed to believe her account of Robespierre as a monster at all.

Towards the end of July she settled in Tönsberg for a while without Fanny and enjoyed walking, riding on horseback, rowing and sea-bathing; she also embarked on the work Johnson had given her. For a while she felt happier under this regime, but by the time she returned to Fanny in August she was nagging at the idea of whether Imlay would live with her again or not, and received three unkind letters from him all at once:

> . . . you tell me that my letters torture you [she wrote back] . . . Certainly you are right; our minds are not congenial. I have lived in the ideal world, and fostered sentiments that you do not comprehend – or you would not treat me thus. I am not, will not be, merely an object of compassion – a clog, however light, to teize you.

She accused him of writing to her after dinner, 'when your head is not the clearest', but her own letters, though evidently always sober, are not always easy to follow:

> What peculiar misery has fallen to my share! To act up to my principles, I have laid the strictest restraint on my very thoughts – yes; not to sully the delicacy of my feelings, I have reined in my imagination; and started with affright from every sensation, (I allude to —) that stealing with balmy sweetness into my soul, led me to scent from afar the fragrance of reviving nature.

It is hard to be certain what exactly was stealing with balmy sweetness into her soul. Her attempt to sort the higher love from the lower left her in the usual difficulties. 'I will not in future confound myself with beings whom I feel to be my inferiors' was perhaps a way of trying to write off the pain of Imlay's sexual preference for girls she despised, but it left her with a decidedly etiolated 'better' love: 'Love in some minds is an affair of sentiment, arising from the same delicacy of perception (or taste) as renders them alive to the beauties of nature, poetry, etc.'

To hate Imlay and his behaviour was beneath her dignity as a rational person, and yet she could not write off her sufferings without writing off the love that had led to them:

> Gracious God! It is impossible to stifle something like resentment, when I receive fresh proofs of your indifference. What I have suffered this last year, is not to be forgotten.

And, most touchingly,

> Love is a want of my heart. I have examined myself lately with more care than formerly, and find, that to deaden is not to calm the mind – Aiming at tranquillity, I have almost destroyed all the energy of my soul . . . Despair, since the birth of my child, has rendered me stupid . . . the desire of regaining peace (do you understand me?) has made me forget the respect due to my own emotions – sacred emotions that are the sure harbingers of the delights I was formed to enjoy – and shall enjoy, for nothing can extinguish the heavenly spark.

To feel that jealousy and despair are wrong was not to extinguish them; she was still caught in the same perpetually recurring cycle of emotion as she travelled to Denmark and on to Hamburg, giving up any hopes that Imlay might meet her in Basle. She may have saved his fortune, but her courage and efficiency did nothing to improve their relations. Once again she returned to England, this time disembarking at Dover; once again he did not meet her, but greeted her with equivocal remarks in London and saw her to her lodgings. Once again, a prey to uncontrollable emotion, she persisted in nosing out the true situation. There was a new girlfriend; this time Mary questioned the servants to find out about her, a procedure she had always held in the utmost contempt. She must have felt that she had almost completed her own moral self-destruction when she was driven to ask a lodging-house cook about the sexual behaviour of the man she had hoped to live with in a new and infinitely more dignified way than the world had yet seen.

[15]

Putney Bridge

By now Mary knew she could not reasonably hope for Imlay ever to become her lover again. Worse still, he was not even ready to keep up appearances like a conventional husband; he was preparing to set up house with his actress, exposing Mary to public humiliation and forcing her to acknowledge openly the failure of her brave social experiment. It is one thing to defy the opinion of the world when you are happy, another altogether to endure it when you are miserable. Mary's Dissenting friends, Johnson, the Newington Green ladies and her family must have wondered at her behaviour and her plight and felt dismay when they realized she was now a discarded mistress saddled with a child. For Mary, the princess, author of *Thoughts on the Education of Daughters,* to be reduced to this was peculiarly painful.

There was this to face; and, equally humiliating, the realization that Imlay found her all too easy to forget and replace. His desire for her had lasted scarcely more than a few months. Mary had protected herself in the past from minding about her sexual failures by claiming indifference to the sexual aspect of love. Now she could no longer do this; the wound was hideous and exposed. And although she never acknowledged it, she must have known that Imlay's desertion was perfectly in accord with their agreed theories about the importance of freedom and the immorality of maintaining a tie once feeling had ceased to sanction it. At the same moment Mary and Imlay were wrestling with their problem, William Godwin was working on the second edition of *Political Justice* and extending his section on marriage with a discussion of inconstancy: it was loathsome, he said, only where it was concealed.[1]

Clearly Imlay tried in his rather feeble way to appeal to such theories in his letters, but Mary would not – could not – take the point. Nor could she quite give up hope that something extraordinary might yet change him again. Till the end of her correspondence with him she harped on the idea that there was a real, better version of Imlay who had somehow become mislaid. Unfortunately the real one, the light-hearted romantic sensualist, a man made to move on with a polite sigh or a well-meant shrug, was liable to turn nasty if demands he could not meet were made on him.

So Mary went round and round in her mind and in her letters until she was again emotionally exhausted. To escape became the most important thing; to escape, and to punish the conscience of those she escaped from. Desire for vengeance, self-hatred and headlong flight from intolerable reality pointed once again to suicide.

The flaw in Mary's courage – or it could be called the sensible loophole she left – was the carefully dispatched letter to Imlay in which she not only announced her intention of killing herself but explained how, and even gave some indication as to where she proposed to carry out the deed. 'I shall plunge into the Thames where there is the least chance of being snatched from the death I seek.' And of course there was a veiled appeal here too: love me enough to come and save me, she was saying. If not, death is to be 'peace' and 'comfort', in contrast with the treatment he has been handing out. 'I would encounter a thousand deaths, rather than a night like the last.'[2]

She had arrived at full romantic status: prepared to die for lack of love. Hitherto heroines had more often died of shame, making their deaths a repudiation of the act of love. Shame was not something she could ever admit to, but she was determined to point a moral to Imlay in the process of dying: 'Should your sensibility ever awake, remorse will find its way to your heart; and, in the midst of business and sensual pleasure, I shall appear to you, the victim of your deviation from rectitude.'[3] The agony was genuine, but the majestic vision of herself appearing Banquo-like before Imlay's Macbeth sets up a faint irritation in the reader. Probably Imlay was infuriated by it; after all, he too felt trapped by the situation, however much he was responsible for it.

For Mary, the way out of a trap was always to fling herself into action, and this is what she now did. In the rainy October afternoon she wrote her note to Imlay and gave it to a servant to be delivered. Fanny – poor Fanny – was hugged and left with Marguerite, who must have known her mistress's state of mind well enough without being able to comfort her; women intent on suicide have sometimes convinced themselves they are performing a service for their children and abandoned them with almost exalted feelings. Mary set off westwards on foot through the streets towards Battersea Bridge. It was a long walk, but she was a good walker, and there is a certain numbing comfort in tramping steadily under drizzling skies: she continued to pace about when she reached Battersea. The low, flat, marshy fields made it a dismal place. Men went there to shoot pigeons or fight duels and not much else. But still it turned out to be too public for Mary's purpose, and after a while she decided it would not do.

She had money in her pocket, and approached a boatman. The apparition of a strange damp woman asking for a boat which she proposed to handle herself in the autumn twilight was unusual, but she persuaded him of her need and began to row upstream towards Putney. There was plenty of time now to remember other days when she had gone to Johnson's country house at Fulham, or to visit her sisters at their Putney school. She may even have called up a wry memory of one of Madame Bregantz's silly pupils who tried to drown herself in the river after getting into debt.[4] But there was nothing in these thoughts to make her abandon her own plan.

By now it was raining harder than ever. She beached her

boat on the bank under the old wooden bridge and decided to go up on to it, high above the water. Why she did not simply drop into the water from the boat is mysterious, but she may have hoped the fall from the bridge would stun her and make drowning easier.

Putney Bridge had a tollgate at either end with a barrier and a bell which prevented anyone from passing without paying their statutory halfpenny.[5] To make her payment she had therefore to be seen again, but once on the bridge she could conceal herself in the bays constructed all along its length to allow foot passengers to keep out of the way of coaches. It was a busy bridge, but she dodged from bay to bay in the darkness until she felt her clothes were completely soaked in rain. Then she climbed on to the railing, a flimsy structure of two wooden bars, not difficult even for a woman in cumbersome clothes to get over, and jumped.

'All is darkness around her. No prospect, no hope, no consolation – forsaken by him in whom her existence was centred . . . blinded and impelled by the agony which wrings her soul, she plunges into the deep, to end her sufferings in the broad embrace of death.' Goethe's seductive account of suicide, which Mary liked to dwell on, was belied by the reality. There was no broad embrace in the river; she found herself still floating and conscious and struggled to press her wet clothes down around her body. She continued with this effort, gasping and choking, the very pain suffered in the process arousing her to a kind of amazed indignation: if this was the price of death, it was surely too high. But finally she became unconscious.*

As it turned out, some watermen had seen her fall. By the time she had floated two hundred yards downstream they reached her and fished her out. They took her to a none too

* She told Godwin afterwards that nothing would have induced her to try to drown herself again after that experience, because the pain had been too great; she would have tried some other method had the occasion arisen.

respectable public house called The Duke's Head, on the Fulham side, where a doctor was called and helped to revive her. Nobody knew who she was, and the locals talked about the incident for some time before they learnt the name of the lady who had jumped from the bridge.[6]

But soon she was fetched, probably at Imlay's behest. He must have received her letter and sent after her. Conscious again, exhausted, sick, wet and wretched, she was bundled into a carriage and driven back to Finsbury Square, where Rebecca Christie had agreed to take her into her house.

Imlay then sent a letter to Mary, saying he did not know how to extricate either of them 'out of the wretchedness into which we have been plunged'; to which she replied tartly that *he* at any rate was long since extricated. In the same letter she defended her suicide attempt as 'one of the calmest acts of reason', and complained of having been inhumanly brought back to life and misery, 'a living death'.[7]

Imlay told her he felt unable to visit her, out of delicacy towards his new mistress, and instead offered her money, which she of course refused. Now, according to Godwin, he very foolishly vacillated once again, suggesting that his new love affair was a casual and light-hearted one of no permanent importance. It was a ham-handed piece of consolation, but she clutched at it. Perhaps he might after all come back later to her and Fanny.

So Mary, for the second time in her life and with very different feelings, suggested a *ménage à trois*. Why should she not join Imlay and his girl in their house? He would at least be a father for Fanny. Imlay, still unable to act decisively, actually took her to inspect the house before making up his mind that such a situation would not do. It is not inconceivable that the actress put her foot down at the prospect of living with her formidable predecessor, especially when she heard Mary had plans for undertaking her education. The project was abandoned.

Thomas Christie may have been inclined to sympathize

with Imlay over a crisis involving two women and a baby, and since he was a business colleague too Imlay was a frequent caller at the Christie house. Mary decided to move out into lodgings, but settled near by in Finsbury Place so as to be close to Mrs Christie, who was *her* friend in the affair. She began to think how she might start earning money for herself once more, and her thoughts naturally turned to Johnson and the *Analytical*. She started reviewing again, prepared a new edition of *Original Stories,* and made up her mind to attempt a play based on her own experiences. This comedy was in fact offered to two producers in a rough draft and then set aside when they rejected it. Unhappily, Godwin later destroyed the manuscript. Whatever its defects, it would have been instructive to see how Mary presented her life in the comic mode.

She also decided to make a book out of the letters she had sent Imlay from Scandinavia. She asked him for their return, and he at once complied. Then on impulse she wrote to Fuseli for her letters to him too:

> I have long ceased to expect kindness or affection from any human creature, and would fain tear from my heart its treacherous sympathies. I am alone. The injustice, without alluding to hopes blasted in the bud, which I have endured, wounding my bosom, have set my thoughts adrift into an ocean of painful conjectures. I ask impatiently what – and where is truth? I have been treated brutally; but I daily labour to remember that I still have the duty of a mother to fulfil.

Only Mary could have been capable of inviting one man who had used her ill to sympathize with her over another's usage. She ended her letter to Fuseli half apologetically, half unable to resist an appeal for reassurance: 'I have written more than I intended, – for I only meant to request you to return my letters: I wish to have them, and it must be the same to you.'[8] But it was not the same to Fuseli, and he paid her the meagre compliment of refusing to return them.

For business reasons, or to escape from the situation and soothe the ruffled feelings of his present mistress, Imlay now set off for Paris. Mary still pursued him with letters in which she castigated his theory of morals, predicted an unhappy old age for him and reproached him for his failure to help her family financially.

He wrote back telling her that she was tormenting him, and pointing out that his conduct was unequivocal. She answered furiously that it had not been so – on the contrary, it had been warm and loving even when he was deceiving her: 'With these assurances, is it extraordinary that I should believe what I wished?' And she still begged him to see her again, until the next to the last letter of all. In that she threw his words in his face: 'forbearance' and 'delicacy' were not what she had found in him.

I have no criterion for morality, and have thought in vain, if the sensations which lead you to follow an ancle or step, be the sacred foundation of principle or affection. Mine has been of a very different nature, or it would not have stood the brunt of your sarcasms. The sentiment in me is still sacred. If there be any part of me that will survive the sense of my misfortunes, it is the purity of my affections. The impetuosity of your senses, may have led you to term mere animal desire, the source of principle . . .[9]

This was the revived voice of the Mary who had written *Thoughts on the Education of Daughters*, her face turned away from the world of the senses. Paris and its lessons were forgotten. She was too outraged not to take refuge in a puritan morality once again.

But with Imlay physically out of the way and some friends about, things did begin to improve at last. In January Johnson published her *Letters Written during a Short Residence in Denmark, Norway and Sweden*, entirely made of letters she had sent Imlay from Scandinavia. She was a good travel writer; although the *Letters* were touched with melancholy personal complaints they were also full of sharply sketched accounts of the people she met and the manner in which they amused or shocked her, the social conditions she found and the northern scenery of rocks, waterfalls and forests in its summer incarnation. Some of her phrases were good enough to provide Coleridge with inspiration.[10]

There was no pretence of a systematic approach; Mary had simply allowed her eye for nature, her curiosity about mankind and her bent towards didacticism to run together in oddly successful harmony. She could end one letter:

> A crescent hangs out in the vault before, which woos me to stray abroad; – it is not a silvery reflection of the sun, but glows with all its golden splendour. Who fears the fallen dew? It only makes the mown grass smell more fragrant.

– and overleaf be transformed into a sociologist: 'The population of Sweden has been estimated from two millions and a half to three millions', going on to discuss the conditions of servants, the taxation system and the beneficial effects of the French Revolution on remaining monarchies.

Reviewers and public praised the book, which showed her not only as a courageous traveller (Anna Seward was particularly struck that she took the baby with her) but as a gentle and thoughtful woman. Amelia Alderson, still an unknown and aspiring young writer, summed up what many readers undoubtedly felt when she wrote to Mary in 1796 saying,

> I remember the time when my desire of seeing you was repressed by fear – but as soon as I read your letters from Norway, the cold awe which the philosopher has excited, was lost in the tender sympathy called forth by the woman. I saw nothing but the interesting creature of feeling and imagination.[11]

By now her personal history was beginning to be fairly widely known, and at this stage people were more inclined to sympathize than condemn her. Coleridge's friend Thomas

Poole, for instance, who had been an admirer of Mary's work for some years, wrote to a young schoolmistress he corresponded with:

> I have heard with pain from my sister Mrs Wolstonecraft's story ... It is a sublime though melancholy instance of the injustice of Providence, that we seldom see great talents, particularly that class which we peculiarly denominate genius, enjoying an even tenour of human happiness ... In their moments of mind ... they form plans which would be practicable only if those moments were of continued duration; but in their career they feel like other mortals the sad burdens of mortality, and these being overlooked in their scheme of life, in the form of various passions they enter the fenceless field, making unbounded havoc. What a striking instance of this is Mrs Wolstonecraft! What a striking instance is my beloved friend Coleridge![12]

Poole concluded that 'people of genius ought imperiously to command themselves to think *without* genius of the common concerns of life' – a thought that would be echoed many, many times by English readers as they surveyed with a mixture of intense disapproval and covert envy the erratic and self-indulgent lives of so many of their writers.

Her name appeared before the public in another context in January, when the letters of John Hurford Stone to his brother William were read out at length in court during William's trial for treason. Sheridan spoke for his innocence, Mr Barbauld stood up stoutly as a character witness, and William, patently innocent of anything worse than trying to dissuade his brother from harebrained schemes of invasion, was acquitted; but John's letters were incriminating enough to make it impossible for him to return to England, and Mary's family no doubt winced as they heard of her presence at revolutionary Christmas festivities in Paris during the Terror.[13] Political feeling in England was running higher and higher. As Mary put in the postscript of a letter to Hamilton Rowan at this time, with more feeling than regard for grammar, 'The state of public affairs here are not in a posture to assuage private sorrow.'[14]

At the end of October 1795, the same time she had made her attempt to drown herself, a small riot had taken place in London in which a crowd surrounded the royal coach and threw a stone at the king. Food was short all over the country, partly because of the bad harvests and partly because of the war. The men who attacked the king were heard to shout: 'Peace', 'Down with George', 'No Pitt', 'No War', and, most pointedly perhaps, 'Bread'. Shortages had swelled the membership of the political clubs, and for a while the fiercer leaders of the London Corresponding Society commanded a good following. When the government was able to prove that a single member of the crowd who had frightened the king was also a member of the Corresponding Society, it used this as a pretext for suppressing all clubs.

In mid-December two acts were passed in Parliament which made political meetings of more than fifty people illegal and speeches or writings against the king or constitution treasonable. The Two Acts outraged all democrats, even though some were less keen on militancy than others. Godwin had written during the autumn a pamphlet, published by Johnson and discreetly signed simply 'By a Lover of Order' (which deceived nobody). 'Be tranquil. Indulge in the most flattering prospects. Be firm, be active, be temperate,' he advised, insisting that all would inevitably turn out well in the long run and that it would be a pity to bring violence to hurry things up, as the French had done. The activities of the Corresponding Society were calculated, in Godwin's view, 'sooner or later to bring on scenes of confusion'.[15] The pamphlet produced a certain breach in the ranks of the radicals, some of whom abandoned all hope of justice in Great Britain. Thomas Christie's uncle left to settle near Priestley in the American wilderness, while Thomas himself found his situation so bad that he too decided to set off on a long business trip to Surinam.

Mary was still undecided about her own future. At the end of January 1796 she was far from calm, as her letter to Hamilton Rowan shows:

> Though I have not heard from you I should have written to you, convinced of your friendship, could I have told you any thing of myself that would have afforded you pleasure – But what can I say to you – I am unhappy – I have been treated with unkindness – and even cruelty, by the person from whom I have had every reason to expect affection – I write to you with an agitated hand – I cannot be more explicit – I value your good opinion – and you know how to feel for me – I looked for something like happiness – happiness! in the discharge of my relative duties – and the heart on which I leaned has pierced mine to the quick – I have not been used well – and I live, but for my child – for am weary of myself – When I am more composed I will write to you again, mean time let me hear from you – and tell me something of Charles – I avoid writing to him, because I hate to explain myself – I still think of settling in France, because I wish to leave my little Girl there – I have been very ill – Have taken some desperate steps – But now I am writing for independence – I wish I had no other evil to complain of than the necessity of providing for myself and child – do not mistake me – Mr Imlay would be glad to supply all my pecuniary wants; but, unless he returns to me himself I would perish first – Pardon the incoherence of my style. I have put off writing to you from time to time, because I could not write calmly. It would afford me the sincerest satisfaction to hear that you are reunited to your family, for I am your affectionate and Sincere friend, Mary Imlay.[16]

It did not occur to her to write a formal or even a discreet letter to Hamilton Rowan; he was not a very old friend, but he was bound to her by their shared experience of crisis in France, and by their common political views. Though she found it intolerable to communicate with her own family, she wanted to establish with him the facts of her virtue and the injury done to her.

At the end of February Imlay returned from Paris and

she inevitably found him at the Christies' one evening when she was calling with Fanny. Rebecca tried to warn her as she came along the corridor, but she entered the room determinedly and led Fanny up to him where he sat. Confronted in public by a bewildered little girl and a reproachful woman, he suggested that all three should retire to another room for a talk, and as usual found it impossible to be as harsh face to face as in a letter. He promised to have dinner with Mary the following day; for the last time she allowed herself to believe that a reconciliation might be possible. But the dinner led to nothing but disappointment, and the next day she left her lodgings and went to stay for a month with a woman friend, a Mrs Cotton, in Berkshire. And at last the affair was finished, and she could write to him, 'I part with you in peace'.[17]

On her return to London in March she met him by chance in the New Road (now the Euston Road). He was on horseback, but he dismounted and walked with her for a while and she found herself able to keep calm. It was their last encounter.*

Now, although she still kept all her furniture in store, she decided to change her lodgings again: it seems probable that, with Christie's departure, Rebecca was less often in town, and apart from her Finsbury Place had no charms for Mary. She moved west, settling with Fanny and Marguerite in Cumming Street, off the Pentonville Road. Here the land begins to rise out of London towards Islington. It was a pretty semi-rural spot then, beside a church which still retains its green graveyard today amid the acres of brick and asphalt that now surround it. Here she was visited by Mary Hays, eager to fill the role of best friend, though she was unable to share Mary's memories of Paris or enter into her grief with quite the same understanding as Rebecca Christie. And here Mary's resolve to forget Imlay led her

* It seems possible that Imlay went with Christie to Surinam, and did not return to England until after Mary's death.

into a characteristically impulsive and direct action: from Cumming Street she set out on the morning of 14 April 1796, to call alone and uninvited on William Godwin at his near-by lodgings in Chalton Street, Somers Town.

[16]

A Social Round

MARY's call at Chalton Street in Somers Town marked her readiness to become a leading lady amongst the London intellectuals once again. There had been a prologue to this moment in January, before her trip to the country, which may have helped to give her courage; Mary Hays had invited her to a small party at her lodgings in order to renew her acquaintance with William Godwin and Thomas Holcroft. Godwin accepted the invitation with the comment that he would be happy to meet Mrs Wollstonecraft (he did not call her Mrs Imlay) in spite of the harsh things she had amused herself with saying about him. Perhaps she had joined in the criticism of his 'lover of order' pamphlet; it had been attacked in the *Analytical* where she was known to work. Nevertheless, both men were pleased to be invited.

They enjoyed the company of women. Holcroft's third wife had died in 1790, and when his ancient father wrote asking if he planned to remarry he had answered despondently that he seemed to have had his share of womankind already, and that it was not easy in any case to find another suitable wife at his age. By 1796 he was fifty-one and still looking; Godwin was only forty and a bachelor. As a young man he seems to have taken no interest at all in women, absorbed in his religious and intellectual life, but lately he had begun to hover about them with a sort of nervous enthusiasm: he had even attempted to seduce a young married woman, Maria Reveley, a couple of years before. Mr Reveley had proved less philosophical about the affair than Godwin expected, and insisted that it be abandoned before resuming his friendship.[1]

Mary Hays's intentions in arranging her party however

were sociable and friendly rather than matchmaking. It is also possible that she was hoping to fire the two eminent writers with a greater enthusiasm than they had so far shown for the cause of women's rights, by renewing their contact with its leading English exponent. But it appears that Mary Imlay held her tongue on that subject for the time being. Possibly she had developed an instinct which told her it was not a theme to dwell on in the company of men, however sympathetic they might be in theory.

Holcroft was a sentimental and idealizing, not at all a practical feminist. He had portrayed a series of high-spirited girls in his plays and novels, girls who did not panic when their horses bolted, girls who could quell would-be rapists by sheer force of personality, girls who browbeat their parents and reformed their foolish lovers, but none of these girls aspired to serious study or useful employment, and all were safeguarded by money.[2] He dodged the real problems for women altogether. Godwin's work showed even less evidence of a feminist sympathy. The attempt to rationalize sexual relations in *Political Justice* simply sidestepped the fundamental issue of economic dependence. Indeed it is possible to see in it a deep uneasiness in the face of something intractable: women threatened to act as pieces of grit in the otherwise smooth-running machinery of the ideal state.

Mary Hays had tried to take Godwin up on his insistence that independence was the first necessity for the good life, asking him how a woman was to arrive at independence:

> Why call woman, miserable, oppressed, and impotent woman – *crushed, and then insulted* – why call her to *independence* – which not nature, but the barbarous and accursed laws of society, have denied her? *This is mockery!* Even you, wise and benevolent as you are, can mock the child of slavery and sorrow![3]

The passage comes from *Emma Courtney*, the novel she

brought out in 1796, in which Godwin figured as the philosopher Mr Francis; some of his actual letters were transcribed. But Mr Francis was unwilling or unable to answer the heroine's (or the author's) anguished demands as to what an unmarried woman who wished to earn an honest living should do. And when Mary Hays complained vehemently and asked more questions, Godwin grew uneasy and warned her she was in danger of becoming unbalanced. To this she produced a very reasonable further reply:

While men pursue interest, honor, pleasure, as accords with their several dispositions, women, who have too much delicacy, sense, and spirit, to degrade themselves by the vilest of interchanges, remain insulated beings, and must be content tamely to look on without taking any part in the great, though often absurd and tragical drama of life. Hence the eccentricities of conduct, with which women of superior minds have been accused – the struggles, the despairing though generous struggles, of an ardent spirit, denied scope for its exertions! The strong feelings, and strong energies, which properly directed, in a field sufficiently wide, might – ah! what might they not have aided? forced back, and pent up, ravage and destroy the mind which gave them birth.[4]

Godwin let the subject lapse; what more could he say? It was not however necessary for him to express perfect sympathy with the views of Mary Hays or Mary Imlay in order to be of interest to them. He was now at the height of his fame. In Hazlitt's phrase, 'he blazed as a sun in the firmament of reputation'.[5] *Political Justice* had made his name as a philosopher, just as he had hoped. His crucial intervention (with a newspaper article that undermined the prosecution) during the treason trials of 1794, when Holcroft, Horne Tooke, Thomas Hardy and a number of other democrats stood in danger of their lives had further increased his stature. Even those who disagreed with his political opinions admired the hypnotic power of his latest book, *Caleb Williams*, a novel set against an English landscape depicted in terms of nightmare. Godwin refused to see his country as the libertarian paradise the establishment insisted it was.

He had a large circle of friends; scarcely a day passed without his being consulted, or receiving admiring callers, or being invited out. He had in fact stepped in to fill the position of intellectual leadership left vacant amongst the English democrats by the death of Price and the emigration of Priestley. He fell short of the moral majesty of their generation: where they had been innocent, he sought, strenuously and sometimes embarrassingly, to be candid; where they were sustained by faith in God, he found himself increasingly disappointed with mankind. Where they had been scientists, mathematicians and ministers, leading quiet personal lives, he was that more vulnerable figure, the man of letters dependent on his pen for his bread. He could be vain, pompous and slippery. He and Holcroft, both firmly persuaded of the power of beneficent mind to overcome physical and emotional problems, displayed in practice a prickly querulousness in their dealings with other people, and were repeatedly wounding one another's feeling too.[6]

Still, Godwin was hugely admired. Holcroft was less popular, and some of his contemporaries found him a blustering bore. He was short-tempered, partly perhaps because of his determination to ignore his own physical symptoms of pain and fatigue: he was a Christian Scientist *avant la lettre*. But he was also a tender and humorous man. His best writing was informal; he kept a notebook in which he entered his observations of human nature, noting with delight (for instance) that the prostitutes of Newman Street, where he lived, invited God's assistance when they prayed for fine weather, the better to walk the streets in comfort.

As a militant atheist, he refused to instruct his children in Christianity; they were to be liberated from all superstition – an insistence that shocked most of his acquaintance. And as it happened he suffered a fearful tragedy with his only son, a clever, restless boy who ran away repeatedly and finally stole money from his father in order to emigrate. Holcroft pursued him to the ship, and the boy shot himself dead before his eyes. Godwin was present when it happened, and the horror of it remained a silent bond between them.

Mary and Holcroft developed a warm affection and respect for one another. She did nothing to provoke his temper, she appreciated his humanity and sense of humour and the strenuous effort of self-education his life had been. Probably she was not shocked by the religious ignorance of his children. Her own little book of lessons for Fanny[7] contained no mention of God or any religious precept. She shared some of his belief that willpower could control bodily pain, and above all she must have sympathized with the bereavements he had suffered.

Still, it was Godwin Mary chose to call on. He was in a better position to be professionally helpful to her; he was the more eminent; he had no children or previous experience of women; he was of the same generation and the same world. She found she had stumbled into a 'situation' of sorts when she was quickly introduced to two other ladies who were dividing between them the attention of both Holcroft and Godwin. One was a widow in her early forties, the actress, playwright and novelist Elizabeth Inchbald; she is supposed to have looked like a perfect blend between a duchess and a milkmaid, and she had a sharp tongue and a ready wit. The other was Amelia Alderson of Norwich, a clever, pretty girl in her twenties, full of what she herself described as 'animal spirits'.[8] Amelia wrote an account of the position she found herself in when she visited London early in 1796, for the delectation of a married friend at home:

> Godwin drank tea and supt here last night; a leave-taking visit, as he goes tomorrow to spend a fortnight at Dr Parr's. It would have entertained you highly to have seen him bid me farewell. He wished to salute me, but his courage failed him. 'While oft he looked back and was loth to depart.' 'Will you give me nothing to keep for your sake, and console me during my absence,'

murmured our philosopher, 'not even your slipper? I had it in my possession once, and need not have returned it!' This was true; my shoe had come off, and he had put it in his pocket for some time. You have no idea how gallant he is become; but indeed, he is much more amiable than ever he was. Mrs Inchbald says, the report of the world is that Mr Holcroft is in love with her, *she* with Mr Godwin, Mr Godwin with *me*, and I am in love with Mr Holcroft! A pretty story indeed! This report Godwin brings to me, and he says Mrs I. always tells him that when she praised *him* I praise Holcroft. This is not fair in Mrs I. She appears to be jealous of G's attention to me, so she makes him believe I prefer H. to him. She often says to me, 'Now you are come, Mr Godwin does not come near me.' Is not this very womanish?[9]

But whether the womanishness was Mrs I's or her own was not clear. Amelia was used to having her own way; she was the adored daughter of a Dissenting doctor in Norwich; her mother had died young, and she had spent her youth writing poetry and plays and organizing amateur theatricals as well as running the house. She had corresponded with Mrs Barbauld and her father, who had encouraged her to write, and when she was twenty-one she published an anonymous novel, *The Dangers of Coquetry*, with the impeccable moral 'that the appearance of impropriety (especially in women) cannot be too carefully avoided'.[10] Godwin had commented on the manuscripts of her plays, and she never failed to call on him when she was in town. Her father's politics were republican, and during the treason trials, which she attended, she knew that he intended to emigrate if the accused were found guilty. Consequently Godwin was a great man to her, even though she had too strong a sense of the ridiculous to be much moved when he began to woo her. A malicious description of him came from her pen, 'his hair *bien poudré*, and in a pair of new, sharp-toed, red morocco slippers, not to mention his green coat and crimson under-waistcoat'.[11] She took to Mary as soon as they met, declaring with her usual vivacity that the only two things in England that had failed to disappoint her were the Cumberland lakes and the author of *Vindication of the Rights of Woman.*[12]

Amelia enjoyed being wooed; Holcroft proposed to her and had to be turned down, but Godwin was trickier. He had put on record his profound objection to the institution of marriage; he wanted love, but not a wife; and in any case he was divided in his feelings.

Elizabeth Inchbald interested him as much as Amelia. Like her, and Godwin himself, she was Norfolk born, but her family were simple farmers, Catholics for generations.[13] She had run away from a widowed mother and houseful of sisters to try her luck as an actress in London. Alone and penniless, beautiful and innocent, she called on theatrical producers asking for work and found that the road to advancement was not what she had expected. She was forced into a quick decision to marry a widowed actor who offered himself, and only through him did she have her first opportunity of joining a touring company. They had no children, he died; she fell in love with the great John Kemble, he would not marry her. Typically, she put him to use in another way, drawing his character in a novel, *The Simple Story*, which was a huge and deserved success.

She acquired many admirers, conducted prolonged flirtations, but did not marry again; either she preferred independence or the men she liked were reluctant to propose to an actress. She turned to writing plays instead of acting, cultivated a ferocious respectability, and was heartbroken when one of her sisters went to the bad and died in sordid circumstances. Vanity and miserliness seem to have become her ruling passions. The few notes she left about her life had more to say of the state of her teeth and her investments than her heart, and she burnt the manuscript of her autobiography on the advice of her confessor. Coleridge has left a description of her, in a letter to Godwin:

> Mrs Inchbald I do not like at all – every time I recollect her, I like her less. That segment of a *look* at the corner of her eye – O God in heaven! – it is so cold and cunning –! thro' worlds of wildernesses I would run away from that look, that heart-picking look. 'Tis marvellous to me that you can like that Woman.[14]

But Godwin was fascinated by that heart-picking look, and Mrs Inchbald was friendly enough to Mary for the moment. Rivalry was in the air, but not a bitter rivalry. Mrs Inchbald's virtue was impregnable, Godwin was known to be resistant to marriage, there seemed no reason why they should not continue in a decorous round of visits and flirtations for as long as they liked without upsetting one another at all.

And now, through this group, a considerable social life began to open up for Mary again. Other great ladies of the stage made her welcome; they all knew what it was to be famous and yet not considered quite respectable, and they were prepared to show her sisterly sympathy. Mrs Siddons befriended her, as did Mary Robinson, who had once dazzled the Prince of Wales as Perdita; now she too was bringing up a daughter alone, and had turned to literature to earn her living. And Mary was often invited to spend her Sundays with the Twiss family, who liked to gather theatrical and literary people under their roof: Frances Twiss was the sister of Mrs Siddons and John Kemble.

Another woman writer who admired Mary was Elizabeth Fenwick;[15] she had just published, anonymously, a novel called *Secresy* (*sic*) which was strongly feminist in tone, and gave a frank account of an idealistic young woman who entered into a marriage relationship without the marriage ceremony and was betrayed as a result. Mrs Fenwick was the wife of Godwin's revolutionary friend John; he took to drink and she was later obliged to separate from him and fend for herself and her children in the usual way: school-teaching, hack writing, governessing. She was also intimate with Mary Hays, and the three women obviously found a good deal to discuss together.

With this sort of encouragement, Mary Imlay began to work on a new novel. It was to be called *Maria, or the Wrongs of Woman,* and it embodied a whole series of case histories illustrating the iniquities of the legal position of women, defending their right to sexual freedom and bitterly attacking society's refusal to allow them proper employment. Mary was less skilful a novelist than Elizabeth Fenwick, Mary Hays or Elizabeth Inchbald; it is probably a pity she allowed herself to be sidetracked from writing a second volume of polemics and chose instead to embody her ideas in fiction. Yet the pressures and drama of her personal experience gave her writing colour and fire. Aspects of her childhood appeared again, and her justifiable resentment against her elder brother produced a sister's aphorism: 'What was called spirit and wit in him, was cruelly repressed as forwardness in me.' She also took the opportunity to sketch a portrait of Imlay: he made his appearance as a sympathetic and charming though somewhat empty-headed lover who seduced a married woman and then drove her by his neglect to attempt suicide with laudanum.

The most striking thing about *Maria* was probably its outspoken assertion that women had sexual feelings and rights, and that the supposed refinement which tried to obscure this was actually degrading:

> When novelists and moralists praise as a virtue a woman's coldness of constitution and want of passion, I am disgusted. We cannot, without depraving our minds, endeavour to please a lover or husband, but in proportion as he pleases us. Men, more effectually to enslave us, may inculcate this partial morality, but let us not blush for nature without a cause!

And to enforce her point about the sexual inflammability of her heroine, she made Maria say: 'I could not coquet with a man without loving him a little and I perceived that I should not be able to stop at the line of what are termed innocent freedoms, did I suffer any.' As in *Mary*, she was trying to explore her own nature as honestly as she could, and with rather more experience to call on now.

She also attempted something new: to see life through the eyes of the poorest sorts of women, without caricaturing them. *Maria* is full of servant girls turned away by their mistresses when found to be pregnant, girls who try to abort their babies or kill themselves, girls bullied by employers, women ill-treated and insulted by landladies, working wives whose husbands take all their earnings, hospital patients whose treatment is experimental and dictated by the convenience of the doctors and students rather than their own wellbeing. The prostitute Jemima, sullen and clever, dragged up in misery and just able to pick up some education from a 'protector', is the finest character in the book, and her attempt to find any work above the most menial is described in detail as the bitter farce any such attempt was bound to be.

Maria was never finished, but left in a disordered and fragmentary state at the time of Mary's death. Even so, and apart from its intrinsic interest, it was important as a contribution to the small body of work by women writers who allowed their pens to dwell on guilt and misery without flinching. Mrs Inchbald's *Nature and Art* also showed a country girl, seduced and left with a baby, becoming a creature everyone else felt free to exploit economically as well as sexually. Mary Hays, both in *Emma Courtney* and in her second novel, *The Victim of Prejudice*, dwelt on the exploitation and helplessness of girls who were not protected by money or family. 'I thought of myself as a wild animal fallen into the hunter's nets' she made one such girl say after a weary effort to find and keep a decent job in London.[16] These were frightening but not fanciful pictures of the dark side of life for women, what they had to fear if eligible husbands failed to appear, fathers' fortunes were lost, rich uncles did not help; then they would indeed find that social superiors were implacably rude and cruel, and that the poor, instead of blending anonymously into the landscape, were individuals like themselves. Together, these novels serve as a reminder of the mass of silent girls who found the world empty of opportunity or happiness. They do something more than this, for they make up the first fictional school of women writing without reference to male tastes or models, and devoted to considering the place of their own sex in society.

In her writing, Mary continued to dwell angrily on the wrongs of her sex, but in her personal life the months that followed her thirty-seventh birthday were more agreeable than any she had passed for a long time. She had many visitors; John Opie, whose divorce finally came through at Easter, took to calling on her so often that there was gossip about his intentions.[17] The portrait he painted of her shows how sympathetic he found her; in it she appears a gentle, rather subdued and motherly-looking woman.

Young men began to worship her too: 'the crude young Jacobins, so soon to ripen into Quarterly Reviewers, were just now coquetting with Mary Wollstonecraft, or making love to the ghost of Madame Roland'.[18] Southey wrote to a friend from London that Mary was the person he liked best in the literary world; he said her face was marred only by a slight look of superiority, and that 'her eyes are light brown, and, though the lid of one of them is affected by a little paralysis, they are the most meaning I ever saw'.[19] Coleridge admired her conversation and character, though he added that her books were ill put together. And if Wordsworth was silent about her it may be that he was uneasy in comparing her situation and reputation with his own avoidance of responsibility towards his French-born daughter. He was in London in June, staying with another young man who was exceedingly fond of Mary – Basil Montagu – and seeing Godwin every few days.[20]

It may well have been through Montagu, who was engaged to Sarah Wedgwood, that Everina was presently found a job as governess to the Wedgwood children. Mary kept in touch with her youngest sister, but she was still totally estranged from Eliza, and there are no letters to any other members of her family from this period. Ned's children were being brought up to regard their aunt as a source of deep mortification.[21] One day her brother James appeared at her lodging, tired of his life at sea and declaring that he had embraced revolutionary principles and wanted to become a French citizen. In spite of the war he managed to make his way to Paris, and François Lanthenas spoke up for him as a suitable candidate for citizenship; was he not the brother of Marie Wollstonecraft? The recommendation was good enough to allow him to settle down as a 'student'.[22]

Mary herself was no longer regretting her life in Paris. She was too busy. She went to the theatre a good deal, and there were dinners and other gatherings at which actors, painters, writers and politicians talked of world affairs and of their work. Sometimes she visited St Paul's Churchyard and Johnson took up his old fatherly role again. And there was one particularly pleasant and memorable evening at John Kemble's when Sheridan, the Irish leader Curran, Elizabeth Inchbald, Godwin and Mary were all present. Everyone was in good spirits, 'the conversation took a most animated turn, and the subject was of Love': a theme on which most of the company was becoming increasingly expert.[23]

[17]

Godwin

IT is tempting to say that Mary's love for Godwin was more mature and in some way worthier than her love for Imlay; the theory satisfies a natural wish to see her life arrive at a happy climax after so much frustration. But there is not really much evidence for this in the letters, and at least one of her friends considered that her 'real' love had gone to Imlay and that Godwin was no more than a consolation prize of a superior kind. Leaving aside the question of whether love can be sized up for quality in this way, it must be said that Godwin was a more intelligent and scrupulous man than Imlay, but that it was Mary's need and his reputation that made the match. An adequate emotion drew her to him and bound him to her, and though there were one or two moments when it promised to grow into something greater, it was only in Godwin's violently emotional retrospect that their wooing and marriage took on the colouring of high romance.

He was susceptible before, during and after his relationship with Mary, and was looking for a woman when she called on him, preferably an intellectual and good-looking one. He was not a man who inspired many women with passion, and it is quite possible that Mary decided to woo him for a husband in cool – if not quite cold – blood. In the *Memoirs* he was at great pains to say that neither wooed the other:

> The partiality we conceived for each other, was in that mode, which I have always regarded as the purest and most refined of love. It grew with equal advances in the mind of each. It would have been impossible for the most minute observer to have said who was before, and who was after. One sex did not take the

priority which long-established custom has awarded it, nor the other overstep that delicacy which is so severely imposed. I am not conscious that either party can assume to have been the agent or the patient, the toil-spreader or the prey, in the affair.

But the image was a curious one, and may perhaps have pointed to some covert sense he had that he had been a prey after all, though willing enough. In one of his angry notes to Mary he claimed that he had 'found a wounded heart, &, as that heart cast itself upon me, it was my ambition to heal it'.[1]

Neither of them was entirely reliable as a witness about the sequence of events in their wooing. When he said, for instance, that she was his 'principal topic of solitary and daily contemplation' on his trip to Norfolk in July 1796,[2] we have to remember that he proposed (presumably marriage) to Amelia Alderson on 10 July, however much he may have been thinking about Mary.[3]

Amelia turned him down, upon which he sat down and philosophically wrote Mary a flirtatious letter. She meanwhile was moving her furniture out of storage and into rooms at 16 Judd Place West, very close indeed to his rooms, so that on his return he found her conveniently installed as a near neighbour.* His letters grew warm; hers, during the early days of August, were studded with arch and anxious references to her rivals, Elizabeth and Amelia. Soon Amelia appeared in London and, in the guise of sweet womanly friendship, spurred Mary into a passion of jealousy by telling her Godwin was ready to 'devour her' and speculating on whether he had ever kissed a woman.[4] Just over a week later Mary became Godwin's mistress, '*chez moi*', as he wrote carefully in his diary.

It was not an altogether ecstatic journey of sexual discovery. He says he 'had never loved till now; or at least had

* Judd Place West, just north of the New Road (now Euston Road), is no longer in existence.

never nourished a passion to the same growth'.[5] He was forty; probably he had never made love to a woman who was a friend before he became Mary's lover, and possibly he had lived a life of absolute chastity, guarding himself as best he could against the assaults of the imagination and the women in the streets – he wrote with authority on the influence of the imagination on the senses of the solitary man.[6]

Whereas Mary was clearly sexually curious, inflammable and enthusiastic. She had already enjoyed one affair with a lover singularly free of inhibition and had been living in torment ever since. However little emotional confidence she had, she was sexually confident and unashamed.

The beginning of the affair cast Godwin into confusion, and the day after she had become his mistress he either acted sick or was genuinely not well enough to greet her as warmly as she had hoped. He attempted a written apology which risked a phrase out of the marriage service but was otherwise less than gallant:

> I have been very unwell all night. You did not consider me enough in that way yesterday, & therefore unintentionally impressed upon me a mortifying sensation. When you see me next; will you condescend to take me for better for worse, that is prepared to find me, as it shall happen, full of gaiety & life, or a puny valetudinarian?[7]

But this crossed with one of Mary's letters in which self-reproach merged into scolding. She offered to withdraw from the situation altogether:

> ... despising false delicacy I almost fear that I have lost sight of the true ... You talk of the roses which grow profusely in every path of life – I catch at them; but only encounter the thorns – I would not be unjust for the world – I can only say that you appear to me to have acted injudiciously; and that full of your own feelings, little as I comprehend them, you forgot mine – or do not understand my character. It is my turn to have

a fever today – I am not well – I am hurt – But I mean not to hurt you. Consider what has passed as a fever of your imagination; one of the slight mortal shakes to which you are liable – and I – will become again a *Solitary Walker*. Adieu! I was going to add God bless you![8]

The tone was painfully reminiscent of her letters to Jane Arden at fourteen, and she certainly did not expect Godwin to accept her adieu any more than her invocation of God's blessing. It is touching to see that he already revealed to her his affliction, the 'slight mortal shakes' he suffered from throughout his adult life, and which were probably a form of epilepsy: it was a gage expressing his confidence in her affection.

Godwin's answer to this letter of Mary's was one of the finest things he ever wrote to her: honest but comforting, he affirmed the strength of his feelings without bullying her, and told her frankly but tactfully for once where he thought she went wrong.

How shall I answer you? In one point we sympathize; I had rather at this moment talk to you on paper than in any other mode. I should feel ashamed in seeing you.

You do not know how honest I am. I swear to you that I told you nothing but a strict and literal truth, when I described to you the manner in which you set my imagination on fire on Saturday. For six & thirty hours I could think of nothing else. I longed inexpressibly to have you in my arms. Why did I not come to you? I am a fool. I feared still that I might be deceiving myself as to your feelings, & that I was feeding my mind with groundless presumptions. I determined to suffer the point to arrive at its own denouement. I was not aware that the fervour of my imagination was exhausting itself. Yet this, I believe, is no uncommon case.

Like any other man, I can speak only of what I know. But this I can boldly affirm, that nothing that I have seen in you could in the slightest degree authorize the opinion, that, *in despising the false delicacy, you have lost sight of the true*. I see nothing in you but what I respect & adore.

I know the acuteness of your feelings, & there is perhaps nothing on earth that would give me so pungent a remorse, as to add to your unhappiness.

Do not hate me. Indeed I do not deserve it. Do not cast me off. Do not become again a *solitary walker*. Be just to me, & then, though you will discover in me much that is foolish and censurable, yet a woman of your understanding will still regard me with some partiality.

Upon consideration I find in you one fault, & but one. You have the feelings of nature, & you have the honesty to avow them. In all this you do well. I am sure you do. But do not let them tyrannise over you. Estimate everything at its just value. It is best that we should be friends in every sense of the word; but in the mean time let us be friends.

Suffer me to see you. Let us leave every thing to its own course. My imagination is not dead, I suppose, though it sleeps. But, be it as it will, I will torment you no more. I will be your friend, the friend of your mind, the admirer of your excellencies. All else I commit to the disposition of futurity, glad, if completely happy; passive & silent in this respect, while I am not so.

Be happy. Resolve to be happy. You deserve to be so. Every thing that interferes with it, is weakness and wandering; & a woman, like you, can, must, shall, shake it off. Afford, for instance, no food for the morbid madness, & no triumph to the misanthropical gloom, of your afternoon visitor [probably he meant Mary Hays]. Call up, with firmness, the energies, which, I am sure, you so eminently possess.

Send me word that I may call on you in a day or two. Do you not see, while I exhort you to be a philosopher, how painfully acute are my own feelings? I need soothing, though I cannot ask it from you.[9]

To this letter Mary, not surprisingly, responded well. Later, when their relations were in a smoother patch, he began to risk conventional expressions of tenderness – '*adorable maîtresse*', for example. But there was usually a feeling of tension: Mary put on the emotional pressure, Godwin hoped for the quiet life.

Like Holcroft in his novels, Godwin could not quite get

over the belief that women were either 'goatish' or else 'without one emotion which celestial purity might not approve';[10] either delicate, or wallowing sensualists. He fell easily into contrasting the 'intercourse of mind' with 'sordid and casual gratification'[11] and was unable to find a vocabulary in which to express the idea of unashamed sexual enjoyment between equal partners. In the *Memoirs* he said of Mary: 'Never was there a woman on the face of the earth more alien to that mire and grossness, in which the sensual part of our species are delighted to wallow.'[12] But Mary had the good sense (or the good luck) not to be ashamed of her own nature; she was even curious and delighted to discuss the effects of love. In November she wrote him a note that began:

> If the felicity of last night has had the same effect on your health as on my countenance, you have no cause to lament your failure of resolution: for I have seldom seen so much live fire running about my features as this morning when recollections – very dear, called forth the blush of pleasure, as I adjusted my hair.[13]

In *St Leon*, the novel he wrote in the year following her death, and which contained his idealized portrait of her, there was a passage which described the rapturous nature of his feeling for her, but even here he felt obliged to preface it with a cautionary reference to purity and refinement:

> To judge from my own experience in this situation, I should say, that nature has atoned for all the disasters and miseries she so copiously and incessantly pours upon her sons, by this one gift, the transcendent enjoyment and nameless delights which, wherever the heart is pure and the soul is refined, wait on the attachment of two persons of opposite sexes ... Ours was a sober and dignified happiness; and its very sobriety served to give it additional voluptuousness. We had each our separate pursuits, whether for the cultivation of our minds, or the promotion of our mutual interests. Separation gave us a respectability in each other's eyes, while it prepared us to enter with fresh ardour into

society and conversation. In company with each other, hours passed over us, and appeared but minutes ... To feel that we are loved by one whose love we have deserved, to be employed in the mutual interchange of the marks of this love, habitually to study the happiness of one by whom our happiness is studied in return, this is the most desirable as it is the genuine and unadulterated condition of human nature. I must have someone to sympathise with; I cannot bear to be cut off from all relations; I desire to experience a confidence, a concord, an attachment, that cannot rise between common acquaintance. In every state we long for some fond bosom on which to rest our weary head, some speaking eye with which to exchange the glances of intelligence and affection. Then the soul warms and expands itself; then it shuns the observations of every other beholder; then it melts with feelings that are inexpressible, but that the heart understands without the aid of words; then the eyes swim with rapture; then the frame languishes with enjoyment; then the soul burns with fire; then the two persons thus blest are no longer two; distance vanishes, one thought animates, one mind informs them. Thus love acts; thus it is ripened to perfection; never does man feel himself so much alive, so truly etherial, as when, bursting the bonds of diffidence, uncertainty and reserve, he pours himself entire into the bosom of the woman he adores.[14]

It was an expressive account of ecstasy. The actual exchanges of Mary's and Godwin's life were naturally not always at this level. In the many notes that passed between them the tone varied from playful attention and teasing, through a good deal of complaining about their health from both of them, to prim and insensitive reprimands from Godwin and nagging, jealous, sometimes hysterical communications from Mary. It is hard to like the way in which she told Godwin that 'little marks of attention are incumbent upon you at present'; his response that 'you spoil little attentions by anticipating them' was equally chilling. Ten days later she could not resist raising the point again: 'You tell me that "I spoil little attentions, by anticipation". Yet to have attention, I find, that it is necessary to demand it.

My faults are inveterate – for I *did* expect you last night – But, *never mind it.* Your coming would not have been worth anything, if it must be requested.'[15]

Quarrels continued to simmer and bubble. Mrs Inchbald was a serious source of trouble: Mary called her Mrs Perfection, and made frequent counter-references to the pleasant times she spent with Opie while Godwin was dancing attendance on her. At other times Mary worried about her own effect on Godwin. She wrote: 'I was endeavouring to discover last night, in bed, what it is in me, of which you are afraid. I was hurt at perceiving that you were';[16] and Godwin several times expressed his sense of being crushed by her cold and bitter moods. They both knew these sprang partly from her fear that he would treat her as Imlay had done. He could be tactless, vain and wilful in a way that might make any woman feel annoyed or jealous, and it is noticeable in *St Leon* that he makes his heroine say she could forgive any failing in a husband except infidelity. Yet he too could be jealous, though he covered up the disreputable emotion better: Mary was asked not to visit Holcroft, on the grounds supposedly that he was Godwin's friend. She did not observe the prohibition entirely.

The quarrels of November were smoothed over with some graceful apologies from Mary; she asked for a 'bill of rights' to be allowed to tease her lover sometimes without his taking it tragically, and he responded. But in December there was further trouble. Mary, not feeling very well, spent an uncomfortable evening at the theatre and had the mortification of seeing her lover below, installed in comfort with Mrs Inchbald: more storms, more reconciliations. She began to suspect she might be pregnant again and in her terror at what this might mean attacked her lover like a wildcat. He wrote her a pitiful letter of expostulation at the harsh words she threw at him: 'You wished we had never met; you wished you could cancel all that had passed between us ...

You wished all the kind things you had ever written me destroyed.'[17]

She must indeed have felt appalled at the thought of having a second illegitimate baby by a different father from the first, and the attack on Godwin was probably based on his failure to propose immediate marriage. All through January she remained deeply dejected: 'Poor Women how they are beset with plagues – within – and without'. She felt ill and resented Godwin's failure to sympathize: 'It is very tormenting to be thus, neither sick nor well; especially as you scarcely imagine me indisposed'.*

A few days later she had to endure another petty humiliation. Her landlady was persecuting her: 'I was glad that you were not with me last night, for the foolish woman of the house laid a trap to plague me. I have, however, I believe put an end to this nonsense.' Her maid Marguerite knew the state of affairs, and presently Mrs Cotton, her Berkshire friend, came to spend a few days with Mary, inspected both Opie and Godwin, and decided Godwin was the man.

On 3 February Mary called on another friend, Dr James Fordyce, no doubt hoping to have her pregnancy confirmed or denied. And in the middle of the month Everina arrived to stay on her way from Ireland to the Wedgwoods. Mary found her company wearisome and embarrassing, and tried to involve her in a round of visits; it was impossible to talk

* She made a curious reference to what she called Godwin's 'chance-medley system' which may possibly have referred to an attempt at contraception on his part: perhaps an endeavour to follow some sort of rhythm method? English eighteenth-century medical books advised women that intercourse in the period immediately after menstruation was most likely to lead to conception; it did not require much imagination to suppose that the time just before might therefore be less likely to produce conception. But her remark is not very clear: 'Women are certainly great fools; but nature made them so. I have not time, or paper, else, I could draw an inference, not very illustrative of your chance-medley system – But I spare the moth-like opinion, there is room enough in the world &c.'

about either her relationship with Godwin or her new pregnancy, which was making her feel unwell, with her sister. Basil Montagu came to the rescue and took her out for a day; Godwin, though patently annoyed when Mary became inaccessible, was still sticking resolutely to his independent way of life. On 6 March Everina departed again. Desultory letters about theatre tickets and reviews were exchanged between the lovers. But two undated notes were probably written at this time and refer to the decision they were working towards. Both are from Godwin: 'I must write, though it will not be long till five. I shall however reserve all I have to say. *Non, je ne veux pas être fâché quant au passé.*' The second reads: 'I will do as you please. Shall I come to consult you; or will you call on me?'[18] And so finally he agreed to abandon his principles and marry her. The ceremony took place, with only Godwin's old and comfortable friend Marshall present, on 29 March, at St Pancras, their local church, a short walk across the fields from either of their lodgings.* Mary signed her name quite correctly as Mary Wollstonecraft, spinster. In the *Memoirs* Godwin states that they had both been unwilling to marry until then, though for different reasons: Mary was tired of being talked about and could not face the thought of more gossip, and Godwin himself was of course famous for his opposition to marriage on theoretical grounds. However these were overcome by the fact of her pregnancy and his developing taste for domestic life. Within a few days of the marriage they moved into a new house, No. 29 the Polygon, facing east towards Evesham Buildings where Godwin took separate rooms in which to work.†

* The church, one of the most ancient in London, was very little used because most of its parishioners lived up in Kentish Town and had built themselves other, more convenient places of worship. At the time of Mary's wedding the river Fleet still flowed at the foot of the hill on which the church stood, with primroses on its banks in spring, and the outlook was quite rural.

† It is clear from contemporary map markings that No. 29 faced

And now Mary proved herself to be a 'worshipper of domestic life. She loved to observe the growth of affection between me and her daughter, then three years of age, as well as my anxiety respecting the child not yet born. Pregnancy itself, unequal as the decree of nature seems to be in this respect, is the source of a thousand endearments ...'[19] She was delighted with her status as a married woman and displayed an almost childish enthusiasm. Two days after the wedding she reminded her husband 'I am to be a partaker of your worldly good – you know!' and a week later she told him: 'when I press anything it is always with a true *wifish* submission to your judgement and inclination'.[20] Wifish submission implied husbandly duties however, and within another few days she was asking him to call on Johnson, send over her spectacles, speak to the landlord about the state of the sink and deal with the tradespeople.

It was difficult for them to announce the marriage to their friends, not just because they feared ridicule or censure but also because both were under financial obligations – Mary to Johnson, Godwin to Wedgwood and possibly others – which made them fear that their benefactors might consider the breeding of a family more than they had bargained for. But everyone seems to have stood up to the shock; Johnson indeed became one of Godwin's most loyal supporters thereafter, largely one imagines on the strength of his love for Mary and protective feelings towards little Fanny.

Holcroft was hurt at not being told the news in advance or supplied with the name of the bride even, but he was

---

east on to Chalton Street, in which Evesham Buildings stood. The Polygon was a ring of houses built around gardens, three stories high and handsomely constructed; they were newly built and intended to attract middle-class families to what was planned as a garden suburb. The project failed in that only a few features, the Polygon being one, were finished, and a slump meant that the houses were sold and let very cheap. Somers Town soon became a notoriously evil slum, but when Mary lived there it was a place for artists and other interesting people to settle.

delighted at the fact of the marriage and able to supply Mary's identity, which Godwin had withheld: 'From my very heart and soul I give you joy. I think you the most extraordinary married pair in existence. May your happiness be as pure as I firmly persuade myself it must be.'[21]

A light-hearted approach was thought best for one of their friends. Godwin wrote to Mary Hays as follows:

> My fair neighbour desires me to announce to you a piece of news, which is consonant to the regard that both she and I entertain for you, you should rather learn from us than from any other quarter. She bids me remind you of the earnest way in which you pressed me to prevail upon her to change her name, she directs me to add, that it has happened to me, like many other disputants, to be entrapped in my own toils: in short, that we found that there was no way so obvious for her to drop the name of Imlay, as to assume the name of Godwin. Mrs Godwin (who the devil is that?) will be glad to see you at No. 29, Polygon, Somers Town, whenever you are inclined to favour her with a call.[22]

This letter was sent on 10 April. On the nineteenth the couple went to the theatre in a party that included Amelia, Maria Reveley, the Fenwicks and Elizabeth Inchbald. But when Mrs Inchbald heard the news from Mary and Godwin she insulted them on the spot. There was a terrific row and another quarrel between husband and wife when they reached Somers Town again. They now had to face laughter and sneers from many of their acquaintances, and Mary was pointedly dropped by most of the theatrical ladies.

Even Mrs Barbauld commented in a letter on the 'numberless squibs' thrown at Mr Godwin:

> ... he winces not a little on receiving the usual congratulations. In order to give the connection as little as possible the appearance of such a vulgar and debasing tie as matrimony, the parties have established separate establishments, and the husband only visits his mistress like a lover, when each is dressed, room in order, &c. And this may possibly last till they have a family,

then they will probably join quietly in one menage, like other folks. He says he submitted to the ceremony in compliance with the prejudices of Mrs Imlay. Now as it is plain she had them not, at one time at least, the excuse will barely serve.[23]

The most revealing statement of Mary's own feelings at the time, outside her letters to Godwin himself, appeared in a letter she wrote to Amelia Alderson soon after the marriage had been announced to the world. Mary was eager to justify herself. She began with a reference to the row at the theatre, and continued: 'I still mean to be independent, even to the cultivating sentiments and principles in my children's minds (should I have more) which he disavows.'[24] That she knew perfectly well she was going to have another child, and this was the reason for the marriage, did not need to be mentioned; Mary had not become so infected with Godwin's belief in perfect frankness. She went on:

> The wound my unsuspecting heart formerly received is not healed. I found my evenings solitary, and I wished, while fulfilling the duty of a mother, to have some person with similar pursuits, bound to me by affection; and beside, I earnestly desired to resign a name which seemed to disgrace me. Since I have been unfortunately the object of observation, I have had it in my power, more than once, to marry very advantageously, and of course, should have been courted by those, who at least cannot accuse me of acting an interested party, though I have not, by dazzling their eyes, rendered them blind to my faults.

It was not a very flattering account of her feeling for Godwin. She went on again:

> I am proud perhaps, conscious of my own purity and integrity, and many circumstances of my life have contributed to excite in my bosom an indignant contempt for the forms of a world I should have bade a long good night to, had I not been a mother.

Honesty again compels the comment that she had twice attempted to bid the world goodnight in spite of being a mother, but she was carried away by her self-justificatory vision:

> Condemned, then, to toil my hour out, I wish to live as rationally as I can; had fortune or splendour been my aim in life, they have been within my reach, would I have paid the price. Well, enough of the subject, I do not wish to resume it. Good night! God bless you.

She signed the letter a little awkwardly, since she had been using the form 'Mary Imlay' until now, as 'Mary Wollstonecraft femme Godwin'. Probably her cool account of her motives in marrying represents the truth of one of her moods if not the whole truth. Godwin was clever and famous and sought after; she was fond of him, wanted a companion and bedmate, a father for Fanny; she had become pregnant by him; he was willing; it was enough. It is difficult at the best of times to write an explanation of one's motives in marrying; if they have to be explained they almost inevitably sound inadequate, undignified or dishonest, or all three.

[18]

Marriage, Childbirth, Death

MARRIAGE allowed them to play some of the games respectable couples indulge in. Fuseli was invited to dinner to see how well they got along, and finding other guests as talkative as himself retired early from the table to join Mary in the drawing room and complain of the wretched company. But the complaints were more often between Mary and her own husband. She found him vain, he thought her bitter. In May they had a dispute which, according to Mary, 'led us both to justify ourselves at the expense of the other', and she went on to attack him on his pet theory:

> Perfect confidence, and sincerity of action is, I am persuaded, incompatible with the present state of reason. I am sorry for the bitterness of your expressions when you denominated, what I think a just contempt of a false principle of action, *savage resentment, and the worst of vices,* not because I winced under the lash, but as it led me to infer that the coquettish candour of vanity was a much less generous motive.[1]

And when Basil Montagu called on her for breakfast one morning with an invitation to join him and the Wedgwoods for a day in the country, and she had to decline because of a prior engagement with dull Hannah Godwin, she took care to let Godwin know about her sacrifice. A fortnight later he, not so interested in moral advantage, set off with Montagu himself on a longer expedition. It was not the most tactful of gestures; Mary had expressed to him the summer before a rather wistful desire that they might together '*vagabondize* one day in the country before the summer is clear gone. I love the country and like to leave certain associations in my memory, which seem, as it were, the landmarks of affection.'[2]

Now she was left alone in London, obviously pregnant, to face friends and household cares while Godwin vagabondized as far as the Wedgwood home at Etruria in Staffordshire, writing long and deeply affectionate letters it is true, but delaying his return in a manner that produced panic in Mary. Fanny was sent out with her toy rake to make hay in the fields surrounding the Polygon, but Mary sat indoors hearing in her mind the alarm bells Imlay had first set jangling; she was not able to control them.

The trouble was trivial enough: Godwin had not only delayed his return, but mentioned to Mary that the cause was his desire to see a 'shew' at Coventry fair, of which the chief attraction was a 'female, representative of lady Godiva ... dressed in a close dress, to represent nakedness'. In fact he missed it because Montagu wanted to visit some gardens, but he still lingered, calling or attempting to call on many old friends and acquaintances. Dr Parr's daughter, who had promised him a 'roasting' when she heard of his marriage, had just eloped to Gretna Green with a rich and foolish pupil of her father's. On hearing this piece of news, Mary adopted her freezing tone: 'Could a woman of delicacy seduce and marry a fool? ... This ignoble method of rising in the world is the consequence of the present system of female education.'[3] Godwin's remarks on Montagu's engagement to Sarah Wedgwood were even more ham-fisted:

> I look upon any of my friends going to be married with something of the same feeling as I should do if they were sentenced for life to hard labour in the Spielburg [a German political prison]. The despot may die, & the new despot grace his accession with a general jail delivery: that is almost the only hope for the unfortunate captive.[4]

In due course Godwin returned to his own personal Spielburg and the quarrel over his prolonged absence was patched up, but there were still other problems. He wished Mary to give up all her religious ideas, she was unwilling. 'How can you blame me for taken [*sic*] refuge in the idea of God, when I despair of finding sincerity on earth?'[5] The need for religion seems to have been brought on by the attentions of a Miss Pinkerton, who was pursuing Godwin and not being fended off with all the vigour required by Mrs Godwin. She wrote him a note on the subject:

You judge not in your case as in that of another. You give a softer name to folly and immorality when it flatters – yes, I must say it – your vanity, than to mistaken passion when it was extended to another – you termed Miss Hay's conduct insanity when only her own happiness was involved – I cannot forget the strength of your expressions – and you treat with a mildness calculated to foster it, a romantic selfishness, and pamper conceit, which will even lead the object to – I was going to say misery – but I believe her incapable of feeling it. Her want of sensibility with respect to her family first disgusted me – Then to obtrude herself on me, to see affection, and instead of feeling sympathy, to endeavour to undermined [*sic*] it, certainly resembles the conduct of the fictitious being, to whose dignity she aspires. Yet you, at the very moment, commenced a correspondence with her whom you had previously almost neglected – you brought me a letter without a conclusion – and you changed countenance at the reply – My old wounds bleed afresh – What did not blind confidence, and unsuspecting truth, lead me to – my very soul trembles, sooner than endure the hundredth part of what I have suffered, I could wish my poor Fanny and self asleep at the bottom of the sea.[6]

Poor Mary: Godwin endured Miss Pinkerton's visits cheerfully enough during the whole summer, flattered by her attentions. He found Mary often unkind, harsh, given to saying 'grating things'; and she continually justified herself by saying she was being disappointed in her expectations. During the last month of the pregnancy however they softened towards one another and took to a new form of address, becoming 'Mama' and 'Papa'. And in the middle of

August Mama was allowed to settle Miss Pinkerton by forbidding her the house, exactly as Fuseli had allowed Sophia to do with Mary.

A few days later they were both absorbed in something more interesting. Mary wrote three notes to Godwin on 30 August:

> I have no doubt of seeing the animal today; but must wait for Mrs Blenkinsop to guess at the hour – I have sent for her – Pray send me the news paper – I wish I had a novel, or some book of sheer amusement, to excite curiosity, and while away the time – Have you anything of the kind?[7]

A few hours later:

> Mrs Blenkinsop tells me that Everything is in a fair way, and that there is no fear of the event being put off till another day – Still, *at present*, she thinks, I shall not immediately be freed from my load – I am very well – Call before dinner time, unless you receive another message from me –

And he did receive one more message, her last note, sent at three o'clock:

> Mrs Blenkinsop tells me that I am in the most natural state, and can promise me a safe delivery. But that I must have a little patience.

And now Mary herself fell silent; from this point the story is told by Godwin. His diary, terse as ever, covers the events of the next twelve days in terms of calls made and received, the arrivals of different doctors, the briefest noting of symptoms and hopes. It is the first, shorthand version of the agony he went over a second time in his *Memoirs*, dwelling on every detail, plucking at the question, could it have been otherwise, could she have been saved had they acted differently?

The answer is almost certainly, no. Mary had insisted on being attended only by a midwife, because she thought it indecorous to have a male doctor in attendance – a point over which Godwin disagreed with her. But all London midwives were obliged to receive two years' training under a physician before they could be licensed,[8] and the woman who came to Mary, Mrs Blenkinsop, was the midwife in charge of the famous Westminster Lying-In hospital. She certainly did not lack experience. Maternal mortality was dropping fast from year to year, even though obstetrics still ignored the danger of infection and surgical intervention was usually fatal to mother and child.

Mary's experience with the birth of Fanny had been so good that she planned to present the new baby to Godwin herself immediately after the delivery, and to get up for dinner the next day. She saw herself as a pioneering example to other women: 'She was so far from being under any apprehension as to the difficulties of child-birth, as frequently to ridicule the fashion of ladies in England, who keep to their chamber for one full month after delivery.'[9] With hindsight, this is unutterably sad; she was sensible and entirely in the right, if only things had been normal.

She felt the onset of labour at five in the morning of the thirtieth of August, a Wednesday; the day before, she and Godwin had taken a walk together and read *Young Werther* aloud in the evening. Godwin slept the night at the Polygon, but departed across the road to Evesham Buildings to work as usual, probably about nine o'clock in the morning, with philosophic calm. Mary was up, excited at the beginning of labour, unable to settle to anything, playing with Fanny perhaps and preparing to send her off to friends for the day, deciding now to send for Mrs Blenkinsop, dispatching her little notes to Godwin. Her pains came slowly. At two o'clock she and Mrs Blenkinsop went up to her bedroom on the second floor. There was one woman attendant besides, and Mary's maid; Marguerite had to stay with Fanny.

Normal labour with a second child was expected to last not much more than eight hours.[10] The midwife's job was to make an internal examination when she judged it timely.

When she thought the birth was imminent she applied butter to smooth the baby's passage, and attempted to grasp its head and help it along, a hazardous undertaking. The mother was supposed to help by managing her breath during the 'throws'. She might have a log of wood set across the foot of her bed to brace her feet against. If she fainted, smelling salts were given; in any case she was expected to groan, cry out and hold her breath enough to become quite hoarse. Hot drinks were therefore prepared to ease her throat after the birth; some families laid in large supplies of alcohol for the mother in order to dull her senses during labour too, but this was not recommended by doctors and certainly not practised in the Godwin household. The best medical writers of the day stressed the importance of just such a cheerful, matter-of-fact approach to childbirth as Mary's. Cleanliness was not much thought of, there was no mention of stitching, but a thick, hot linen cloth was prepared to lay soothingly over the newly delivered woman.

Mary's labour proved slow and, according to what she told Godwin the next day, extremely painful in the later stages. He did not go up to her room during the afternoon, at her request; in fact he dined at the Reveleys' and then went back to Evesham Buildings. The Fenwicks and Marshal ate supper with him; at ten he returned a little anxiously to the Polygon to wait downstairs. At 11.20 he must have heard the baby cry. Probably the maid came down to tell him that, though the baby was fine and sturdy, it was not the little William they had hoped for but a girl, and probably he felt a small pang of disappointment as he prepared himself to go up to see Mary and the new Mary.

Only now Mrs Blenkinsop sent down a message to say, not yet. Godwin waited and waited. At three in the morning he was told that the placenta had not come away and asked to go for Doctor Poignand, the chief obstetrician at the Westminster Lying-In. Very frightened, Godwin set off on foot through the summer night.

Once the baby is delivered, the mother is no longer in pain; the delivery of the placenta is a trivial anticlimax. But when it fails to appear there is anxiety amongst the attendants, because a retained placenta means the womb cannot contract into a tight ball and will go on bleeding steadily. If it is not removed, infection becomes likely. Nowadays it is relatively common to have retained pieces of placenta scraped out under anaesthesia, even as late as ten or twelve days after birth. In 1797 a retained placenta, if not dealt with very quickly, meant certain death. Dr Poignand's job therefore was to extract the whole thing as swiftly as he could, by hand and (of course) with no anaesthetics.

Godwin went up to Mary's candle-lit room with the doctor, saw her bleeding and half-conscious and withdrew in distress. Exhausted from her long and painful labour and weak from loss of blood, she now had to lie on her back with her shoulders held by Mrs Blenkinsop and her maid whilst Dr Poignand ferreted around as best he could, inserting his hand into her womb and feeling for the placenta with his fingertips. Probably she was past understanding exactly what was happening, but perhaps she sensed the dismay when it was found that the placenta was broken up into pieces, making the doctor's job infinitely more difficult. He worked through the dawn. The sun rose at six and he was still toiling at eight, when Mary's condition made him give up, but he was hopeful that he had removed all the pieces, and told Godwin so. Almost certainly he had introduced infection in the process. Mary slept for a while, her first sleep in over twenty-four hours. The baby lay in her cradle.

Perhaps Godwin now slept too. When he awoke he went straight to Mary and found her transformed; she smiled and joked, saying that although she had been through the worst pain she had ever known, she had no intention of leaving him a widower. She also expressed a wish to be visited by a doctor they both liked, James Fordyce, an amiable and somewhat eccentric man with no special knowledge of obstetrics.

Dr Poignand returned before noon, and said he saw no need to call in another doctor. Nevertheless Godwin did call in Fordyce, who examined Mary and pronounced that all was well. Godwin scarcely left her side on Thursday; she seemed to improve steadily and they both allowed themselves to feel cheerful. The passage in *St Leon* in which he describes the birth of a child is obviously based on these shared moments in which they examined their tiny daughter happily together. Were it not for the pathos, there would be something wonderfully funny about this hymn to family life from the pen of the man who had so recently advocated communal child-rearing, inspired by love for a woman who had spoken so fiercely against indissoluble bonds:

> Never shall I forget the interview between us immediately subsequent to her first parturition, the effusion with which we met each other after all danger seemed to have subsided, the kindness which animated us, increased as it was by the ideas of peril and suffering, the sacred sensation with which the mother presented her infant to her husband, or the complacency with which we read in each other's eyes a common sentiment of melting tenderness and inviolable attachment!
>
> This, she seemed to say, is the joint result of our common affection. It partakes equally of both, and is the shrine in which our sympathies and our life have been poured together, by presents and tokens; we record and stamp our attachment in this precious creature, a creature of that species which is more admirable than anything else the world has to boast, a creature susceptible of pleasure and pain, of affection and love, of sentiment and fancy, of wisdom and virtue. This creature will daily stand in need of an aid we shall delight to afford; will require our meditations and exertions to forward its improvement, and confirm its merits and its worth. We shall each blend our exertions for that purpose, and our union confirmed by this common object of our labour and affection, will every day become more sacred and indissoluble.[11]

To outward appearance things continued to go well, so much so that on Friday morning Godwin returned to his usual routine and went out for the day. Mary lay and dozed, played with her baby, began to suckle her, chatted to her attendants. Fanny must by now have been brought up to see her and inspect her little sister with three-year-old gravity. She did not like her mother to stay in bed, but was reassured by the sight of her, and was used to being looked after by Marguerite. In the evening, after Godwin's return, Johnson also called and there was a generally cheerful and congratulatory atmosphere.

On Saturday Maria Reveley offered to have Fanny to stay for a few days and came to collect her; Fanny said good-bye to her mother for the last time. All day Mary heard the door knocker going busily. Basil Montagu arrived, then Godwin's bachelor friends Tuthil and George Dyson; Anthony Carlisle, an excellent doctor and member of Godwin's and Holcroft's circle, paid a social call. He went up to Mary's room to talk to her. Fordyce had been telling his colleagues how well she had done in her labour with only a midwife in attendance, and Carlisle was interested in any evidence of the influence of mental attitudes over bodily states. Whether he was impressed or alarmed by what he now saw is not on record. Godwin meanwhile had decided to go out for a long walk with Montagu; they went as far as Kensington, several hours away on foot, and during their absence Mary began to feel ill and asked anxiously for her husband. He did not get back till dinner time and was met by apprehensive faces. Mary had suffered a fit of shivering so bad that the bed frame shook. The shivering was unreadable, untreatable and therefore mysteriously frightening; we know now that it pointed to the onset of septicaemia.

Godwin, feeling guilty at his long absence, sent a message telling Hannah and her friend, who had been invited to dinner, not to come; and Mary, in her feverish state, asked for dinner not to be laid in the room below hers as usual, where she could hear the voices and bustle, but on the ground floor. In the evening she had another fit of shivering. Godwin was with her this time: 'every muscle of her body trembled, the teeth chattered, and the bed shook under her. This continued probably five minutes. She told me, after it was over, that it had been a struggle between life and death, and that she had been more than once, in the course of it, at the point of expiring.'[12] Clearly she herself persisted in the idea that she might hold off death by an effort of will, much as Holcroft believed possible; perhaps this is what Thomas Cooper had in mind when he spoke later of her distressing reluctance to quit the world. Carlisle was also of the opinion that her will could either cooperate with the disease or combat it, and that it was better for her not to believe she was dying.

There is something peculiarly horrible about this third death of Mary's, buzzed about by doctors and well-meaning intellectuals, painful, long drawn out and lacking in peace or dignity. Twice she had willed herself to die and been brought back to life: friends had awoken her from a drugged sleep and roused her to look at her child; watermen had fished her out of the river and delivered her back through one sort of agony to another. Now a dozen pairs of hands tried to pluck her back from death to be with her two children and her husband, but could do nothing to save her.

Godwin refused to succumb to despair. Both Fordyce and Poignand came on Sunday; it was Poignand's last visit. He withdrew on the pretext that Fordyce had taken over the case, but he probably knew from experience that it was past cure. Mrs Blenkinsop returned and Eliza Fenwick volunteered to act as nurse. Mary expressed a wish to have Mrs Cotton sent for, but this was not done. Probably the doctors thought she could not arrive in time to be of use. On Monday Mary was able to joke feebly again when puppies were applied to her breasts; Fordyce had ordered the removal of the baby, and she had an overflowing supply of milk. According to Godwin, the puppies were meant to draw off the milk; if so, it was an odd procedure, since milk can usually be expressed quite easily by hand, and the suckling of puppies would stimulate the breasts to produce still more milk. Possibly they were in fact intended to help the womb contract and expel the remaining pieces of placenta. Mary smiled and spoke affectionately to Godwin through these blackly farcical moments, and he clung to such evidence of her resistance to the fever. By now she must have been suffering from the general blood poisoning and possibly the onset of gas gangrene. On Tuesday afternoon Fordyce brought in a colleague called Clarke, a surgeon who was to consider performing a further operation in the hope of removing the rest of the placenta. But it could not have made any difference at this point; the infection was there and there was no treatment for that. In any case Mary was too reduced to stand any more, and the operation was not attempted.

It was now a whole week since the birth. Godwin knew things were very bad. Carlisle told him to give Mary wine in order to dull her suffering, and from four in the afternoon he sat by her bedside offering her sips from a glass. The baby had been taken to Maria Reveley to join Fanny, so they were alone. At seven, as it began to dusk, Mary's maid came in and Godwin asked her what she thought of her mistress's state. The woman answered that 'in her judgement, she was going as fast as possible'. This reply sent Godwin into a state bordering on madness; he went downstairs and begged Basil Montagu to go for Carlisle again.

Montagu fetched him from a great distance – he was dining on the other side of town – and Carlisle from then on became Godwin's best support. He remained in the house until Mary's death, talking with him and doing the little he could to make her comfortable. On Wednesday night she rallied slightly again; on Thursday evening Carlisle warned them to expect her death soon, but still she lived for the whole of Friday and Saturday. Godwin's friends sat dishevelled about the house, eager to go on helpful errands, whilst the terrible slow process dragged on. She was no longer coherent in her expressions, but tried to do as she was told, attempting to sleep for instance, though she could not do more than feign the breathing of a sleeping person for a minute or so. She asked her nurses not to bully her, she did not mention religion apart from one exclamation: 'Oh Godwin, I am in heaven', to which he is supposed to have answered anxiously, 'You mean, my dear, that your symptoms are a little easier.'[13] She was not able to discuss the children when he at last approached the subject, but simply said 'I know what you are thinking of' and could add nothing.[14]

The shivering fits had ceased after Thursday. On Sunday night Carlisle told Godwin to go to bed, at six in the morning he called him, and at twenty to eight she died. 'She had died a death' as one respectable clergyman was soon to remark 'that strongly marked the distinction of the sexes, by pointing out the destiny of women, and the diseases to which they were peculiarly liable.'[15]

Her death coincided with the falling-off of many things she had believed in. She had embodied the spirit of the age faithfully, its political optimism, its faith in willpower, self-improvement, education. She had hoped that courage and good intentions might triumph over dead convention, and that the whole structure of society might be reformed and renewed by philosophers. She had imagined generously that what she wanted for herself might be welcomed by all her own sex and at least understood by the other. She had hated prudence, bigotry and cant. Had she lived on, she would have seen plenty of all these; she would have seen the flight to reaction, the apostasy of one after another of her radical friends, and their spiritual decay. In its own way that was to be as painful as her end. 'I could weep,' wrote Southey, 'To think that *she* is to the grave gone down'; but for her own sake it may have been almost as well.

[19]

Aftermath and Debate

UNABLE to write the fact of her death in his diary, Godwin entered simply the words '20 minutes before 8' and filled in three lines with strokes of his pen.

But then the diary resumed its neat, factual function. The dinner guests for the same day appear: Basil Montagu, Marshal (the old friend who had witnessed the wedding), Hannah Godwin and little Fanny, brought over from the Reveleys to comfort and be comforted as best possible. Carlisle went home for a few hours but soon returned to do what he could for the bereaved, and during the next few days Johnson, Holcroft, Opie and the Fenwicks all came to mourn with Godwin. He began to write letters, some anguished, some hectoring. There was an angry exchange with a friend who felt he could not as an unbeliever properly attend the funeral, since it was a religious ceremony. Godwin, despite his own atheism, was deeply offended, but when the time came for the funeral on Friday (the fifteenth) he was too upset to go himself.

She was buried in the churchyard of St Pancras, where she had been married five months before. Godwin saw to the preparation of a large, square memorial block of grey stone, inscribed:

MARY WOLLSTONECRAFT
GODWIN
Author of
A Vindication
of the rights of Woman

Born 27th April 1759
Died 10th September 1797

And presently a pair of weeping willows were planted, one on each side of her grave.

Godwin was eager to persuade old friends who had broken with Mary at the time of their marriage to acknowledge her virtue again now she was dead. Elizabeth Inchbald received several letters from him, 'but they are more like distracted lines than anything rational' she observed coldly, and neither changed her mind nor renewed her friendship with him. To the end of her life she made mocking remarks when his name arose, especially in connection with his matrimonial affairs.[1]

Others reacted more kindly. Maria Reveley kept the baby for a few days, then handed her to Elizabeth Fenwick who looked after her for a while longer. Mrs Fenwick also wrote to Everina, hoping to heal the breach there by stressing Godwin's goodness to Mary and her affection for him. Meanwhile Godwin sat in his rooms in Evesham Buildings, trying to read and writing more letters. To Holcroft he wrote:

> I firmly believe that there does not exist her equal in the world. I know from experience we were formed to make each other happy. I have not the least expectation that I can now ever know happiness again. Do not – if you can help it – exhort me, or console me.[2]

And to Carlisle:

> One of my wife's books now lies near me, but I avoid opening it. I took up a book on the education of children, but that impressed me too forcibly with my forlorn and disabled state with respect to the two poor animals left under my protection, and I threw it aside ... If you have any ... consolation in store for me, be at pains to bestow it.[3]

After ten days, when he felt he could bear it, he moved all his things to the Polygon and settled there. First Fanny and then the baby were fetched; henceforth they were to be in the care of a friend of Hannah Godwin's, Louisa Jones, an unremarkable creature who could not replace Mary either with Godwin or with the children.

Marguerite's name was heard no more. Perhaps she had had enough of upheavals and tears, and wanted to settle into a steady French domesticity and forget the strange ways of English intellectuals. This meant that before she was four, Fanny had lost father, mother and the nurse she had known for as long as she could remember. Godwin loved her dearly and brought her up to think of herself as his eldest daughter, and indeed to call herself Fanny Godwin: so she always signed herself and was addressed by her step-sisters, and one of the British Museum copies of *Original Stories* has 'F.G.' inscribed in it in large childish letters. Godwin's description of his eldest daughter in *St Leon* suggests how he studied Fanny's nature, and shows a sad prescience:

> Uncommonly mild and affectionate, alive to the slightest variations of treatment, profoundly depressed by every mark of unkindness, but exquisitely sensible to demonstrations of sympathy and attachment. She appeared little formed to struggle with the difficulties of life and frowns of the world; but, in periods of quietness and tranquility nothing could exceed the sweetness of her character and the fascination of her manners. Her chief attachment was to her mother ...

He was sensitive to her emotions, but quite unable to make up for her losses. Coleridge noted the 'cadaverous silence ... quite catacombish' prevailing at the Polygon over a year later,[4] and the baby quickly grew to dominate her sister and perhaps ride a little roughshod over her.

A Lavaterian study of Mary's physiognomy, carried out when she was only a few days old, pronounced her the possessor of memory, intelligence, quick sensibility and a certain lack of patience. Like much fortune telling, it turned out to be a self-fulfilling prophecy. But Fanny remained meek to the point of martyrdom. Her true father was never heard of again.*

Opie either gave or sold Godwin his portrait of Mary, finished during the last year of her life; it was hung above the desk where he worked. Fuseli had been informed of her death within hours, in a note from Francis Jeffrey: 'One who loved you and whom I respected, is no more. Mrs G died this morning.'[5] And Fuseli in turn wrote to Roscoe, no more than the words 'Poor Mary' in a postcript; his sarcasm for once deserted him.[6]

Mary Hays contributed an obituary in the *Monthly Magazine* which extolled her friend's 'ardent, ingenuous and unconquerable spirit' and referred to her as 'a victim to the vices and prejudices of mankind'. Even the *Gentle-*

* A Gilbert Imlay was buried in November 1828 in the churchyard of St Brelade's, Jersey. His epitaph, engraved on his tombstone, read as follows (the version is a copy made in 1833 and cited by Richard Garnett in 1903):

> Stranger intelligent! should you pass this way
> Speak of the social advances of the day –
> Mention the greatly good, who've serenely shone
> Since the soul departed its mortal bourne;
> Say if statesmen wise have grown, and priests sincere
> Or if hypocrisy must disappear
> As phylosophy extends the beam of truth,
> Sustains rights divine, its essence, and the worth
> Sympathy may penetrate the mouldering earth,
> Recall the spirit, and remove the dearth,
> Transient hope gleams even in the grave,
> Which is enough dust can have, or ought to crave.
> Then silently bid farewell, be happy,
> For as the globe moves round, thou will grow nappy.
> Wake to hail the hour when new scenes arise,
> As brightening vistas open in the skies.

It is certainly odd, and leads one to question the fidelity of the copyist; but it is also touching and suggests that Imlay's interest in philosophy and human rights had been genuine, if not very studiously followed up.

man's Magazine spoke politely of her 'soundness of understanding and sensibility of heart'. News of her death travelled without further details; several months later Anna Seward reacted with shock and concern and inquired of what disorder she died. Had her question remained unanswered, Mary's posthumous reputation might have stood higher than it did thereafter. But Godwin's reaction to his grief was to write and publish; within two weeks of his wife's death he had begun work on a tribute to her. The *Memoirs* were fired by the same sort of intensity of feeling that inspired *Caleb Williams,* and distinguished by the candour that was Godwin's most cherished tenet. It is impossible to read them without being moved by his pain, especially in the last section when he lingers over the days, hours and minutes of her dying: the outpouring of grief is like a belated love offering of the kind he had found hard to make while she still lived, and he seems to be writing in order to fix for himself what he now felt and could not hope to feel again.

But the *Memoirs* were written at high speed, and inevitably there were omissions, inaccuracies and misrepresentations. Godwin used a few of Mary's letters, notes made during his conversations with her, a discreet account of her London years from Johnson, some communications from Hugh Skeys and a letter from a young friend of Paine's which gave a very brief sketch of a few meetings with her in Paris. He wrote to her sisters in Dublin – Everina had not stayed long with the Wedgwoods – and in December he received an unhelpful missive from her, withholding the letters in her and Eliza's possession and supplying a tart reprimand instead: 'I am sorry to perceive you are inclined to be minute when I think it is impossible for you to be even tolerably accurate.'[7]

He seems to have made no attempt to approach her father in Wales or her brother Ned in London. Of the Paris circle, Christie had died in Surinam and Rebecca and Jane Christie either were not consulted or kept silent.* The Barlows, Stone and Helen Williams were relatively inaccessible in France, and in any case the continuing war and political climate of England made Godwin reluctant to dwell on her French years, and they were dismissed with a few generalized comments.

When Godwin applied to Fuseli for her letters, the painter opened a drawer, showed him the packets and then shut the drawer again, saying, 'Damn you, that is all you will see of them.'[8] The two men were never able to speak to one another without falling into ironic tones, and the death of Mary, painful to each in different degree, could not be expected to draw them together. They were as clumsy in distress as they had been in love.

The *Memoirs* appeared in January 1798, headed by an etching which gives Mary chubby cheeks and a rosebud mouth; otherwise there were not many concessions to conventional piety. Godwin freely discussed her love affairs, suicide attempts and pregnancies, and praised her (not altogether accurately) for her rejection of Christianity. At the same time he and Johnson brought out four small volumes of her *Posthumous Works* containing, amongst other papers, her letters to Imlay and the fragments of *Maria, or the Wrongs of Woman*. Both her personal behaviour and her insistence on the need for divorce reform and the excusa-

* Thomas Christie died of a fever in Surinam in the same month as Mary. A letter announcing his death from Theophilus Lindsey to a friend in Dundee suggests that he was, like Holcroft, a believer in the power of mind over matter: 'through his own obstinacy at last in refusing to take the usual remedies in his case' he died. (MS. letter in Dr Williams's library.) He left less than £1,000 to his widow and died intestate: see Public Record Office, letters of administration for March 1798. The fate of his daughter Julie is not known, and though the French historian Robinet mentions Christies in Montrose in the 1890s who talked of their famous revolutionary forebear, there seem to be none left today.

bility of adultery were thus publicly established through her own words as well as Godwin's.

The public's reaction was made up of fascination and horror in more or less equal parts. Neither Godwin nor even the careful Johnson had apparently foreseen this. Indeed Johnson, being aware as a magazine publisher of the public's appetite for gossip about the famous, and the readiness of partisan journalists to supply it with titbits, may have encouraged Godwin to give a plain unvarnished version of Mary's life before a scandalously distorted one could appear. But all they succeeded in doing was scandalizing the public themselves, and in the process striking a severe blow at the feminist cause. People who were prepared to consider the doctrines of the *Vindication* seriously simply could not swallow the account of Mary's character that emerged from the later books.

> Hard was thy fate in all the scenes of life,
> As daughter, sister, parent, friend and wife
> But harder still in death thy fate we own,
> Mourn'd by thy Godwin – with a heart of stone.[9]

wrote Roscoe, and there were many others who felt Godwin had done her a terrible disservice in telling the world what any decent biographer would have concealed most carefully.

Wordsworth, who had called on Godwin in December 1797, wrote in March 1798 to a friend, 'I have not yet seen the life of Mrs Godwin [*sic*]. I wish to see it, though with no tormenting curiosity';[10] and in April his sister Dorothy noted that 'Mary Wollstonecraft's life, etc, came'. Tormenting curiosity or no, Wordsworth was closely involved with those who surrounded Mary at the time of her death, since he and Dorothy were caring for Basil Montagu's child, and cannot have failed to hear of the circumstances from him, even if his conversation with Godwin remained formal. But the poet did not deliver himself of any opinion on Mary's beliefs or her behaviour, absorbed as he was in coming to terms with his own guilt feelings: he was preparing, after all, to behave very much as Imlay had done.*

Godwin received almost no praise, and soon public attacks began to come in, notably from the ranks of Tory journalists, rallying to their cry of 'common sense' against the nonsense of 'philosophers'. Mary's misfortunes combined with her experience of Godwinian marriage were too good to be missed; she had once defended her friend Mary Hays against the allegation that *she* was a 'philosophess and Godwinian',[11] but no one could successfully defend Mrs Godwin now.

Of the very few attempts to make a fair and serious estimate of her in the light of Godwin's biography, the most interesting appeared in a pair of articles, printed in February and March 1798 in a woman's magazine called *The Monthly Visitor*, which seem to be the work of a personal friend. The first article was prefaced by an engraving of Mary which the writer declared a better likeness than the etching from Opie: 'Those who have seen the late Mrs Godwin will be able to judge of the improvements we have endeavoured to effect.' The article went on to point out how different Mary's ideas were from Godwin's: 'In soul, in information, in understanding, and in manner, they are eminently distinct.' What is more, her feelings had not been what he supposed: 'that she ever loved Mr Godwin, is at least improbable'.

After these confident assertions, the author continued:

> She had strong passions, and a strong understanding. She was a great genius; but like most great geniuses she was uncommon. Uncommon in her ideas of society and those rules which, for

* The poem *Ruth*, about an English girl wooed and abandoned by a young American, which Wordsworth wrote in Germany in 1799, had other sources of inspiration, but there are passages in it which evoke both Mary's and Imlay's story, as well as Wordsworth's carefully hidden remorse for his own treatment of Annette.

the general good, must be borne with in particular instances ... She was ... much at variance with your common maxims of prudence; and exclaimed, 'there are arguments which convince the reason, whilst they carry death to the heart!' But indeed she was no modern philosopher ... And, in all probability, had she been married well in early life, she had then been a happy woman, and universally respected. She was a woman of high genius; and, as she felt the whole strength of her powers, she thought herself lifted, in a degree, above the ordinary trammels of civil communities. She inveighed bitterly against a code of regulations which she deemed derogatory to her sex; nor did she for an instant reflect that unless women were equally qualified with herself to act on the grand principles of all morality, independent of tuition and restraint, the doctrine she inculcated if received, must overturn the basis of every civilized state.[12]

Compared with the crude abuse and smoking-room jokes of the Tory press, which enjoyed depicting Mary as a whore and Godwin as a pimp, this was at least considered and well-intentioned, and it is probably representative of the opinion of Mary's Dissenting and radical friends, who admired her for her talent but thought she had in the end gone too far.* At the same time, being aimed at the very audience of literate women who had most to learn from Mary's ideas, the article was damaging, both because it ignored her arguments, and also in its assertion that a demand for sexual equality threatened the very basis of civilization. Some of the next generation of Unitarian ladies paid the price of this dismissal of Mary's feminism on account of her sexual transgression: Harriet Taylor certainly

* The most likely candidate for authorship of the article is Mrs Barbauld, who never shared Mary's feminist views but equally never joined in the abuse other women heaped on her. As late as May 1797 the Barbauld family evidently regarded Mary with respect, as is clear from a letter written by their adopted son to Mrs Barbauld from Etruria, in which he mentions the Wedgwoods' governess, 'a sister of Mrs Wollstonecraft (now Mrs Godwin is she not!) ... She has much of her sister's good sense but is more reserved.' The manuscript letter is in Stoke Newington library.

felt obliged to put an extraordinary restraint upon her own sexual behaviour. Harriet Martineau, not herself troubled by sexual problems, simply declared categorically that 'the Wollstonecraft order do infinite mischief; and for my part, I do not wish to have anything to do with them'.

Another of Mary's Dissenting friends, Amelia Alderson, turned against her with a distinctly malicious enthusiasm. Here there were personal motives at work: in May 1798 she married John Opie, and she may have felt sensitive about the fact that he was a divorced man, that he had once been an admirer of Mary's, and that he and Godwin had also been close friends. At all events, by 1799 Godwin told Holcroft that Opie was 'no friend of mine' any longer, and Mrs Opie set to work on a series of novels designed to make her own respectability absolutely clear.[13] In *Father and Daughter* (1800) she showed the ostracism endured by an unmarried mother, a form of cruelty she felt called on to defend:

> It is the *slang* of the present day, if I may be allowed this vulgar but forcible expression, to inveigh bitterly against society for excluding from its circle, with unrelenting vigour, the woman who has once transgressed the salutary laws of chastity; and some brilliant and persuasive writers of both sexes have endeavoured to prove that many an amiable woman has been for ever lost to virtue and the world, and become the victim of prostitution, merely because her first fault was treated with ill-judging and criminal severity.
>
> This assertion appears to me to be fraught with mischief; as it is calculated to deter the victim of seduction from penitence and amendment, by telling her that she would employ them in her favour in vain ... But it is not to be expected that society should open its arms to receive its prodigal children till they have undergone long and painful probation, – till they have practised the virtues of self-denial, patience, fortitude, and industry. And she whose penitence is not the mere result of wounded pride and caprice, will be capable of exerting all these virtues, in order to regain some portion of the esteem which she has lost.

This was a direct hit at her old friend's views, and in her next novel Amelia went much further and produced something like a *roman à clef*: *Adeline Mowbray* was a travesty of the story of Godwin and Mary, but there is no doubt that it used their experience and held them up to ridicule for their theoretical rejection of marriage. Adeline was made to say, as Mary did, that 'it is the individuality of the attachment that constitutes its chastity'; both she and her lover, who had written attacking marriage and outlined a plan for an ideal form of society, were hurt and amazed when they found themselves insulted and shunned by respectable people. The superior way of life they had imagined was found to be a chimera, and they experienced nothing but misery and humiliation, especially when Adeline became pregnant. The grand deterrent to behaviour like theirs, Mrs Opie suggested, was the cruel treatment meted out to illegitimate children themselves, as well as their mothers. The length of the book did not prevent it from being widely read at the time, and it is hard to forgive Amelia Opie for the cool way in which she thus made use of the woman who had certainly done her no harm and who had left daughters, legitimate and illegitimate, who could have done with some kindness from their mother's friends.

A further piece of really malign bad luck offered Mary's detractors fresh ammunition against her. Her old employers, the Kingsboroughs, were involved in a family scandal centring on their daughter Mary and Robert himself. Mary King had been a child of eight when in Miss Wollstonecraft's charge, but ten years later she was able to cause trouble of exactly the kind that allowed people to shake their heads and murmur that she had been corrupted. What happened was this: she had been staying in London with her mother in September 1797 (the time of Mary's death) when she disappeared. The frantic family posted bills and had rivers dragged, but in fact she had eloped with a Colonel Fitzgerald, an illegitimate half-brother of her mother's, brought up at Mitchelstown but now married and living in England; she was pregnant by him and they were planning to escape to America together.

The subsequent behaviour of the family probably owes something to the fact that Fitzgerald was committing not just adultery but also incest, though perhaps unknown to little Mary, who had grown up in a houseful of near and distant relations and may not have been told the truth about all of them. At all events, she was traced and, after some bizarre episodes, Fitzgerald was shot dead. There can be no doubt that it was murder, but the murderers – Robert Kingsborough and one of his sons – stuck to their version of the story, which made it killing in self-defence. The old Earl died conveniently at this point, so that Robert, succeeding to the earldom, was able to claim a trial in the Irish House of Lords. It turned into a splendid occasion for pageantry. Tickets were sold and there was general sympathy for the accused from the galaxies of peeresses and lords temporal and spiritual who gathered to witness the scene. Robert was acquitted without any witnesses being called. Mary King's baby was disposed of, and the whole affair blew over.* Except in one respect: the coincidence of the trial occurring at the time the *Memoirs* of Mrs Godwin were circulating had its effect. Bishop Percy took the trouble to send his wife a copy of the shocking book from Dublin, and to repeat the gossip about its subject having been involved with Robert Kingsborough during her days as a governess. Another Irish bishop preached a sermon in which the names of Voltaire and Mrs Wollstonecraft Godwin were linked together in infamy. Only Margaret Mountcashel spoke up in her

* A mass of gossip and legend has gathered around Mary King; according to some her baby was killed by her family. What is certain is that she lived to marry a Gloucestershire gentleman, G. G. Meares, in 1805, bore three sons and three daughters in wedlock, and died relatively young, in 1819, leaving no account of her history.

defence, but since she herself was an outspoken republican and atheist, she only made matters worse and so the Kingsboroughs had their revenge in turn, and contributed to the horror in which the establishment held the memory of their governess.

Godwin produced a second edition of the *Memoirs* within months of the first. It contained a few modifications and explanatory passages to appease the public; the *Posthumous Works* were allowed to rest. In their own way, even the *Memoirs* had diminished and distorted Mary's real importance: by minimizing her claim to be taken seriously for her ideas, and presenting her instead as the female Werther, a romantic and tragic heroine, he may have been giving the truth as he wanted to see it, but he was very far from serving the cause she had believed in. He made no attempt to discuss her intellectual development, and he was unwilling to consider the validity of her feminist ideas in any detail. Instead, he stressed the way in which her mind had complemented his:

> One of the leading passions of my mind has been an anxious desire not to be deceived, and as long as I can remember, I have been discouraged, when I have endeavoured to cast the sum of my intellectual value, by finding that I did not possess, in the degree of some other men, an intuitive perception of intellectual beauty ... what I wanted in this respect, Mary possessed in a degree superior to any other person I ever knew. The strength of her mind lay in intuition. She was often right, by this means only, in matters of mere speculation ... and yet, though perhaps, in the strict sense of the term, she reasoned little, it is surprising what a degree of soundness is to be found in her determination. But if this quality was of use to her in topics that seem the proper province of reasoning, it was much more so in matters directly appealing to the intellectual taste. In a robust and unwavering judgement of this sort, there is a kind of witchcraft.[14]

Mary had bewitched the materialist philosopher, it

seemed, not only by her sexual appeal but by the very processes of her mind, the traditionally feminine intuition that allowed her to overleap logic. Godwin had nothing to say about her reasonable discussions of the manner in which women's upbringing, social expectations and deprivation of the chance of work affected the development of their natures. In his view, he was devoted to reason and she reliant on a kind of witchcraft. And when the *Memoirs* were followed a year later by *St Leon*, in which Marguerite, supposedly a portrait of Mary, appeared as an almost totally passive and dependent wife and mother without a thought or ambition outside the domestic circle, his determination to present the world with an unrecognizably softened Mary, a Mary with her sting drawn, was confirmed. Her memory was to be honoured by effacing and ignoring, not by defending and preaching her ideas; by dwelling on the sad and gentle averted gaze of the Opie portrait, not the fierce and challenging glare of the champion of female rights. But as Condorcet had said, 'Il est difficile même à un philosophe de ne pas s'oublier un peu lorsqu'il parle des femmes.'[15]

But now another voice was raised, concerned neither to explain away Mary's character defects nor establish her as a tragic heroine but rather to keep alive her message. Mary Hays, who had spent many hours in conversation with her friend during the last two years of her life, and who had already made 'the moral martyrdom of those who press forward' her theme in a novel, took up her pen briskly and finished the book she had started six years earlier: she called it an *Appeal to the Men of Great Britain in Behalf of the Women*. Like the *Vindication* it was a straightforward polemical work, and had Mary Wollstonecraft supplied the second volume she promised, it would probably not have been completed.

Johnson encouraged Miss Hays, despite his own severe difficulties in 1798; the government finally succeeded in sending him to prison for six months for selling a seditious pamphlet by one of his Dissenting authors, and he was obliged to withdraw his support from the *Analytical*, which folded almost at once. But he was allowed to entertain as much as usual in prison, Mary Hays was a frequent visitor,[16] and her book appeared in print in 1798. It was issued anonymously, something Johnson commonly did to shield authors when in doubt about their reception, and it must have been a very small edition, since no copies appear to have survived. Were it not for the *Analytical*'s summary and review, its contents would be quite lost.*

Mary Hays made a determined effort to follow up and extend her dead friend's arguments. She began by discussing the way in which agitation for general political reform had led women to consider the particular oppression they had to endure. Although her sex was denied unversity education or a place at any of the academies, it could no longer be denied knowledge because books were now cheaply available to all. There needed to be changes in the law, in property ownership and civil rights. The lack of any decent alternative to marriage, and the hypocrisy of masculine insistence on female chastity, were both deplored. She pointed out that the progress of the human species as a whole must depend on the emancipation of women, on their access to education and careers, and had some sensible things to say about 'the tacit acquiescence of the injured party' in the sex war and the importance of women being charitable towards one another. Once again she raised the cry that 'mind is of no sex' and that the inculcation of a sly submissiveness in girls from early childhood was equally harmful to both sexes.

* The authorship of the *Appeal* is easily established: in 1825, when Mary Hays was still alive, William Thompson referred to her as its author in the Preface to his own *Appeal of One Half the Human Race, Women, against the Pretensions of the Other Half, Men, to restrain in Political and thence in Civil and Domestic Slavery*.

One quotation will show the tone and spirit of the book well enough:

You may talk to woman to eternity of the supreme felicity of pleasing you, though at her own expence, at the expence of her liberty, her property, her natural equality; at the expence of almost every gift with which God may have endowed her, and which you pretend to prune, to garble or to extirpate at will; I say, you may preach thus to eternity, but you will never convince ... while the voice of nature pleads within us, and clearly intimates, – that a greater degree, a greater proportion of happiness might not be the lot of women, if they were allowed as men are, some vote, some right of judgement in a matter which concerns them so nearly, as that of the laws and opinions by which they are supposed to be governed. And of which it is but reasonable to suppose that they themselves must be very competent judges.

This was fully worthy of her predecessor; it was also exactly what should have been expected from intelligent women brought up in Dissenting circles at that date. But, except in the *Analytical*, she found no support at all. Her friends were silent, and she became another butt for Tory sarcasm:

This is one of the impertinent effusions of modern theorists and visionary reformers, who, instead of attributing the miseries and distresses of life to the real causes, the wickedness and mischievous passions of human nature ... ascribe them to the incorrect *organization of society*, and the abuses of established institutions.[17]

It was by now the stock all-purpose response to any suggestion that living conditions were less than perfect for any section of English society. When the *Lady's Monthly Museum* reviewed the *Appeal* it went a stage further and produced a perfectly circular anti-feminist argument: the author, it suggested, might lose any hope of winning a husband if she continued to advocate 'unqualified equality' between the sexes.[18]

There may have been an element of malice here; Mary Hays did make life difficult for herself by putting into practice her belief in sexual equality in a way that rendered her vulnerable to ridicule. She pursued men noisily, persistently and (worst of all) unsuccessfully. She had lost a fiancé who died suddenly when she was twenty, grieved for him painfully – she said she felt like a widow – and longed to find another; she harried both the Cambridge radical William Frend and later the young poet Charles Lloyd, much her junior. For this lack of delicacy she was mocked. Time-honoured terms of abuse reserved for plain, pushing women were brought out, and even Coleridge was unable to express his dislike for her views without automatic reference to her ugliness and her petticoats, for neither of which could she be held responsible. And it was doubly unfortunate that Mary Wollstonecraft's one ardent female disciple should have been vulnerable to mockery in this way, because it lent weight to generalizing arguments about the sort of women who took up feminism, and their motives in doing so.

After the *Appeal*, Mary Hays published her second feminist novel, and then wilted; her six-volume *Female Biography* (1803) was written in a much less polemical spirit. She lived on to see the ascendancy of almost every idea she had castigated in her *Appeal*, but her own fighting spirit had been defeated long before her death in 1843.

The wave of defection from revolutionary ideas of any kind built up until it swept along almost everyone in England. It was to be expected, perhaps, that men would brush aside women's claims and dismiss Mary Wollstonecraft and Mary Hays as graceless, grabbing creatures who had preached to their intellectual and social superiors about matters they could not understand.* But the steady cam-

* See, for example, Beloe's outcry in 1817, which finished: 'Daughters of England, be not beguiled; be assured that the study of politics is not essential to female accomplishments, that the

paign of denigration from women writers, who might have seen their own interest in supporting the Marys, is harder to explain. Of those women who took it upon themselves to lay down standards for their own sex, one after another approached the question of women's rights, examined its various aspects, and retreated with expressions of disapproval or contempt. Amelia Opie's contribution to the debate has already been discussed; other apparently sensible and well-educated women produced comparable stuff. Maria Edgeworth, for instance in her *Practical Education*, published (by Johnson too) in 1798, stressed the need for passivity in girls:

> In the education of girls we must teach them more caution than is necessary to boys ... they *must* trust to the experience of others, they cannot always have recourse to what *ought to be*, they must adapt themselves to what is.[19]

Far better to fit girls to existing conditions than to encourage them to discontent or rebellion which might expose them to disappointment or disgrace. The message was repeated many times:

> We cannot help thinking that their happiness is of more consequence than their speculative rights, and we wish to educate women so that they may be happy in the situation in which they are most likely to be placed.

---

possession of the Machiavellian knowledge will neither make you better mothers, wives or friends; that to obtain it, a long life, severe study, and the most laborious investigation are indispensably necessary. Must it not excite the strongest emotions of contempt, to hear pert misses, just escaped from boarding-schools, harangue in a more peremptory tone than Selden would have assumed, and with the slightest reading, and most superficial knowledge, presume to pass judgment on the political rights and conditions of nations?'

And, still more awfully, Lord Castlereagh, speaking in the House in 1819, expressed his belief that it was enough to restrain women from attending political meetings 'to let them know that when the French Republicans were carrying on their bloody orgies, they could find no female to join them except by ransacking the bagnios or public brothels'.

Girls must very soon perceive the impossibility of their rambling about the world in quest of adventures.

A just idea of the nature of dignity, opposed to what is commonly called *spirit,* should be given early to our female pupils.

So much depends upon the temper of women, that it ought to be most carefully cultivated in early life; girls should be more inured to restraint than boys, because they are more likely to meet with restraint in society.

Miss Edgeworth's attitude was to some extent politically inspired: the demand for rights, whether by men or women, terrified her because of the terrible examples of France and Ireland (where she witnessed some violent revolutionary activity in 1798). She blamed Madame Roland's tragic ending on her deficient education, and went on to write several fictional attacks on women who made claims she thought dangerous. *Madame de Fleury* showed a good French girl assisting her aristocratic patroness during the Revolution whilst her thieving and lying cousin Manon (actually given Madame Roland's name) believes in the rights of man and woman, and becomes the mistress of an ex-hairdresser turned revolutionary leader. *Belinda,* written at the same time (in 1801), contained a character called Harriot Freke who advocated women's rights, encouraged her friends to adultery and female duelling, and behaved so indelicately altogether that she disgusted the heroine with the whole idea of such rights. And the principal character of *The Modern Griselda,* an argumentative and dissatisfied wife, after insisting on a divorce, was made to complain that all she had really wanted was for her husband to master her.*

* Maria, exceptionally dependent on her father's approval, wrote this story especially to please him. It seems possible that her insistence that women's lives must be envisaged in terms of restraint

Much later in her life, in 1834, when she published *Helen*, Miss Edgeworth did speak up for a slightly amended point of view:

> Let me observe to you, that the position of women in society, is somewhat different from what it was a hundred years ago, or as it was sixty, or I will say thirty years since. Women are now so highly cultivated, and political subjects are at present of so much importance, of such high interest, to all human creatures who live together in society, you can hardly expect, Helen, that you, as a rational being, can go through the world as it now is, without forming any opinion on points of public importance. You cannot, I conceive, satisfy yourself with the common namby-pamby little missy phrase, 'ladies have nothing to do with politics'.

But of course there *had* been some women forty years since who had taken a lively interest in politics. It was one of the things Miss Edgeworth's equally influential contemporary, Hannah More, particularly objected to in her *Strictures on the Modern System of Female Education* (1799) in whose opening chapter on 'Influence' she was at pains to express her horror of 'female politicians' and her conviction that women should use their powers only to improve the general moral tone of society, and not to meddle in public matters. This led her quite naturally a few paragraphs further on to attack Mary Wollstonecraft for her

---

and endurance owes something to her feelings about her father, just as Mary Wollstonecraft's feminism may have owed something to her contempt for her father and brother. A man of brilliant inventiveness, Richard Lovell Edgeworth created amongst his other achievements the role of Victorian paterfamilias. His wives were perpetually pregnant and ailing, each one replaced within months of her death, until Maria had a 'mother' younger than herself and over twenty siblings; and she, the eldest daughter who always felt insufficiently loved, created an ideal of womanhood that could blossom only at the centre of a domestic circle, the children not even being sent to school, but carefully educated at home. See Marilyn Butler's excellent account in *Maria Edgeworth* (1972).

direct vindication of adultery . . . for the first time attempted by a *woman*, a professed admirer and imitator of the German suicide Werter. The Female Werter, as she is styled by her biographer, asserts in a work, intitled 'The Wrongs of Woman,' that adultery is justifiable, and that the restrictions placed on it by the laws of England constitute part of the *wrongs of woman.*

Miss More's politics were thoroughly reactionary, and she proceeded from the narrowest of nonconformist assumptions about human nature, a world away from Mary's Unitarian friends. She believed in the innate wickedness of children and saw education as primarily concerned with crushing this wickedness and ferreting out the evil impulses of the human heart, male or female. Thus the prevalence of adultery caused her more concern than the starvation suffered by the poor as a result of the French wars, since starvation could be attributed to the will of God. Her point of view made her popular with the government; she was employed to write calming tracts for the rural poor and ridiculed quietly in London for her concern over the sinfulness of Society.[20]

The link between feminism and radical ideas was also seized on by Elizabeth Hamilton, a popular novelist living in Edinburgh. In 1800 she published *The Modern Philosophers,* a satirical attack on any demand for rights in either sex, which went into several editions, including an Irish one renamed *The London Philosophers.* She made an attempt to exclude Mary Wollstonecraft from her satire, referring to her as 'the very sensible authoress' and concentrating her fire instead on Mary Hays, with a sublime disregard of the essential similarity of the two women's views – perhaps she had not read *Maria.* Ugly, stupid and undomesticated Bridgetina Botherim was clearly meant for Miss Hays, with her perpetual quoting of Godwin and her unavailing pursuit of men. To her suggestion that unmarried women needed work and married ones were sometimes oppressed, a beautifully simple answer was provided: Christian faith was in itself enough to prevent single women from feeling unhappy or frustrated, and no true Christian husband would ever oppress his wife. A similar point of view was expressed by Wilberforce, who was pleased with the notion that unmarried women 'may always find an object in attending to the poor', rather as though God had thoughtfully provided them for one another's benefit.

To this particular brand of optimism even Maria Edgeworth was clear-sighted enough to see possible objections, though she went no further than recommending that governesses should be paid well enough to ensure their dignity and ultimate independence. She suggested a salary of £300 a year, but nobody took her advice.[21] Another woman writer, the north London Quaker Priscilla Wakefield, did plead for a greatly enlarged range of employments for women and made the truly revolutionary suggestion that there should be equal pay for male and female servants performing equal labours. Her *Reflections on the Present Condition of the Female Sex, with Suggestions for its Improvements* (published by Johnson in 1798) was careful not to offend in any way against delicacy or rigid notions of the class structure: thus she called for female undertakers in order to preserve the modesty of female corpses, and women teachers in all subjects so that schoolgirls should not have to meet men at all, and she wished to protect girls of the lower classes from novels and indeed all beautiful works of art in case they should lead them to expect too much of life. But in her own way Mrs Wakefield was at least drawing attention again to the practical problems discussed by the Marys and casting about for a solution, even if there was no question of referring to their ideas or example.

Another well-known novelist, Jane West, took up overtly didactic writing at the turn of the century, possibly under the influence of her friend Bishop Percy, the old man who was so fascinated by the gossip about Mary Wollstonecraft at the time of Robert King's trial. It may have been he who caused her to harp so insistently on Mary's vicious example:

> Among the writers whose extravagant doctrines have not only been published in this country, but circulated with uncommon avidity, loaded with extravagant praise, transfused into a thousand shapes, and insinuated into every recess, the name of Mary Wollstonecraft has obtained a *lamentable* distinction.

This and several other similar references occurred in her *Letters to a Young Man* (published in 1801: it went into six editions before 1810). A few years later she produced *Letters to a Young Lady*: men were always men, but females were either ladies or women, and Jane West had nothing to say to the second category. By now she felt even more strongly about the influence of Mary and her fellow-radicals – the doctrine of human perfectibility was dangerous, moral revolution was the precursor of political revolution, and God had designed ladies especially to be 'conservators of morals'.* Their work as conservators had to be carried on, however, entirely in the domestic sphere, and while it was acceptable enough that they should write as amateurs, they were guilty of a serious sin if they attempted to rival men and make a profession of literature: 'Literature is with us an ornament, or an amusement, not a duty or profession; and when it is pursued with such avidity as to withdraw us from the especial purposes of our creation, it becomes a crime.' The especial purposes of creation were domesticity, marriage and motherhood. Ladies must practise absolute obedience to their husbands, give up even their female

* Thomas Spence, a humble radical bookseller who wrote a pamphlet advocating easy divorce in 1801, also expressed clearly how people associated any idea of a change in the status of women with political revolution: 'The subject is so feelingly understood in this country, that it is supposed the Chains of Hymen would be among the first that would be broken ... in case of a Revoution.' (Quoted by Edward Thompson in *The Making of the Engish Working Class*.)

friends if so required, cultivate the passive virtues, 'humble resignation and cheerful content', because 'the lords of creation' liked to find smiling faces awaiting them at home. It is tempting to discover some irony in Mrs West's phrases here, but she was speaking as unequivocally as the *sans-culotte* husbands of 1793.

A true lady would avoid marrying a man with Whig principles, according to Mrs West, since they made notoriously bad husbands. She might show disapprobation of her husband's conduct on occasion, though she should do so quietly, but she should not expect much or feel too keenly. 'If we wish our girls to be happy – we must try to make them docile, contented, prudent, and domestic' – and, of course, chaste.

Her views on what constituted the perfect lady were backed by extreme disapproval of the lying, rapacious and envious poor who, apart from their notorious sexual immorality ('Bastardy is scarcely reckoned a disgrace, and criminality before marriage is too common even to excite surprise'), had been stirred up by Tom Paine and his crew to expect all the luxuries of life, which God had very properly denied them. It would be pleasant to believe her attitudes represented an extreme rather than a norm, but the fact is she was a popular and admired writer: Jane Austen's 'good Mrs West'.[22]

The most poignant and curious of the responses to Mary's views came from an unexpected voice: that of Fanny Burney, herself reared in the rationalism of the eighteenth century, but always somewhat subject to creeping attacks of perfect ladyship. Her last novel, *The Wanderer, or Female Difficulties*, appeared in 1813, though it had been planned and begun in the Nineties.[23] Its principal theme was a conflict between the ladylike Juliet and Elinor, the anti-heroine, enthusiast for the Revolution and the rights of men and women alike. The book was not a success then and is undoubtedly too long and frequently absurd: Juliet is pushed about from difficulty to difficulty through no less than five volumes without for one instant losing the delicacy which makes a move in almost any direction other than flight an infringement of the moral ideals she sets herself. But although Fanny Burney clearly felt obliged to endorse Juliet officially, she could not help giving the better speeches to the opposition. When, for instance, Juliet refused point-blank to support herself by becoming an actress, Elinor points out:

> You only fear to alarm, or offend the men – who would keep us from every office, but making puddings and pies for their own precious palates! Oh woman! poor, subdued woman! thou art as dependent, mentally, upon the arbitrary customs of man, as man is, corporally, upon the established laws of his country!

Elinor actually proposes marriage to the man she loves, in conformity with her principles, though she cannot help blushing as she does so. He rejects her and her ideas, but she continues to pursue him throughout the book, and makes repeated suicide attempts in order to capture his attention. Her behaviour is made ludicrous and unbelievable, but her words remain sensible:

> Why, for so many centuries, has man, alone, been supposed to possess, not only force and power for action and defence, but even all the rights of taste; all the fine sensibilities which impel our happiest sympathies, in the choice of our life's partners? Why ... is woman to be excluded from the exertions of courage ... to be denied deliberating upon the safety of the state to which she is a member, and the utility of the laws by which she must be governed: – must even her heart be circumscribed by boundaries as narrow as her sphere of action in life? Must she be taught to subdue all its native emotions? To hide them as sin, and to deny them as shame? Must her affections be bestowed but as the recompence of flattery received; not of merit discriminated? Must everything that she does be prescribed by rule?

Again,

> This Woman, whom they estimate thus below, they elevate above themselves. They require from her, in defiance of their examples! – in defiance of their lures! – angelical perfection. She must be mistress of her passions; she must never listen to her inclinations; she must not take a step of which the purport is not visible; she must not pursue a measure of which she cannot publish the motive; she must always be guided by reason, though they deny her understanding!

And here, for the last time, Elinor addresses the man who prefers to marry Juliet on the subject

> which you have long since, in common with every man that breathes, wished exploded, the Rights of Woman; Rights, however, which all your sex, with all its arbitrary assumption of superiority, can never disprove, for they are the Rights of human nature; to which the two sexes equally and inalienably belong . . . But I must leave to abler casuists, and the slow, all-arranging ascendance of truth, to raise our oppressed half of the human species, to the equality and dignity for which equal nature, that gives us Birth and Death alike, designs us.

In giving her formal blessing to the perfect lady, Fanny Burney made no real attempt to answer her own imperfect but articulate Elinor; she remains as a curious tribute to the feminism her creator was determined to disapprove of.

One more female critic must be considered: Mary's mother-in-law, Mrs Godwin, whose remarks were kinder than most of her educated contemporaries:

> My dear Wm – I'm a poor letter writer at best, but now worse than ever. After thinking of yo. for yr. genteel present of the *Memoirs* of yr. wife. Excuse me saying Providence certainly knows best, the fountain of wisdom cannot err. He that gave life can take it away, and none can hinder, and tho we see not his reasons now, we shall see them hereafter. I hope yo. are taught by reflection your mistake concerning marriage, there

might have been two children that had no lawful wright to anything yt. was their fathers, with a thousand other bad consequences, children and wives crying about ye streets without a protector. You wish, I dare say, to keep yr. own oppinion, therefore I shall say no more but wish you and dear babes happy. Dose little Mary thrive? or she weaned?[24]

'Children and wives crying about ye streets without a protector': this was the essential objection for Mrs Godwin and many other women too no doubt. The flaw in Mary's attitude to natural sexuality (as well as Godwin's theories of marriage) was the lack of effective birth-control, and as long as women could not protect themselves against conception, the 'naturalness' admired by Mary was too loaded with danger. Her emphasis on sexual freedom seemed likely, to most of the women of her day and for several generations afterwards, to produce the very conditions in which women were most helpless, most disadvantaged, least free.* She might make a prostitute into a heroine in *Maria*, and have herself fished out of the Thames by watermen and revived in a public house, but how could anyone want to follow her example and take her risks? And the idea that one false step was irretrievable was after all based on the fact that seduction, like marriage, led almost inevitably to the birth of a child. Mrs Opie made Adeline Mowbray's mother prepare to forgive her but give up the idea again when she found she was pregnant, causing a friend to ask

* Steven Marcus's discussion, in *The Other Victorians* (1966), of the way in which nineteenth-century prudery, by encouraging girls to discipline and self-restraint and making their sexuality inaccessible even to themselves, produced rigid and thwarted women, but also allowed them to extend their humanity in other ways, seems relevant here. There remains the question as to why more women did not welcome the early birth-control campaigns, and the answer to this looks like deliberate, persistent and villainous suppression by the established male preserves of Church and State. See Peter Fryer, *The Birth Controllers* (1965) and N. Himes, *Medical History of Contraception* (1936).

naively, 'Is it a greater crime to be in the family way, than to live with a man as his mistress?' Society agreed with Adeline's mother. Mary King's baby had to be got rid of before she could be embarked on a new life, and Fanny Imlay's realization of her true parentage probably determined her (at least in part) to kill herself. 'One whose birth was unfortunate' she called herself in her last note, from which she tore the signature. Given the prevailing ideas of the time, she was right.

Instead of the perfectible woman, the perfect lady: instead of inaugurating an age of natural rights restored and equal partnership with enlightened men, Mary died just in time to avoid the ludicrous sight of her sex being hoisted on to a new and supremely uncomfortable pedestal (those members of her sex, that is, whose menfolk could afford so to elevate them). Ladies, though intellectually inferior, were henceforth to be morally superior, so that for them it was a privilege to make sacrifices, to submit to authority with good grace, and to deny themselves what they really wanted, if indeed they ever arrived at the point of knowing what there might be to want. A piece of chivalric nonsense was revived to do duty as a literal truth. Even the term 'better half', which had once applied to a spouse of either sex, was now applied exclusively to the wife, with the natural result that it soon acquired the jocular and contemptuous connotation it still bears.

By the time Lecky came to publish his *History of Morals* in 1869, he was able to advance as an evident and generally accepted truth that:

> Morally, the general superiority of women over men, is I think, unquestionable ... There are two great departments of virtue: the impulsive, or that which springs spontaneously from the emotions; and the deliberative, or that which is performed in obedience to the sense of duty; and in both of these I imagine women are superior to men.[25]

In the same year, John Stuart Mill published a dissenting view:

> As for moral differences, considered as distinguished from intellectual, the distinction commonly drawn is to the advantage of women. They are declared to be better than men; an empty compliment, which must provoke a bitter smile from every woman of spirit, since there is no other situation in life in which it is the established order, that the better should obey the worse.[26]

And where Lecky pointed to the smaller number of crimes committed by women, Mill answered:

> I doubt not that the same thing may be said, with the same truth, of negro slaves ... I do not know a more signal instance of the blindness with which the world, including the herd of studious men, ignore and pass over all the influence of social circumstances, than their silly depreciation of the intellectual, and silly panegyrics on the moral nature of women.

But Mill was speaking for the very few; Lecky's opinion was undoubtedly the standard one in England.* English fiction writers of the mid-nineteenth century made their own commentary on the situation. Thackeray polarized the female sex into the virtuous and stupid on the one hand, and the intelligent, ambitious and sexually developed on the other.

* Though not in France. In 1843 Mill had corresponded with Auguste Comte at length on the subject of feminism; Comte had assured him that the championing of women was a passing phase he himself had been through twenty years before, and that Mill would soon see its fallaciousness, since women were clearly inferior to men: biologically, intellectually and morally they were closer to children. Comte even confessed that 'je me rappelle très bien, quant à moi, le temps où l'étrange ouvrage de miss Mary Wollstonecraft (avant qu'elle eût épousé Godwin) me produisait une forte impression'; but Mill refused to be drawn on the subject of Miss Wollstonecraft, here or anywhere else. No doubt he approved her views but was disturbed by her behaviour. There is a pleasant passage in this correspondence when Mill teases Comte gently about the supposed 'femininity' of the French character in general, a point that Mary had made more than once.

Becky in *Vanity Fair* is driven to use her sexuality for advancement because brain alone does not give her the chance; a belief in women's rights is presented only as one of the quaint follies of the villainous Miss Crawley. Writing in 1847 about 1815, he made the point lightly, a stock joke that needed no further consideration.

The women novelists, when they approached such questions at all, either drew back in dismay at the reception they received, as Mrs Gaskell did with *Ruth*, a plea for kindness to unmarried mothers that met with a very harsh response in 1853; or muffled their anger in Christian resignation: Charlotte Brontë's *Shirley* (1849) contained some stirring but finally crushed feminism. George Eliot, deeply nervous of feminism, was unable to present a heroine who was not defeated, diverted from her ambitions and obliged to settle for much less than she had hoped and striven for, both sexually and intellectually. Maggie had to be drowned; Romola played husband to her own dead and faithless husband's childlike mistress and cared for her children. Dorothea's 'full nature ... spent itself in the channels which had no great name on earth'.[27] And it is impossible to believe that Gwendolen Harleth would have done better had she, instead of marrying Grandcourt, become the governess of Mrs Momperts's daughters. There was no satisfactory way out of the trap for women in the mind of Marian Evans.

Dickens, with the most far-ranging and finely tuned imagination of all the novelists of his time, devoted one of his best books, *David Copperfield* (1850), to exploring alternative ways of being for women: Rosa Dartle savagely refused to be treated as a doll by Steerforth, whereas little Em'ly, Dora, Annie Strong and David's mother knew no other possibility than that of dolls, child-wives, child-mistresses; and Betsy Trotwood embodied the deliberate masculinization of a woman who finds no scope for her talents and energy in the ordinary social pattern. The attempt to create something more satisfactory in Agnes foundered: Dickens saw the situation with perfect clarity, but he could not provide a solution in the shape of a convincingly mature and attractive woman.*

In effect, women with Mary's breadth and experience and outspokenness were lacking in England throughout the hundred years that followed her death. She had presented an ideal, but it had been turned almost at once into a bogey, flanked by the spectres of revolution, irreligion and sexual anarchy. The women who began to fight over particular feminist issues – their legal position, questions of employment and education, birth control, the vote – did not often invoke her name. When at the very end of the century some began to take an open interest in her and write about her, they tended to adopt defensive tones and gloss over the aspects of her life and personality that might bring discredit or ridicule on their causes: the episode with Eliza was transformed into a heroic piece of rescue work, the Fuseli affair denied, the relationship with Godwin romanticized. Her awkwardness has persisted, and she has shrugged off calumny and whitewash and resisted some strenuous efforts at feminist canonization. She was often bitter in her lifetime, but she might have laughed if she had been able to foresee the vagaries of her reputation after death.

* This aspect of *David Copperfield* is discussed by Q. D. Leavis in a remarkable interpretative essay in *Dickens the Novelist* (1970).

Epilogue

Except in her younger daughter, Mary's talent did not appear again in the family, and none of the Wollstonecrafts flourished. Her father died in 1803 in Laugharne. He had not altered the will he made in 1791 in which he asked her to settle his debts for him, and he left nothing but a horse and a few cows. The only one of his children who tried to claim anything was James; he had been rudely rejected by his adopted country in the autumn of 1798 and imprisoned in the Temple, from which Mary had seen Louis driven to his trial six years before. Appeals to Talleyrand and John Hurford Stone were of no avail: 'ainsi me voilà renvoyé dans mon pays, que mes opinions m'ont fait quitter, et rejeté d'une patrie devenue la mienne par adoption,' he complained.[1] He returned reluctantly to England, managed to rejoin the Navy in spite of his opinions, and died at sea three years after his father.

In 1809 Joseph Johnson died: Fuseli wept bitterly at the news.[2] Johnson directed that a bond for two hundred pounds in his possession should be returned to William Godwin 'to be applied by him to the use of Fanny Imlay who is minor in his care'.[3] Probably Fanny saw little enough of the money. When she was twenty-two she killed herself, swallowing laudanum in a Swansea inn she had travelled to alone, after Everina and Eliza had refused to take her to live with them and her existence in the Godwin household had become intolerable to her. It was a more efficient and whole-hearted enactment of her mother's suicide attempts.

Fanny's younger half-sister Mary had some of her parents' brilliance, and some of their gift for scandal and tragedy. Her marriage to Shelley left her with one small son, Percy, to whom she determined to give as conventional an education as possible. When it was urged that he should be taught to think for himself, she exclaimed, 'Oh God, teach him to think like other people,' and sent him to Harrow and Trinity College, Cambridge.

Everina and Eliza ran a school together in Dublin, quarrelling and complaining a good deal, until Eliza's death in the 1830s. Everina then returned to London and took lodgings in Pentonville. Mary Shelley felt obliged to be kind although she disliked her; once she even took her to visit Godwin. Joseph Johnson's protégé Rowland Hunter was also attentive, lending her books and talking over his memories with her. She continued to lament Mary's residence in Paris and her subsequent union with Godwin; she never mentioned Fanny in her letters, but commented that young Percy Shelley at least seemed to be free from 'immoral failings'. In 1841 she announced that she was writing a book, but by this time her handwriting had grown enormous, suggesting failing eyesight, and she was not clear in her mind either. She died in 1843.

Ned's two children, Elizabeth and Edward, who had suffered so badly from the notoriety of their aunt Mary, both grew up into strait-laced conservatives. After the early deaths of their parents Edward went out to Lisbon and then to South America on business, sending his sister querulous letters and the present of a parrot to cheer her up. He then decided to go into partnership with another young Englishman, Alexander Berry, whom he had met in Lisbon, and the two of them agreed to settle in New South Wales and run a timber and tobacco business, using convict labour. Presently they sent for Elizabeth to join them; she married Berry in 1827, when she was forty-six. According to Berry's testimony she regarded herself as his 'monitor and conscience'. Edward died unmarried in 1832, of a painful illness which made his temper deteriorate until it became intolerable during the last years. After his death Elizabeth made some effort to keep in touch with her surviving relations; she corresponded with Everina, who sent her mementoes of the once-dreaded Aunt Mary – a copy of the Opie portrait, a lock of hair, some inoffensive examples of her work: *Mary* and the *Letters from Sweden*. And when Elizabeth died in turn, Berry himself embarked on a correspondence with Mary Shelley. She always answered him kindly enough, but must have been amused at his fiercely reactionary tone; in 1848 he told her that the French were a hopeless lot, 'now reaping the matured and bitter fruits of their first Revolution'. He continued to write to her daughter-in-law after her death in 1851, and was still lamenting the decline of the English into a nation of shopkeepers as late as 1871.[4]

Mary's favourite brother Charles, who had settled in America during her lifetime, helped Hamilton Rowan to run a bleaching works in Philadelphia for a while, then joined the Army and rose to the rank of major. He went south to New Orleans and married Sally Garrison, the daughter of a judge; they had a daughter, Jane Nelson, in 1806. Three years later Charles detected his wife in adultery and, after some violent displays of rage, sent her home to her father without her child. He divorced her in 1811 and married a second wife, Nancy, with whom he lived till his death from yellow fever in 1817. Nancy had the care of Sally's child, but Sally kidnapped her daughter back and there was a threatened lawsuit which came to the ears of Edward Wollstonecraft in London; he sent for an account of the affair and kept it amongst his papers.

Nancy managed to keep Jane Nelson and later took her to Cuba, where the trail disappears. Perhaps Jane Nelson Wollstonecraft's descendants are even now making their contribution to Castro's revolutionary society.

Godwin's life story is well known; debts, disciples, a second marriage to a woman his friends detested and who brought him troublesome step-children; more debts, more troubles, hack work, still more debts. Finally he took a government pension; he died in 1836 and was buried beside Mary. In due course the second Mrs Godwin joined them also, but before long their bodies were all dug up in order to make way for the railway line coming in to King's Cross. They now lie in Bournemouth, where Sir Percy Shelley decided to install them beside his parents. Only the stone which Godwin set up still stands in old St Pancras churchyard, flanked by railway lines, gasometers, a hospital for tropical diseases, a children's playground and a municipal convenience. Few if any flowers are laid upon it, but it is worth a visit on a sunny day.

Percy Shelley died childless in 1888, having done his best to protect his grandmother's reputation by buying and destroying her letters to Fuseli. His education had achieved the desired effect and he lived a blameless life, his chief pursuits yachting and amateur theatricals.

A Sydney suburb is named after Edward Wollstonecraft; a block of council flats in Somers Town is called Godwin Court; not a house Mary lived in in London is still standing, and not a street or college is named after her.[5] 'The English Mignon' Carlyle called her, echoing Godwin's sentimentality, even though he condemned the *Memoirs* for contriving to imprison 'Ariel in a brickbat'. But there is after all something more solid to Mary than an Ariel. She was tough – the role of governess came naturally to her; her ideas were enduring and, in practical terms, more successful than Carlyle dreamed. If she was not the perfect heroine, she was at least, like Fanny Burney's Elinor, an anti-heroine to be reckoned with. She got herself an education as best she could, she wooed her own men, and was sometimes selfish and insensitive, sometimes comical. She endured ridicule and beat it down by sheer force of personality; she faced extreme unhappiness with the outrage of one determined to impose her will on fate; and, while the world busied itself with great concerns, she spoke up, quite loudly, for what had been until then a largely silent section of the human race.

Notes

Chapter 1

1 Information about Spitalfields from Malcolm's *Londinium Redivivum* (1802–7), Sabin's *Silk Weavers of Spitfield,* Charles Knight's *London* (1842) and Dorothy George's *London Life in the Eighteenth Century* (1925).

2 Parish rate books for 1712, Guildhall Library.

3 Parish registers of St Botolph's Without Bishopsgate, Guildhall Library. See also family tree (Appendix II).

4 However his name is not amongst those weavers who declared their loyalty to George II in 1745 in a printed address.

5 LCC survey of Wood-Michell Estate; the building lease for No. 21 Brown's Lane was granted to 'Edward Wollstonecraft of Primrose Street, Bishopsgate, Gentleman'.

6 Parish register.

7 Godwin's *Memoirs of the Author of a Vindication of the Rights of Woman,* 1st ed. (1798), p. 5.

8 Vaudeville to *Le Mariage de Figaro* by Beaumarchais, published in 1785 but written earlier.

9 Parish register.

10 Godwin's *Memoirs,* p. 60.

11 Parish register.

12 The will is in the Public Record Office.

13 *Maria,* her posthumous novel, vol. 1 in *Posthumous Works* (1798), p. 172.

14 *Ballyshannon* by Hugh Allingham (1879) gives information about the Dixons being in the wine trade, and sometimes spelling their name Dickson.

15 Everina referred to Dixon cousins in the army and navy in her letters now in the Mitchell Library, Sydney, New South Wales. Edward Sterling Dickson rose to be a rear-admiral; his name is in the navy lists.

16 Information from *The Gascoyne Heiress* by Carola Oman (1968), p. 27.

17 *Mary*, her first novel, p. 11.
18 *Mary*, p. 10.
19 Information about Beverley from T. Allen's *Yorkshire* (1831), Chs. VI–IX; also from N. Higson, county archivist, who found evidence of the Wollstonecraft leasing of the house in Wednesday Market.
20 All the quotations from letters addressed to Jane Arden are taken from *Shelley and his Circle*, ed. Cameron, vol. II, pp. 933–84.
21 Information about the Ardens from Everilda Anne Gardiner's *Recollections of a Beloved Mother* (1842), p. 2.
22 See for example James Burgh's views on education of girls in his *Thoughts on Education* (1747), pp. 51–6.
23 *Mary*, p. 14.

Chapter 2

1 All the quotations from letters to Jane Arden are taken from *Shelley and his Circle*, ed. Cameron, vol. II, pp. 933–84.
2 *Maria*, p. 152, vol. I.
3 Godwin's *Memoirs*, p. 20.
4 *Mary*, p. 21.
5 ibid., p. 21.
6 Letter to Jane Arden, Cameron, p. 966, vol. II.
7 In *The Wanderer, or Female Difficulties.*
8 Letter to Jane Arden, Cameron, p. 978, vol. II.
9 ibid., pp. 976–7.
10 ibid., p. 966.
11 ibid., p. 983.
12 Abinger MS., my transcript.

Chapter 3

1 Parish register for St Andrew's, Enfield, gives Elizabeth Wolstingcroft, buried on 19 April 1782. Godwin was wrong in his dating of Mrs Wollstonecraft's death.
2 According to the parish register for St Katharine by the Tower, Edward (Ned) and his wife Elizabeth had a daughter Elizabeth born in 1782 and a son Edward born in 1783.
3 *Mary*, pp. 39–40.

4 His wife is named in his will, which is in the Public Record Office.
5 *Maria*, p. 173, vol. I.
6 Abinger MS., my transcript.
7 *Mary*, p. 44.
8 Abinger MS., my transcript.
9 Abinger MS., my transcript.
10 His profession is given in the parish records of Bermondsey in GLC archives.
11 Parish register of St Katharine by the Tower, Guildhall.
12 Letter given in *Shelley and his Circle*, p. 983, vol. II.
13 St Mary Magdalene, Bermondsey, parish register in GLC archives.
14 All Mary's letters to Everina are from the Abinger MS. They were evidently preserved by Sir Percy and Lady Shelley because they felt they were to Mary's credit; those that were not they had destroyed. I have used my transcripts.
15 Parish register for St Mary Magdalene, Bermondsey.

Chapter 4

1 This is what the Dean of Gloucester, Josiah Tucker, accused 'the younger Dissenters, both clergy and laity' of in his pamphlet *A Series of Answers to Popular Objections &c*, in 1776, p. 69, footnote.
2 Information about Richard Price from R. Laboucheix's *Richard Price* (1970), Peter Brown's *The Chathamites* (1967), J. T. Rutt's *Life and Correspondence of Joseph Priestley* (1831).
3 First published in 1754, it went into several editions including one published by Joseph Johnson in 1767.
4 Ann Jebb, 1753–1812, wrote under the name 'Priscilla' in the *London Chronicle* in the years 1772–4, corresponded with the reformer Cartwright in the Eighties and was still an ardent democratic pamphleteer in the Nineties.
5 Abinger MS., my transcript.
6 ibid., my transcript.
7 There has been much speculation about the identity of 'Neptune'. I have now established that Neptune was a family name over several generations of the Blood family

and that there was one contemporary with Mary. I owe this information to Mr Brian Inglis, whose mother was a Blood.

8 Abinger MS., my transcript.

9 ibid., my transcript.

10 ibid., my transcript.

11 Burgh was responsible for *Thoughts on Education* (1747) and *Direction for the Use of the Youth at a Boarding School* (1749) as well as his *Dignity of Human Nature*, which was substantially devoted to education.

12 e.g., Priscilla Wakefield, a Quaker lady from Tottenham, who published her *Reflections on the Present Condition of the Female Sex* with Joseph Johnson in 1798 and was an early advocate of equal pay as well as enlarging employment opportunities for women. Maria Edgeworth, also in 1798, suggested that governesses should be paid £300 a year in order that they might save and retire in dignified independence. Mary Anne Radcliffe, in 1799, in her *Female Advocate, or an Attempt to Recover the Rights of Women from Male Usurpation*, claimed that female employment was on the decline. By 1804 a Ladies' Committee had been set up to consider this particular problem – nearly twenty years after Mary's book.

13 Abinger MS., my transcript.

14 ibid., my transcript.

15 ibid., my transcript.

16 See *Vindication of the Rights of Woman*, final pages.

17 It was Joseph Priestley's, on leaving the employ of his aristocratic patron Lord Shelburne, a job arranged for him by his friend Richard Price: see J. T. Rutt, op. cit., p. 205, vol. I.

18 Information from *Shelley and his Circle*, ed. Cameron, pp. 843–4, vol. IV.

Chapter 5

1 See *Portrait of a Whig Peer*, Brian Connell (1957), p. 128.

2 From *Shelley and his Circle*, ed. Cameron, p. 982, vol. II.

3 The details about the King family come largely from Captain Douglas King-Harman's *The Kings* (1959), which is based on unpublished family papers in his possession.

4 Printed by E. McAleer in *The Sensitive Plant* (1958), pp. 4–8. Lady Mountcashel wrote this document for her two illegitimate daughters by George Tighe, in 1818.
5 Arthur Young's *Autobiography*, ed. Edwards (1898), pp. 76–80.
6 This and all further quotes from Mary's letters in this chapter from Abinger MS., my transcript.
7 As 4.
8 Bishop Percy told his wife that this was the gossip in Dublin in 1798, when the Kings were much in the news; see British Museum additional MS. 32.335 f. 15–17. I am indebted to Thomas Pakenham for this reference, which is discussed further below on p. 295.
9 Godwin's *Memoirs*, p. 58.
10 *Mary*, p. 110.
11 ibid., p. 145.
12 Letter given in *Shelley and his Circle*, p. 860, vol. IV.
13 Mary refers to this in letters to George Blood, Abinger MS., my transcript.
14 See 4.
15 Bishop Percy again.

Chapter 6

1 Howells, *State Trials*, vol. XXIV (1818), p. 511.
2 William Cowper's *Letters*, ed. Frazer (1912), vol. II, p. 294, letter CCLXXXIV.
3 *Unpublished and Uncollected Letters of William Cowper*, ed. T. Wright (1925), p. 55.
4 *Gentleman's Magazine* for 1809.
5 The printed order form can be seen in Dr Williams's Library, used on its reverse side for a letter by Theophilus Lindsey.
6 Abinger MS., my transcript.
7 Letter by Thomas Campbell cited by M. MacGregor in her *Amelia Opie* (1932), p. 36.
8 She is referred to in a letter in Dr Williams's Library, dated 1782, MS. copy by Rutt.
9 Quoted in Eudo Mason's *The Mind of Henry Fuseli* (1951), p. 130.

10 See below, p. 115
11 Philip Magnus, *Edmund Burke* (1939), p. 150.
12 Peter Gay, *The Enlightenment* (1966), p. 431–2, vol. II.
13 See Johnson's will in Public Record Office.
14 Letter printed in *Posthumous Works* (1798), p. 83, vol. IV.
15 ibid., p. 80, vol. IV.
16 Abinger MS., my transcript.
17 See J. E. Stock's *Life of Beddoes* (1811) for account of his political and feminist views, pp. 68, 144; Mrs H. Sandford's *Thomas Poole & His Friends* (1888) for Beddoes's medical lectures to women; also his own introductory lecture to an anatomy course, published by Johnson in 1797.
18 Information from Nicolas Barker.
19 *Letters* of Anna Seward (1811), p. 3, letter I, vol. IV.
20 Abinger MS., my transcript.
21 See R. Laboucheix, *Richard Price* (1970), pp. 201–2, footnote 101.
22 *The Sexagenarian* (1817), pp. 314–15, vol. I. Beloe is not always reliable, but there is no need to doubt this particular piece of information.
23 See Rutt's *Life and Correspondence* of Priestley (1831), p. 280, vol. I.
24 Godwin mentions Anderson as a particular friend of Mary's at this time; information from DNB. He died young and suddenly, and in the year he died it proved impossible to produce any figures for the India Office, so indispensable had he become.
25 Information about Christie from DNB; obituary in *Gentleman's Magazine*; Rutt's *Life of Priestley*; MS. letters in Dr Williams's Library; Meikle, *The French Revolution in Scotland*; Public Record Office; etc.
26 *Letters* of Anna Seward, p. 311, letter 67, vol. I.
27 *Letters Written during a Short Residence in Denmark, Norway & Sweden*, 2nd ed., 1802, pp. 26, 27, 28.
28 See Dowden's *Life of Shelley* (1866), pp. 23–4, vol. II.
29 Berry papers, Mitchell Library, Sydney, Australia.

Chapter 7

1 So she told Johnson, who told Godwin, *Memoirs*, p. 63.

2 Information on Fuseli, who was born Johann Heinrich Fuessli, from Knowles, *Life and Writings of Henry Fuseli* (1831); Allan Cunningham, *Lives of the Painters* (1829); Eudo Mason, *The Mind of Henry Fuseli* (1951); Ruthven Todd, *Tracks in the Snow* (1947); J. T. Smith, *Nollekens and his Times* (1829), as well as various catalogues, BM print room, etc.
3 Professor Gert Schiff, who is preparing a complete catalogue of Fuseli's work, states categorically that there is no drawing of Mary.
4 Quoted by Eudo Mason and translated by him, op. cit., p. 97.
5 ibid., p. 152.
6 ibid., p. 155.
7 Godwin's *Memoirs*, p. 92.
8 Knowles, op. cit., p. 380, vol. I.
9 Abinger MS., my transcript.

Chapter 8

1 Mary Anne Schimmelpenninck, *Life* (1858), p. 216, vol. I.
2 *Letters* of Anna Seward (1811), p. 28, letter 8, vol. II.
3 *Correspondence of Josiah Wedgwood*, 1781–94 (1906), pp. 94–6,
4 See *Life & Correspondence of Joseph Priestley*, ed. J. T. Rutt (1831), p. 50, vol. II.
5 Quoted by R. Laboucheix in *Richard Price* (1970), p. 203.
6 Rutt, op. cit., pp. 80–81, vol. II.
7 ibid., p. 88, footnote, vol. II.
8 *A Vindication of the Rights of Men*, p. 24.
9 Godwin's *Memoirs*, p. 77.
10 Rutt, op. cit., p. 106, vol. II.
11 Quoted in *William Roscoe of Liverpool* by George Chandler (1953), pp. 389–90.
12 Information from *The Chathamites* by Peter Brown (1967).
13 Rutt, op. cit., pp. 170–71, vol. II.
14 *Diaries of Samuel Rogers*, ed. Clayden (1888), pp. 126–7, 140.
15 Thomas Christie, *Letters on the French Revolution* (1791), p. 121. Christie quotes Mary's answer to Burke, calling her an 'animated writer'.

16 Information on Barlow from Victor Clyde Miller's *Joel Barlow, Revolutionist, London 1791–2* (Hamburg, 1932).
17 Schimmelpenninck, op. cit., pp. 217–18, vol. 1.

Chapter 9

1 The number of her house in Store Street is unknown; one eighteenth-century house still stands in the street.
2 See *Complete Works* of Caritat, Marquis de Condorcet, edited in twelve volumes by O'Connor and Arago (1847). Information about Condorcet from *Condorcet et la Révolution française* by L. Cahen (1904), and Robinet's *Condorcet* (1893) – in which the historian takes it on himself to refute Condorcet's feminist arguments.
3 My translation.
4 Roscoe letters, Liverpool City Libraries, my transcript.

Chapter 10

1 *The Letters of Horace Walpole* (1905), p. 337, letter 2956, vol. xv.

At Covent Garden, the Prologue to Mrs Inchbald's new comedy, *Everyone Has His Fault*, referred to the book of the moment:

Our Author, who accuses great and small,
And says so boldly, there are faults in all;
Sends me with dismal voice, and lenthen'd phiz,
Humbly to own one dreadful fault of *his*:
A fault, in modern Authors not uncommon,
It is, – now don't be angry – He's – *a woman*.

. . .

The Rights of Women, says a female pen,
Are, to do everything as well as Men.
To think, to argue, to decide, to write,
To talk, undoubtedly – perhaps, to fight.
(For Females march to war, like brave Commanders,
Not in old Authors only – but in Flanders.)

I grant this matter may be strain'd too far,
And Maid 'gainst Man is most uncivil war:
I grant, as all my City friends will say,
That Men should rule, and Women should obey:
That nothing binds the marriage contract faster,
Than our – 'Zounds, Madam, I'm your Lord and Master.'
I grant their nature, and their frailty such,
Women may make too free – and know too much.
But since the Sex at length has been inclin'd
To cultivate that useful part – the mind; –
Since they have learnt to read, to write, to spell; –
Since some of them have wit, – and use it well; –
Let us not force them back with brow severe,
Within the pale of ignorance and fear,
Confin'd entirely to domestic arts,
Producing only children, pies, and tarts.

The fav'rite fable of the tuneful Nine,
Implies that female genius *is divine*.
Then, drive not, Critics, with tyrannic rage,
A supplicating Fair-one from the Stage;
The Comic Muse perhaps is growing old,
Her lovers, you well know, are few and cold.
'Tis time then freely to enlarge the plan,
And let all those write Comedies – that can.

2 Roscoe letters, Liverpool City Libraries, my transcript.
3 Brian Connell, *Portrait of a Whig Peer* (1957), p. 259.
4 *Love Letters of Mary Hays*, ed. A. Wedd (1925), p. 5.
5 See J. E. Stock's *Life of Thomas Beddoes* (1811), p. 68. Beddoes was obliged to leave Oxford in the summer of 1792 because of his political opinions; he remained a feminist. I have not been able to find a copy of his *Letters to a Lady*.
6 *Letters* of Anna Seward, p. 117, letter xxxv, vol. III.
7 Note in Abinger MS., my transcript.
8 Knowles, op. cit., p. 170, vol. I.
9 Mary referred to the first Mrs Opie's behaviour in a letter, Abinger MS.; she eloped with an army officer soon afterwards.
10 Abinger MS., my transcript.
11 ibid., my transcript.

12 The evidence for this love affair and the birth of the child in London in the summer of 1792 is found in A. Douarche, *Les Tribunaux civils de Paris* (1905–7), vol. I, pp. 637–8.
13 Printed by Victor Clyde Miller, op. cit., appendix.
14 Information on Talleyrand from Duff Cooper's *Talleyrand* (1932), p. 53, Cape paperback.
15 *The Early Life of Samuel Rogers*, diaries edited by Clayden (1888), pp. 244–5.
16 Information on Madame de Genlis from her *Memoirs* and other contemporary sources.
17 *Speeches of Edmund Burke*, edited by J. Burke (1853), pp. 414–24.
18 This description is taken from Amelia Opie's *Adeline Mowbray*, p. 47, vol. I, a novel devoted to attacking her erstwhile friends' ideas. See above, p. 293.
19 The phrase is in the Roscoe MS. letters, my transcript.
20 Rutt, op. cit., pp. 183–4, vol. II.
21 Roscoe letters, my transcript.
22 According to Halévy, *La Formation du radicalisme philosophique* (1901), p. 35, vol. II.

Chapter 11

1 Roscoe MS., Liverpool Public Libraries, my transcript.
2 *Thraliana*, Mrs Piozzi's diary, ed. K. C. Balderstone (1942), p. 797, vol. II.
3 Brian Connell, *Portrait of a Whig Peer*, p. 262.
4 Abinger MS., quoted by Kegan Paul, vol. I, p. 208.
5 *Posthumous Works*, pp. 94–5, vol. IV.
6 According to family tradition, reported in Robinet, *Danton émigré* (1887), p. 29.
7 Howells, *State Trials*, vol. XXIV, p. 536.
8 H. W. Meikle, *The French Revolution in Scotland* (1912), p. 98.
9 ibid.
10 *Diaries and Letters of Madame D'Arblay* (1842–6).
11 Mrs Piozzi's comment. Information about Helen Williams from L. D. Woodward's *Hélène Maria Williams et ses amis* (1929).
12 Abinger MS., my transcript.

13 *Souvenirs de la Révolution française* by Helen Maria Williams, Paris (1827), p. 19.
14 *Letters* of Georg Forster, p. 436, letter 410, vol. II, translated here by Martina Mayne.
15 Clark Durant gives these lines in his Supplement to Godwin's *Memoirs*, p. 248.
16 See Ph. Sagnac, *La Législation civile de la Révolution française* (1898), pp. 279–93.
17 Crabb Robinson diaries, ed. E. Morley (1938), p. 209, vol. I.
18 Abinger MS., quoted by Ralph Wardle.
19 Quoted by V. C. Miller, op. cit., p. 40.
20 ibid., p. 46.
21 Cited by M. Sydenham, *The Girondins* (1961), p. 192.
22 See Claude Mazauric's account of Babeuf's ideas in *Babeuf et la conspiration pour l'égalité* (1962); Bancal's ideas in F. Mège, *Le Conventional Bancal des Issarts* (1887); and Mary's *Historical and Moral View of the French Revolution*, in which she prophesies the crumbling and disappearance of Paris under a well-established republican government, p. 508.
23 Information from letter to Mrs Barlow printed in *Shelley and his Circle*, p. 866, vol. IV.
24 See Léopold Lacour, *Trois Femmes de la Révolution* (1900).
25 *Lettres de Madame Roland* (1900); information about Manon from her own *Mémoires*, ed. Perroud (1905).
26 *Historical and Moral View of the French Revolution* (1794), pp. 309–10.
27 Both Mège, p. 163, and Woodward, pp. 47–52, accept this explanation.
28 Published in the letters of Madame Roland to Bancal, quoted by Mège, p. 164.
29 ibid., p. 164.
30 *Autobiography* of Eliza Fletcher (1875), p. 70.
31 See *Shelley and his Circle* for documentary evidence of this, p. 127, vol. I.
32 The letter is in the Archives de France.

Chapter 12

1 See her *Historical and Moral View of the French Revolution*, p. 282.
2 Information about Imlay from Ralph Rusk's *Adventures of Gilbert Imlay*, Indiana University Studies (1923).
3 Mary's description in a letter, Abinger MS., my transcript.
4 *Common Reader*, vol. II, p. 160.
5 Godwin's *Memoirs*, pp. 112–13.
6 *Letters to Imlay*, pp. 106 and 128, letters XLIV and LV (1908 ed.).
7 ibid., p. 53, letter XXV.

Chapter 13

1 MS. letter in Archives de France.
2 Quoted by Dauban in *La Démagogie à Paris en 1793* (1868), pp. 276–7; my translation.
3 See Ph. Sagnac, *La Législation civile de la Révolution française* (1898), p. 246.
4 Information on feminism from Michelet, *Les Femmes de la Révolution* (1955); L. Lacour, *Trois Femmes de la Révolution* (1900); Aulard, article in *Revue bleue* (March 1898); Frank Hamel, *A Woman of the Revolution* (1911); Dauban, op. cit.; Sagnac, op. cit., etc.
5 Quoted by Lacour, op. cit., p. 261; my translation.
6 Hamel, op. cit., p. 287.
7 See proceedings of Comité d'instruction publique.
8 Hamel, op. cit., p. 173.
9 Lacour gives the text of her letter, pp. 344–5.
10 De Genlis, *Memoirs* (1882), p. 106, vol. IV; my translation.
11 Quoted by Lacour, op. cit., p. 60.
12 ibid., p. 61.
13 From Letters of Georg Forster, here in Hamel's translation, p. 341.
14 Information from Dauban, op. cit., p. 297.
15 See *Complete Works* of Condorcet for all these references.
16 Information about Condorcet from L. Cahen, *Condorcet et la Révolution française* (1904).
17 *Observations philosophiques sur la réforme de l'éducation*

publique by J. Courdin, Montpellier (1792), footnote to p. 101.

18 *De l'Amour*.

Chapter 14

1 Godwin gives this story in his *Memoirs*, p. 116. Amelia Opie tells a similar story about a woman character in her novel *A Wife's Duty*, which has scenes set in Paris during the Terror; possibly she had had Mary's account directly from her and used it.

2 *Letters to Imlay*, here given in 1908 edition, ed. R. Ingpen, p. 19, letter x. All further quotes in this chapter where no other indication is given are from Ingpen.

3 Stone's remarks occur in letters to his brother William in Hackney, given in Howells's *State Trials*, vol. xxv, pp. 1215 and 1216.

4 See *Four New Letters of Mary Wollstonecraft and Helen Maria Williams*, ed. Kurtz & Autrey (1937), p. 39, letter I.

5 *Reflections on the French Revolution*, Burke.

6 *Historical and Moral View of the French Revolution*, M.W., p. 6.

7 ibid., p. 518.

8 ibid., p. 460.

9 ibid., p. 484.

10 ibid., pp. 485–6.

11 Abinger MS., my transcript.

12 *Historical and Moral View*, p. 311.

13 Archives de la ville du Havre.

14 See Coleridge's *Letters*, ed. Griggs, September 1794, p. 99, letter 55, vol. I.

15 Abinger MS.

16 See Richard Holmes's introduction to the Penguin edition (1987) of *Letters Written during a Short Residence in Sweden, Norway and Denmark*, which is informative and persuasive about the book's influence on the Romantics. He says that it 'entered into the literary mythology of Romanticism within a single generation'; and indeed Johnson printed a second edition in 1802.

Chapter 15

1 This particular comment does not appear in the first edition and was evidently the product of his thinking in 1794 and 1795.
2 *Letters to Imlay*, p. 158, letter LXIX.
3 ibid., p. 159, letter LXIX.
4 A letter written in 1792 (in the Abinger MS.) refers to this story; Mary dismissed the victim very contemptuously.
5 Information about Putney Bridge from *Fulham Old and New* by Charles J. Féret (1900) and also from GLC archives.
6 D. Lysons, *Environs of London* (1799), vol. II, p. 365.
7 *Letters to Imlay*: his words are quoted in her letter, p. 160, letter LXX.
8 Letter printed by Knowles, op. cit., p. 169, vol. I.
9 *Letters to Imlay*, p. 176, letter LXXVII.
10 See Livingston Lowes's suggestion in *The Road to Xanadu* that some of the images in *Kubla Khan* were inspired by Mary's descriptive writing in the *Letters from Sweden*, pp. 30 and 161.
11 Abinger MS., my transcript.
12 Letter given in *Thomas Poole and his Friends* by Mrs H. Sandford (1888), p. 133, vol. I. Poole ordered his books from Johnson, and headed his list for the book club he founded in his Somerset village in January 1793 with a request for a copy of *A Vindication of the Rights of Woman*.
13 See above, p. 212.
14 Letter given in full by Clark Durant, pp. 300–301.
15 *Considerations on Lord Grenville's and Mr Pitt's Bills* (1795).
16 *Life* of Archibald Hamilton Rowan, pp. 250–51.
17 *Letters to Imlay*, p. 177, letter LXXVII.

Chapter 16

1 Coleridge refers to this scandal in his letters, and there are entries in Godwin's diary which indicate a crisis. When he later tried to woo the widowed Mrs Reveley he referred back to her having admitted to loving him on an earlier occasion.

2 See, e.g., Olivia in *Hugh Trevor*; Anna St Ives in the novel named for her; and the philosophic Lucy Peckham in his play *The School for Arrogance*.

3 *Memoirs of Emma Courtney* by Mary Hays (1796), p. 107.

4 ibid., p. 169.

5 *The Spirit of the Age* by William Hazlitt (1825), p. 182 (Everyman).

6 See for instance Holcroft's *Autobiography* (1816) with its verbatim transcript of a quarrel he and Godwin had about an over-frank criticism of a play, pp. 122–6, vol. III.

7 Printed in her *Posthumous Works*, p. 169 et seq., vol. II.

8 Information about Amelia Opie from Cecilia Brightwell's *Memorials of the Life of Amelia Opie* (1854); Margaret MacGregor's *Amelia Alderson Opie, Worldling and Friend*, Smith College Studies in Modern Languages (1932); also from Ada Earland's *John Opie and his Circle* (1911).

9 Brightwell, op. cit., pp. 59–60.

10 Review in *The Critical Review*, LXX (1790), p. 339, quoted by MacGregor, op. cit., p. 13.

11 Brightwell, op. cit., p. 43.

12 See Kegan Paul, *William Godwin and his Friends* (1876), p. 158, vol. I.

13 Information about Mrs Inchbald largely from Boaden's *Life* (1833).

14 Coleridge *Letters*, ed. Griggs, p. 589, letter 333, vol. I.

15 Information about Mrs Fenwick from *The Fate of the Fenwicks* by Annie Wedd (1927). Elizabeth Fenwick knew Holcroft and Francis Place, who spoke well of her; the British Museum has lately acquired a copy of *Secresy*. John Fenwick devoted himself to defending the Irish conspirator O'Coigly, who was executed for treason.

16 The only version of this novel I have seen is a French translation published in Paris in 1799, in the BM.

17 Faringdon Diaries.

18 See *Household Words* for 27 April 1850, p. 113, article on Francis Jeffrey's life by John Forster, the friend and biographer of Charles Dickens, who was a close friend of Jeffrey. Jeffrey in turn had known and admired Mary.

19 Southey's *Letters*, ed. C. C. Southey (1849), p. 305, vol. I.
20 See *Life of William Wordsworth* (The Early Years) by Mary Moorman (1957), pp. 296–7.
21 See Australian DNB for entry on Edward Wollstonecraft, Mary's nephew.
22 L. D. Woodward, op. cit., p. 138.
23 So Godwin told Hazlitt; see *The Spirit of the Age*, p. 194.

Chapter 17

1 *Letters of Godwin to Mary Wollstonecraft*, edited by Ralph Wardle (1967), letter 120, p. 75. I have used this excellent edition throughout this chapter.
2 Godwin's *Memoirs*, p. 152.
3 Evidence of Godwin's diary.
4 *Letters*, op. cit., p. 12, letters 6 and 7.
5 Godwin's *Memoirs*, p. 154.
6 In *Political Justice*.
7 *Letters*, op. cit., p. 14, letter 10.
8 ibid., p. 15, letter 12.
9 ibid., pp. 16–17, letter 13.
10 The phrases are taken from Holcroft's *Hugh Trevor* (1794–7).
11 *Memoirs*, 2nd edition, quoted by Clark Durant, p. 100.
12 ibid., p. 129.
13 *Letters*, op. cit., p. 46, letter 64.
14 *St Leon* by William Godwin (1799), pp. 39–40, Chap. IV (1831 ed.).
15 *Letters*, op. cit., p. 53, letter 75.
16 ibid., p. 43, letter 56.
17 ibid., p. 60, letter 87.
18 ibid., p. 72, letter 113.
19 Godwin's *Memoirs*, p. 167.
20 *Letters*, op. cit., p. 73, letter 116.
21 Kegan Paul's *William Godwin* (1876), p. 240, vol. I.
22 *Love Letters of Mary Hays*, ed. Wedd, p. 241.
23 Quoted by Clark Durant in his supplement to Godwin's *Memoirs* (1927), pp. 313–14.
24 See Cecilia Brightwell, op. cit., pp. 61–2.

Chapter 18

1 *Letters of William Godwin and Mary Wollstonecraft*, ed. Wardle (1967) used throughout, p. 76, letter 123.
2 ibid., p. 31, letter 34.
3 ibid., p. 93, letter 131.
4 ibid., p. 91, letter 130.
5 ibid., p. 111, letter 140.
6 ibid., p. 112, letter 140.
7 ibid., p. 119, letter 158.
8 See Dorothy George, *London Life in the Eighteenth Century* (1925), p. 61 (Penguin ed.).
9 Godwin's *Memoirs*, p. 173.
10 Information on childbirth in the eighteenth century from William Buchan's *Domestic Medicine* (1796) and from *The Ladies Dispensatory*.
11 *St Leon* by William Godwin (1799), p. 43, Chap. IV (1831 ed.).
12 Godwin's *Memoirs*, p. 181.
13 The story comes through Basil Montagu's family.
14 Godwin's *Memoirs*, p. 192.
15 The Rev. Richard Polwhele, himself a poet and friend of Anna Seward: *The Unsex'd Females* (1798).

Chapter 19

1 See *Memoirs of Mrs Inchbald* by J. Boaden (1833), p. 15, vol. II.
2 Quoted by C. Kegan Paul in *William Godwin and his Friends* (1876), p. 276, vol. I.
3 ibid., p. 285, vol.I.
4 *Letters* of Coleridge, ed. Griggs.
5 Abinger MS., my transcript.
6 Roscoe papers.
7 Abinger MS., my transcript.
8 Clark Durant prints this note, p. 185.
9 Roscoe MS., 3958A.
10 See vol. I of Wordsworth's *Letters*, ed. de Selincourt, revised C. Shaver, 1967 edition, p. 188.
11 Quoted in introduction to *Love Letters of Mary Hays*, ed. A. Wedd, p. 9.

12 The only copy I have seen of this article is in the GLC archives: the British Museum *Monthly Visitors* were burnt during the Second World War.
13 See *John Opie and his Circle* by Ada Earland (1911) for friendship of Godwin and Opie; Kegan Paul, op. cit., for Godwin's letter to Holcroft, p. 347, vol. I.
14 Godwin's *Memoirs*, pp. 195–8.
15 In *Sur l'admission des femmes au droit de Cité* (1790).
16 See Crabb Robinson's diaries for this; he often accompanied her, and also refers to contemporary disapproval of her 'zealous espousal' of M.W.'s views and warm friendship with her, p. 5, vol. I.
17 *Gentleman's Magazine*, April 1799. I am indebted for this reference to Mark Cousins.
18 *Lady's Monthly Museum*, August 1798.
19 This and four following quotations are all from *Practical Education* (1798), and all taken from chapters written by Maria herself, pp. 699, 168, 336, 168, 168.
20 For a further account of Hannah More, see M. Gladys Jones's *Life* (1952).
21 In *Practical Education*, pp. 548–9.
22 See Jane Austen's *Letters*, ed. Chapman (1932), p. 466.
23 The germ of the book is in her diaries for August 1791. The influence of Madame de Staël and Fanny's sister Susanna, who was more of a feminist than Fanny, must be taken into account; the suicide attempts may refer to M.W. and de Staël's threats to her lover Narbonne; and the similarity between the names of F.B.'s Albert Harleigh and Mary Hays's hero August Harley may be a sign that Miss Burney had read *Emma Courtney*.
24 Letter given by Kegan Paul, op. cit., p. 325, vol. I.
25 p. 359 in Longman's 1911 ed.
26 This and the next quotation are both from *On the Subjection of Women*, published in 1869, pp. 292–3 (Everyman ed.).
27 See final page of *Middlemarch* (1871–2).

Epilogue

1 Lionel Woodward, op. cit., p. 138.

2 Knowles, p. 299, vol. I; Johnson left his portrait of Priestley by Fuseli to his great-nephew, John Miles; it would be interesting to know where it is now.

3 Johnson's will can be seen in the Public Record Office.

4 Information from Berry manuscripts in the Mitchel Library, Sydney, Australia.

5 A plaque has been put up on the site of Polygon, Somers Town, since this book was first published.

References in the Notes to letters that were unpublished or from scattered sources when the book was first published have not been adjusted in this edition; interested readers can now find them in Ralph M. Wardle (see under 'Works of Mary Wollstonecraft' in the Bibliography).

Appendix I

Eighteenth-century References to Votes for Women

A reference to votes in local government (i.e., parish council meetings) occurs, by pleasant coincidence, in the register of Mary Wollstonecraft's native parish of St Botolph Without Bishopsgate, in the minutes of a meeting held in December 1765, when she was six:

> NB There was several Disputes concerning whether women who kept House and paid to the Poor, has a Right to Vote for Parish Officers.
>
> It was agreed to be unprecedented, therefore their Votes were not Counted in ye Division.

This suggests that women were actually present at the parish council meeting, though their names are not entered. Perhaps they were weavers' widows, used to working and earning in their own right; but the weaving industry was going into a decline, and no more seems to have been heard of their claim.

In 1776 Josiah Tucker, the Dean of Gloucester, raised the question of female suffrage in what was intended as a heavily satirical passage (in his *Series of Answers to Certain Popular Objections, against Separating from the Rebellious Colonies, being the Concluding Tract of the Dean of Gloucester*, R. Raikes & Cadell):

> ... were Taxation and Representation so essentially connected, and so absolutely inseparable, as Mr Lock and his followers would make us believe; – then most certainly every Man's Consent (the Consent of every *moral* Agent of every Sex and Con-

dition) ought to be previously obtained for divesting him, her or them of any Part of his, her, or their natural Rights and Liberties in any Respect whatever. For indeed our personal Rights are nearer and dearer to us, and are more essentially our own (our own Property) than any adventitious Accession of Lands or tenements, Goods or Chattels.

John Cartwright responded to this joke in his *Legislative Rights of the Commonwealth Vindicated; or, Take Your Choice!* published in the same year.

For want of arguments against an equality of representation, some authors have been driven to the sad expedient of attempting to be *witty* on the subject. A dignitary of our church, and a writer also who takes upon him to assert the rights of Great Britain, have in particular been pleased to advance that provided this equality be due to men, it must equally appertain to women; and that then of course all the women, as well as all the men, must be free to vote at elections.

It might be want of politeness to ask these gentlemen if they seriously meant what they say; but, as I am serious myself, I will beg leave to refer the Dean to the Scriptures, and the other gentleman to the *law of nature* and the *common law of England*, and both of them to the fair sex, in order to settle this point. Man and wife are called in scripture *one flesh*, in law *one person*; and by both, the temporal dominion is given to the man. With regard to God and his salvation, the sexes are equal in dignity. Now the matron is the highest of her sex in temporal dignity; and yet, as a wife, she is commanded 'to submit herself to her husband in *everything*'; and *he*, both in scripture and in law, is considered as her representative, her *lord*, her *head*. If this be the condition of the matron, it will be difficult, even for a Dean, to show that her inferiors should enjoy a privilege denied to her. But, were the Rev Dean and the bold assertor to receive no greater thanks from the ministry than they are likely to obtain from the fair sex for such attempts to serve them, poor indeed would be their reward. Women know too well what God and nature requires of them to put in so absurd a claim for a share in the rights of election. Their privilege and power are of another kind; they know their sphere.

Who the women consulted by Cartwright were he does not say, though it is possible that one was Ann Jebb. I have not been able to trace the other writer mentioned.

Bentham's notes on female suffrage are discussed in the text, p. 134.

Appendix II

Family Tree of

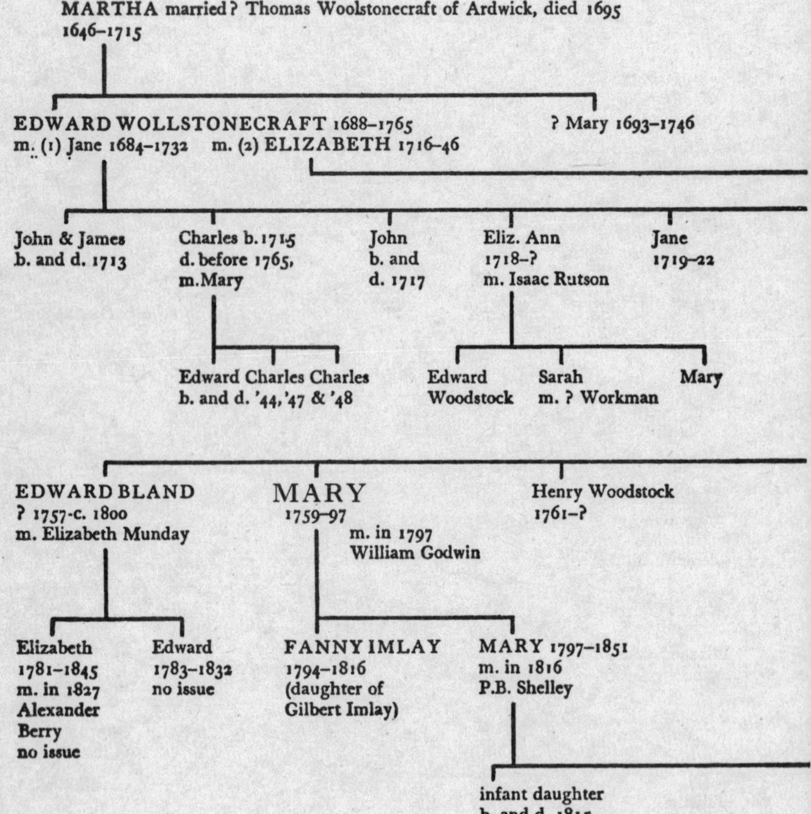

the Wollstonecrafts

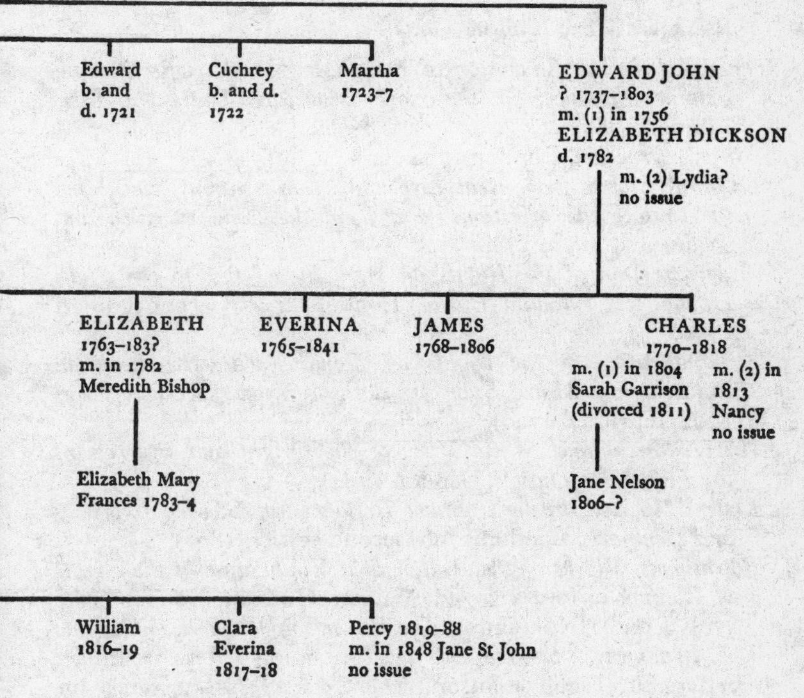

Bibliography

This is a slightly revised bibliography, in view of the fact that the book was written twenty years ago; essentially it remains an indication of the sources I used, though I have added some titles published since I wrote.

1 *Works by Mary Wollstonecraft*

Thoughts on the Education of Daughters: With Reflections on Female Conduct, in the more important Duties of Life, London 1787.

Mary: A Fiction, London 1788.

Original Stories from Real Life, with conversations, calculated to regulate the affections, and form the mind to truth and goodness, London 1788.

A Vindication of the Rights of Men, in a letter to the Right Honourable Edmund Burke, London 1790 (second edition 1790).

A Vindication of the Rights of Woman, with Strictures on Political and Moral Subjects, London 1792 (second edition 1792, reprinted 1796).

An Historical and Moral View of the Origin and Progress of the French Revolution, London 1794.

Letters Written during a Short Residence in Sweden, Norway and Denmark, London 1796 (second edition 1802).

Posthumous Works of the Author of a Vindication of the Rights of Woman in four vols, ed. William Godwin, London 1798 (vols I and II containing *The Wrongs of Woman, or Maria; A Fragment*; vols III and IV containing letters to Imlay, letters to Joseph Johnson, *The Cave of Fancy*, notes for work on infant management and some lessons, headed by Mary 'The first book of a series which I intended to have written for my unfortunate girl', probably begun in October 1795 and continued later).

Of these, only *A Vindication of the Rights of Woman* has remained in print steadily throughout the two hundred years since it first appeared. The two novels were reprinted together by Oxford in 1976, ed. Gary Kelly, and an Oxford paperback of this edition followed in 1980; a Penguin edition by Janet Todd will appear in 1992. Mary's letters to Imlay were reprinted in London in 1879 by Charles Kegan Paul and in 1908 by Roger Ingpen. *Letters Written during a Short Residence in Sweden, Norway and Denmark* was republished in the US in 1976 by the University of Nebraska Press, ed. Carol Postan, and in the UK in 1987 in Penguin Classics, edited and introduced by Richard Holmes (together with Godwin's memoir of his wife); I have drawn gratefully on the information assembled by Holmes to supplement my account of the book.

A *Collected Letters of Mary Wollstonecraft* appeared in 1979, edited by Ralph M. Wardle, from Cornell University Press.

The Works of Mary Wollstonecraft in a magnificent (and very costly) seven-volume edition, edited by Janet Todd and Marilyn Butler assisted by Emma Rees-Mogg, was published by Pickering & Chatto, London 1989. This contains all her printed works, including translations, journalism (mostly book reviews) and some, though not all, of her letters. There is an introduction by Marilyn Butler.

2 *General Historical Background*

J. G. Alger, *Englishmen in the French Revolution*, London 1889.

Analytical Review, London 1788–99.

H. N. Brailsford, *Shelley, Godwin and their Circle*, London 1913.

P. A. Brown, *The French Revolution in English History*, London 1918; New York 1965.

James Burgh, *Thoughts on Education*, London 1747; New York.

James Burgh, *The Dignity of Human Nature*, London 1754.

Ed. K. N. Cameron, *Shelley and his Circle*, London and Cambridge, Massachusetts, vols 1 and 2 1961, vols 3 and 4 1970.

Thomas Christie, *Letters on the French Revolution*, London 1791.

Coleridge, *The Watchman*, ed. L. Patton, London and Princeton 1970.

Condorcet, Marie-Jean-Antoine-Nicolas Caritat, marquis de, *Œuvres Complètes*, ed. O'Connor and Arago, 12 vols, Paris 1847.

C. A. Dauban, *La Démagogie à Paris en 1793*, Paris 1868.

A. Douarche, *Les Tribunaux Civils de Paris*, Paris 1905–7; New York.

Maria Edgeworth, *Practical Education*, London 1798.

Peter Gay, *The Enlightenment*, 2 vols, London 1967 & 1970; New York 1973.

Dorothy George, *London Life in the Eighteenth Century*, London 1925; Peregrine edition, Harmondsworth 1966.

Thomas Gisbourne, *An Enquiry into the Duties of the Female Sex*, London 1797.

Élie Halévy, *Formation du radicalisme philosophique*, 3 vols, Paris 1901–4.

Mary Hays, *Appeal to the Men of Great Britain in Behalf of the Women*; published anonymously by Joseph Johnson in 1798, it was thought to have disappeared at the time I wrote, but a copy turned up in America and was published in 1974 in a facsimile edition by Garland Publishing, New York.

W. Hazlitt, *The Spirit of the Age*, London 1825.

T. S. Howells, *State Trials*, vols XXIV and XXV, London 1823.

Georges Lefebvre, *The French Revolution from its Origin to 1793*, London and New York 1962.

D. Lysons, *Environs of London*, London 1792–9; New York.

J. P. Malcolm, *Anecdotes of the Manners and Customs of London*, London 1808.

Dorothy Marshall, *The English Poor in the Eighteenth Century*, London 1926; Clifton, New Jersey.

H. W. Meikle, *The French Revolution in Scotland*, London 1912.

J. Michelet, *Les Femmes de la Révolution*, Paris 1855.

Hannah More, *Strictures on the Modern System of Female Education*, London 1799.

F. A. Mumby, *Publishing and Bookselling*, London 1930; New York.

Per Nyström, *Mary Wollstonecraft's Scandinavian Journey*, Acts of the Royal Society of Arts and Sciences of Gothenburg, Humaniora No. 17, 1980. Per Nyström of Gothenburg established the facts of Imlay's attempted silver smuggling out of France and his claim against Ellefson when he was in turn defrauded.

Mary-Anne Radcliffe, *The Female Advocate, or an Attempt to Recover the Rights of Women from Male Usurpation*, London 1799.

Constance Rover, *Love, Morals and the Feminists*, London 1970.

Ph. Sagnac, *La Législation civile de la Révolution française*, Paris 1898.

M. Sydenham, *The Girondins*, London 1961; Connecticut 1973.

E. P. Thompson, *The Making of the English Working Class*, London 1963.

J. M. S. Tompkins, *The Popular Novel in England 1770–1800*, London 1932; Gloucester, Massachusetts.

Priscilla Wakefield, *Reflections on the Present Conditions of the Female Sex; with Suggestions for its Improvement*, London 1798.

G. F. A. Wendeborn, *A View of England*, London 1791.

Jane West, *Letters to a Young Man*, London 1801.

Jane West, *Letters to a Young Lady*, London 1806.

3 *Letters*

Letters of Jane Austen, ed. R. W. Chapman, Oxford 1932; New York 1952.

Collected Letters of Coleridge, ed. E. L. Griggs, Oxford 1956; New York.

Letters of William Cowper, ed. Thomas Wright, London 1904; New York.

Letters of George Forster, ed. his widow Thérèse, Germany 1829.

Love Letters of Mary Hays, ed. A. Wedd, London 1925.

Letters of Madame Roland, ed. Perroud, Paris 1900.

Letters of Anna Seward, Edinburgh 1811; New York.

Letters of Richard Brinsley Sheridan, ed. C. Price, London and New York 1966.

Letters of Horace Walpole, ed. Mrs Toynbee, Oxford 1903–5.
Correspondence of Josiah Wedgwood 1781–94, London 1906.
Letters of Wordsworth, ed. de Selincourt, revised C. Shaver, London 1967.

4 *Unpublished Sources*

Parish records in the Guildhall Library, London, the General London Council archives and St Andrew's, Enfield, Middlesex, have been consulted, as well as wills in the Public Record Office and letters lodged in Doctor Williams's Library, London, and Stoke Newington Library. Wollstonecraft family papers preserved in the Mitchell Library, Sydney, Australia, have helped to give some account of the fate of Mary's brothers and sisters. The French national archives, while they failed to yield any of Mary's lost letters, contained references to Godwin and Christie, and the archives at Le Havre produced the birth certificate of Françoise Imlay. The Bentham manuscripts in University College, London, were consulted for his notes on female suffrage, and Bishop Percy's letters in the British Museum manuscript room for references to Mary's involvement with the Kingsboroughs.

5 *Diaries*

H. Crabb Robinson, ed. Edith Morley, London 1938.
Diaries of Fanny Burney, London 1842, 7 vols; and vols 1 and 2 of Joyce Hemlow's 1972 edition.
Thraliana, the diaries of Mrs Piozzi, ed. K. Balderstone, Oxford 1942.
Portions of Samuel Rogers's diary appear in *The Early Life of Samuel Rogers*, ed. P. Clayden, London 1887; US 1973.
Nancy Woodforde's diary for 1792, amongst the Woodforde papers, London 1932.

6 *Biographies of Mary Wollstonecraft*

William Godwin, *Memoirs of the Author of a Vindication of the Rights of Woman*, two editions London 1798, the second slightly altered.
Elizabeth R. Pennell, *Mary Wollstonecraft*, London 1885;

New York 1972. A straightforward and sympathetic life, drawing on Kegan Paul's material (in *Godwin and his Friends* and the preface to his edition of *Letters to Imlay*) and Godwin's *Memoirs*. Mrs Pennell, an American writer who lived in London for several years, asked the Shelley family if she could see Mary's letters but was not allowed to.

E. Rauschenbusch-Clough, *A Study of Mary Wollstonecraft and the Rights of Woman*, London 1896. The emphasis is on the intellectual background.

G. Stirling Taylor, *Mary Wollstonecraft, a Study in Economics and Romance*, London 1911; US. Enthusiastic and readable.

W. Godwin, *Memoirs*, new edition with supplement by W. Clark Durant, New York 1927. A scholarly labour of love.

Marthe Severne Storr, *Mary Wollstonecraft et le mouvement féministe*, Paris 1932. Most thorough in its account of Mary's feminist predecessors: a French academic thesis.

H. R. James, *Mary Wollstonecraft, a sketch*, London 1932; US. The author died before he could revise this slight and personal book.

Ralph Wardle, *Mary Wollstonecraft*, Kansas 1951. The first adequately researched life, meticulous and always interesting, but not much concerned with the feminist debate or Mary's contemporaries.

Margaret George, *One Woman's Situation*, Illinois 1970. A brilliant discussion of Mary's failure to find a role as a free woman in a bourgeois society.

Edna Dixon, *Mary Wollstonecraft*, London 1971. A romantic biography, marred by factual errors.

Eleanor Flexner, *Mary Wollstonecraft*, New York 1972. An excellent book; my own book duplicates some of the research, but my conclusions are not always the same.

7 *Memoirs, biographies and autobiographies*

William Beloe, *The Sexagenarian*, published anonymously in London in 1817. A mass of gossip by a violently reactionary anti-feminist.

Ed. M. Betham-Edwards, *Autobiography of Arthur Young*,

London 1898; New York 1926. Useful account of his time with the Kingsboroughs ten years before Mary.

J. Boaden, *Life of Mrs Inchbald*, London 1833. Mrs Inchbald, a Catholic, burnt her autobiography on the advice of her confessor; Boaden's attempt to replace it is dull.

Boswell, *Life of Johnson*, ed. Chapman, London 1953.

Cecilia Brightwell, *Memorials of the Life of Amelia Opie*, Norwich 1854.

Ford K. Brown, *The Life of William Godwin*, London and Toronto 1926. Corrects and fills in Kegan Paul.

Peter Brown, *The Chathamites*, London 1967. Useful section on Price.

Marilyn Butler, *Maria Edgeworth*, London 1971; New York 1972. Especially interesting in its full account of Maria's relations with her father and stepmothers.

L. Cahen, *Condorcet et la Révolution française*, Paris 1904; New York.

George Chandler, *William Roscoe of Liverpool*, London 1953. Describes his friendship with Mary, Fuseli and Johnson.

A Narrative of the Life of Charlotte Charke by herself, London 1755. Charlotte Charke was the youngest daughter of Colley Cibber, quarrelled with her family, liked to dress as a man and had to support herself and daughter after she separated from her husband. Vivid and absorbing account of her struggles, a generation before Mary.

Ed. Brian Connell, *Portrait of a Whig Peer*, papers of second Viscount Palmerston, London 1957. Palmerston was in Paris in 1792, and the letters and diaries printed here give a good picture of the attitudes of his class.

J. Cottle, *Reminiscences of Southey and Coleridge*, London 1847.

Allan Cunningham, *Lives of Painters*, London 1829. The section on Fuseli, malicious in its account of his relationship with Mary, is not necessarily invalid; Cunningham knew many of Fuseli's friends.

Edward Dowden, *Life of Shelley*, London 1886; US. The full two-volume version is one of the most entertaining biographies ever written, and is informative about Fanny Imlay.

Ada Earland, *John Opie and his Circle*, London 1911.

Eliza Fletcher, *Autobiography*, Edinburgh 1875. Mrs Fletcher was a young and ardent Edinburgh radical during the 1790s.

Everilda Anne Gardiner, *Recollections of a Beloved Mother*, London 1842. The mother was Mary's childhood friend, Jane, who became a schoolmistress of extreme piety and prevented her pupils from reading the works of Byron.

Stéphanie de Genlis, *Memoirs*, London 1825.

Frank Hamel, *A Woman of the Revolution*, London 1911. Well-documented life of Théroigne de Méricourt.

Archibald Hamilton Rowan, *Autobiography*, London 1840; New York 1973. A United Irishman and friend of Mary and her family, he gives an account of his meeting with her in Paris.

Ed. (and compiled by) Hazlitt, *Autobiography of Thomas Holcroft*, London 1816. Godwin made Hazlitt cut references to Mary and Imlay in Holcroft's diary; the chapters Holcroft dictated from his deathbed are probably the best he ever wrote, and remind one of Dickens in their insight into the mind of a boy whose sensibility is finer than that of those who surround him.

Ed. F. P. Hett, *Memoirs of Susan Sibbald, 1783–1812*, London 1926; New York. Describes a conventional middle-class country and boarding school upbringing.

M. Gladys Jones, *Life of Hannah More*, Cambridge 1952. One of Mary's opponents; shows Miss More's dependence on the devoted services of her sisters.

Charles Kegan Paul, *William Godwin and his Friends*, London 1876; US. Pious in its attitudes to Mary especially, and unreliable, but another classic of Victorian biography.

R. D. King-Harman, *The Kings, Earls of Kingston*, Cambridge 1959. A privately printed book that draws on unpublished family letters and gives a vivid picture of the characters of Mary's employers.

Charles Knight, *Shadows of Old Booksellers*, London 1865.

J. Knowles, *Life and Writings of Henry Fuseli*, London 1831.

R. Laboucheix, *Richard Price*, London 1971.

J. Lackington, *Memoirs*, London 1810. Contains an account of the rise of female literacy, by a bookseller.

Leopold Lacour, *Trois Femmes de la Révolution*, Paris 1900. Olympe de Gouges, Théroigne de Méricourt and Rose Lacombe, a socialist and feminist.

E. McAleer, *The Sensitive Plant*, London and North Carolina 1958. Lady Mountcashel, née Margaret King, is the subject; a hostile account of Mary and her relationship with the family is given.

Margaret MacGregor, *Amelia Alderson Opie, Worldling and Friend*, Smith College Studies in Modern Languages, 1932.

Philip Magnus, *Edmund Burke*, London 1939; New York 1973.

Eudo Mason, *The Mind of Henry Fuseli*, London 1951. Extremely useful selection of his writings, personal and official, with translations of German letters, bibliography, etc.

Claude Mazauric, *Babeuf et la conspiration pour l'égalité*, Paris 1962.

F. Mège, *Le Conventional Bancal des Issarts*, Paris 1887.

Victor Clyde Miller, *Joel Barlow, Revolutionist*, London 1791–2, Hamburg 1932. Succinct account of Barlow's activities.

Mary Moorman, *William Wordsworth: a biography*, Oxford 1957.

E. Morchard Bishop, *Blake's Hayley*, London 1951; New York 1972.

J. Nichols, *Literary Anecdotes of the Eighteenth Century*, London 1812–15.

Laetitia Pilkington, *Memoirs*, London 1784. Another woman obliged to support herself after being divorced for adultery. She tried to earn her living as a writer in London; one of her patrons in Ireland (where she was born and to which she returned) was the uncle of Mary's Robert Kingsborough.

J. F. E. Robinet, *Condorcet*, Paris 1893. Robinet takes it on himself to refute Condorcet's feminist ideas.

Madame Roland, *Memoirs*, various editions include two English translations printed by Joseph Johnson in London, 1795 & 1796.

Ralph Rusk, *Adventures of Gilbert Imlay*, Indiana University Studies 1923.

Ed. J. T. Rutt, *Life and Correspondence of Joseph Priestley*, London 1831.

William St Clair, *The Godwins and the Shelleys*, London 1989.

Mrs H. Sandford, *Thomas Poole and his Friends*, London 1888; US 1973. Gives Poole's reading lists and letters demonstrating his interest in feminism at the time he first knew Coleridge.

Mary Anne Schimmelpenninck, *Life*, London 1858. Valuable account of the Priestley family and their Unitarian friends during the 1790s. The author is a perfect specimen of those who rejected eighteenth-century rationalism for a comforting piety; she thought the Unitarians expected too much of themselves and others.

Edward Smith, *The Story of the British Jacobins*, London 1881. A sympathetic account.

J. T. Smith, *A Book for a Rainy Day*, London 1845, and *Nollakens and his Times*, London 1829 – both rich sources of anecdote and information.

Ed. (his son) C. C. Southey, *Life and Correspondence of Robert Southey*, London 1849.

A. Stephens, *Memoirs of John Horne Tooke*, London 1813; New York 1968. Shows Horne Tooke as an old-fashioned radical, uninterested in feminism. He never married, but adopted his two illegitimate daughters and expected them to cheer his old age; they were taught a little art so that they might support themselves. The illegitimate son was shipped off to India.

Claire Tomalin, *Shelley and his World*, London 1980 and Penguin 1992.

A. Wedd, *The Fate of the Fenwicks*, London 1927.

Helen Maria Williams, *Souvenirs de la Révolution française*, Paris 1827.

L. D. Woodward, *Hélène Maria Williams et ses amis*, Paris 1930.

8 *Fiction*

Jean-Jacques Rousseau, *La Nouvelle Héloïse*, 1760, first London edition 1784 (a Dublin one in 1761).

Goethe, *The Sorrows of Young Werther*, 1774, English translation London 1779.
These two novels were favourite reading of Mary and her circle.

Thomas Holcroft, *Anna St Ives*, London 1792; New York 1970. The heroine looks forward to an ideal future in which marriage will no longer be necessary, determines for the present to marry for the good of society rather than merely to please herself; she quells a would-be rapist by sheer force of personality and marries her father's steward's son.

Mary and Elizabeth Hays, stories in *Letters and Essays Moral and Miscellaneous*, London 1793. They demonstrate the superiority of educated women over ignorant, and imagine ideal settlements in the American woods.

Gilbert Imlay, *The Emigrants*, London 1793. Pictures American life and advocates easy divorce.

Thomas Holcroft, *Hugh Trevor*, London 1794–7; New York 1973. Rambling political novel, discussing exploitation of women as well as poor, talented young men.

Elizabeth Fenwick, *Secresy*, London 1795. Gothic novel with feminist ideas and criticism of marriage.

Robert Bage, *Hermsprong*, London 1796. A radical hero and two spirited, independent and well-read heroines; several references to Mary Wollstonecraft.

Elizabeth Inchbald, *Nature and Art*, London 1796. Another radical novel, with a bold account of the ruin of a village girl through seduction and her inability to restore herself to a tolerable existence thereafter.

Mary Hays, *Memoirs of Emma Courtney*, London 1796. The sad life of an active and educated young woman who wants to find work and woo her own husband; portrait of Godwin and almost certainly his actual letters quoted.

William Godwin, *St Leon*, London 1799; New York. Written in the aftermath of Mary's death, it contains an idealized portrait of her.

Mary Hays, *A Victim of Prejudice*, London 1799. The persecution of the illegitimate daughter of a young woman who has died (the only copy in the BM is a French translation, Paris 1799).

Elizabeth Hamilton, *The Modern Philosophers*, London 1800. Crude satire on radicals and feminists, featuring Bridgetina Botherim (meant for Mary Hays) and the hairdresser Valloton, turned orator and planning an ideal community in central Africa.

Amelia Opie, *Father and Daughter*, London 1801. Another young woman with an illegitimate child; she drives her father mad with grief and is ostracized.

Maria Edgeworth, *Belinda*, London 1801. Attacks feminists in the person of Harriot Freke, whose behaviour is coarse and who encourages her women friends to adultery.

Anne-Louise-Germaine de Staël, *Delphine*, 1802, and *Corinne*, 1805: both books describe women struggling against the limitations imposed on them by society, but are strictly novels of high life.

Maria Edgeworth, *The Modern Griselda*, written about 1803, satirizes a dissatisfied wife who insists on a divorce and then regrets it.

Amelia Opie, *Adeline Mowbray*, London 1805. Supposedly based on the story of Godwin and Mary, it depicts an idealistic young couple who resolve to live together without marriage on principle and suffer hideously as a result; except perhaps for the physical description of the heroine, it cannot be taken seriously as an account of Mary.

Amelia Opie, *A Wife's Duty* (date unknown; the only copy I have seen is in the London Library in a nineteenth-century reprint collection). The story is set during the period of the French Revolution and the wife behaves as Mary reported herself when she found herself beside the guillotine. The message is that wives should endure patiently any amount of provocation from husbands.

Maria Edgeworth, *Madame de Fleury*, a story printed in *Tales of Fashionable Life*, was written about 1805. It contrasts a good, submissive heroine with her wicked cousin who supports the Revolution and comes to a deservedly bad end.

Fanny Burney (Madame d'Arblay), *The Wanderer, or Female Difficulties*, published in London in 1814 but planned and begun 'before the end of the last century', shows clearly that its author had brooded over the question of women's rights, influenced no doubt by Madame de Staël and her own sister Susanna as well as the English feminist writers.

Jane Austen, *Sense and Sensibility* (London 1811; New York 1913), also planned and drafted in the 1790s, contains in Marianne a heroine who is brought to say, 'Had I died, – it would have been self-destruction.' It is perhaps worth pointing to a link between Jane Austen and Mary Wollstonecraft which suggests that Miss Austen probably knew Mary's story: Sir William East, a neighbour of the Mrs Cotton with whom Mary stayed in Berkshire in 1796 after her second suicide attempt, is said to have shown her much kindness. The son of Sir William East was a resident pupil in the house of Jane Austen's father.

Chronology

1689 Birth of Edward Wollstonecraft, Mary's grandfather.

c. 1700 Arrival of Edward Wollstonecraft in London.

1713 Birth of Edward's first children, twin sons John and James, by his first wife Jane.

1750 Edward John, son of Edward and his second wife Elizabeth, apprenticed weaver to his father.

1757 Edward John married to Elizabeth Dickson of Ballyshannon, Ireland. Their eldest child is a son, Edward (Ned).

1759 21 April, birth of Mary Wollstonecraft.

1763 The family acquire a farm at Epping.

1765 Death of Edward, Mary's grandfather. The Wollstonecrafts move to Barking in Essex.

1768 Family moves to Beverley, Yorkshire.

1773 Mary's first surviving letter, to Jane Arden.

1774 Family returns to the London suburb of Hoxton.

1775 Mary meets Fanny Blood and falls in love with her.

1776 Family moves to Laugharne in Wales.

1777 Return to London, this time to the London suburb of Walworth, near the Blood family.

1778 Mary goes to Mrs Dawson as a companion, spending time in Bath, Windsor and Southampton. Her family moves to Enfield; Ned, qualified as an attorney, marries.

1781 Birth of Ned's daughter Elizabeth.

1782 19 April, death of Mrs Wollstonecraft.

20 October, marriage of Eliza to Meredith Bishop, a Bermondsey lighter-builder.

Mary goes to live with the Bloods.

Her father marries again, a woman called Lydia, and settles in Laugharne.

1783 10 August, birth of Eliza's daughter Elizabeth Mary Frances.

1784 Mary summoned by Meredith to tend Eliza, who has had a nervous breakdown. Mary and Eliza run away, first to Hackney and then to Islington where they attempt to set up a school with Fanny Blood, but failing in this move to Newington Green.
Mary meets Richard Price and Dr Johnson.
Eliza's daughter dies.
Everina joins her sisters.

1785 Fanny goes in February to Lisbon to marry; in November Mary follows to find her dying in childbirth.

1786 Mary arrives back in London to find the school has failed. She writes *Thoughts on the Education of Daughters*. Her sisters are found teaching posts. Mary goes as a governess to Lord and Lady Kingsborough at Mitchelstown, near Cork, Ireland.

1787 With the Kingsboroughs in Dublin until August, when they go to Bristol, where Mary is dismissed. She goes to Joseph Johnson. In France, Condorcet makes case for female suffrage in *Lettres d'un bourgeois de Newhaven.*

1788 Mary living at the house Joseph Johnson has taken for her, 49 George Street, Blackfriars. She sends Everina to Paris. *Analytical Review* founded by Joseph Johnson and Thomas Christie. In all probability Mary meets Fuseli, who marries in June Sophia Rawlins.
Joseph Johnson publishes Mary's novel *Mary* and her *Original Stories*.
Jeremy Bentham prepares essay on suffrage for Mirabeau, with discussion of female suffrage.

1789 Mary works at the *Analytical* and on translations.
Her brother Charles, failing to get on as apprentice to Ned, turns to her for help and she sends him to Cork to learn farming.
In France the Revolution begins in July, and in November Dr Price gives his Old Jewry discourse.

1790 Mary still working on the *Analytical*; Johnson publishes her translation of *Elements of Morality* by Salzmann, with illustrations by Blake. Burke publishes his *Reflections on the Revolution in France*, and Mary's answer, *A Vindication of the Rights of Man,* is published anonymously in December. Everina and Eliza both now at Putney school.

1791 Second edition of Mary's *Vindication of the Rights of Man*, with her name, published.

Paine's *Rights of Man*, part 1, published.

Dr Price dies in April.

Fox and Burke quarrel in May. In July, the Birmingham riots; Priestley comes to London, dines with Sheridan but refuses to enter directly into political activities.

Joel Barlow arrives in London.

William Roscoe visits London and commissions a portrait of Mary.

In September she moves to Store Street and starts writing *Vindication of the Rights of Woman*. In November she meets William Godwin at Johnson's; he has just started work on his *Political Justice*.

In France, the Legislative Assembly is formed; Olympe de Gouges's *Déclaration des droits de la femme et de la citoyenne* appears.

1792 Publication of *Vindication of the Rights of Woman*.

Talleyrand visits London, calls on Mary and dines at Hackney with a party of Dissenters and English radicals.

Part 2 of Paine's *Rights of Man* published.

London Corresponding Society founded. Friends of the People founded. Barlow's pamphlets published by Johnson, also George Dyer's poems.

In August Mary, Johnson and the Fuselis set off for Paris but turn back; crisis with Fuseli.

September, Paine goes to Paris; October, Charles Wollstonecraft sets off for US. Mary Hays and Mary W. meet. November, Barlow to Paris; Johnson ill. December, Mary sets off for Paris alone.

Imlay's *A Topographical Description of the Western Territory of Northern America* published in London.

In France, Etta Palm addresses Legislative Assembly on women's rights, especially public education and divorce, and the first divorce laws are passed.

1793 *Political Justice* published in London; Godwin sends copies to Paris.
Execution of Louis XVI; war declared between England and France.
Mary meets Imlay.
Imlay's *The Emigrants* published in London.
In June, the Girondins proscribed. Mary moves to Neuilly.
In July, Charlotte Corday kills Marat and is guillotined. Condorcet goes into hiding. Olympe de Gouges arrested.
In August, Mary conceives baby; in September she returns to Paris and is registered at US embassy as Imlay's wife; he goes to Le Havre.
In October the Terror brings the arrest of most of the English.
Manon Roland, Olympe de Gouges and the queen guillotined.
Théroigne de Méricourt confined to madhouse.
Women's clubs closed.
Mary spends Christmas in Paris with Helen Williams, John Hurford Stone, the Barlows; she is writing her book on France.
Condorcet, in hiding, is writing his *Esquisse d'un tableau historique des progrès de l'esprit humain* and a fragment, *Sur l'Atlantide*, both containing further statements of his feminist views.

1794 Mary goes to Le Havre, where Fanny is born in May.
In August Imlay goes first to Paris and then to London.
Mary spends the winter in Paris.
In London, the Treason Trials occupy the autumn; Godwin publishes *Caleb Williams*, Coleridge and Southey discuss their Pantisocracy scheme.
Publication of Mary's *Historical and Moral View of the Origin and Progress of the French Revolution.*

1795 Mary returns to London and makes her first suicide attempt, probably with laudanum. In June she takes Fanny and her French maid Marguerite to Scandinavia with her on Imlay's business, returning via Hamburg

in September. In October she makes a second suicide attempt, jumping off Putney Bridge.
Rioting in London leads the government to pass the Two Acts which make meetings of more than fifty people illegal and certain publications seditious.
Mary lives in Finsbury Square and tries to write a play.
In France, Madame Condorcet publishes the *Esquisse*.

1796 Publication of Mary's *Letters Written during a Short Residence in Sweden, Norway and Denmark*.
Mary's name mentioned at trial of William Stone for treason.
She moves to Cumming Street and calls on Godwin.
Godwin proposes to Amelia Alderson and is turned down.
Godwin and Mary become lovers.
Death of Christie in Surinam.
In December, Mary conceives her second child.

1797 In March, Mary and Godwin marry at St Pancras church and she moves to the Polygon.
In August, Mary Godwin born; 10 September, death of Mary Wollstonecraft.

1809 Death of Joseph Johnson.

1816 Suicide of Fanny Imlay.

1828 Supposed death of Gilbert Imlay.

Index

CLAIRE TOMALIN

CHARLES DICKENS: A LIFE

A major new biography of our greatest novelist, published for the 200th anniversary of his birth

Charles Dickens was a phenomenon. A demonically hardworking journalist, the father of ten children, a tireless walker and traveller, a supporter of liberal social causes, but most of all a great novelist – the creator of characters who live immortally in the English imagination: Sam Weller, Mr Pickwick, the Artful Dodger, David Copperfield, Little Nell, Lady Dedlock, Mrs Gamp, Pip, Miss Havisham and many more.

At the age of twelve he was sent by his affectionate but feckless parents to work in a blacking factory. By the time of his death in 1870 he drew adoring crowds to his public appearances, had met princes and presidents on both sides of the Atlantic, and had amassed a fortune. He was truly 'the inimitable', as he jokingly described himself. When he died, the world mourned, and he was buried – against his wishes – in Westminster Abbey.

Charles Dickens: A Life is the examination of Dickens we deserve. It gives full measure to his heroic stature - his huge virtues both as a writer and as a human being - while observing his failings in both respects with an understanding but unblinking eye. Claire Tomalin has written a full-scale biography of the writer, a story worthy of Dickens' own pen: a comedy that turns to tragedy as the very qualities that made him great, his indomitable energy, boldness, imagination, showmanship and enjoyment of fame, finally destroyed him. The man who emerges is one of extraordinary contradictions, whose vices and virtues were intertwined as surely as his life and art.

Published in Viking hardcover 6 October 2011